PARIS

TOP SIGHTS, AUTHENTIC EXPERIENCES

Lonely Planet's

Paris

Plan Your Trip

Top Experiences 35

Dining Out 115

Treasure Hunt 143

Bar Open 163

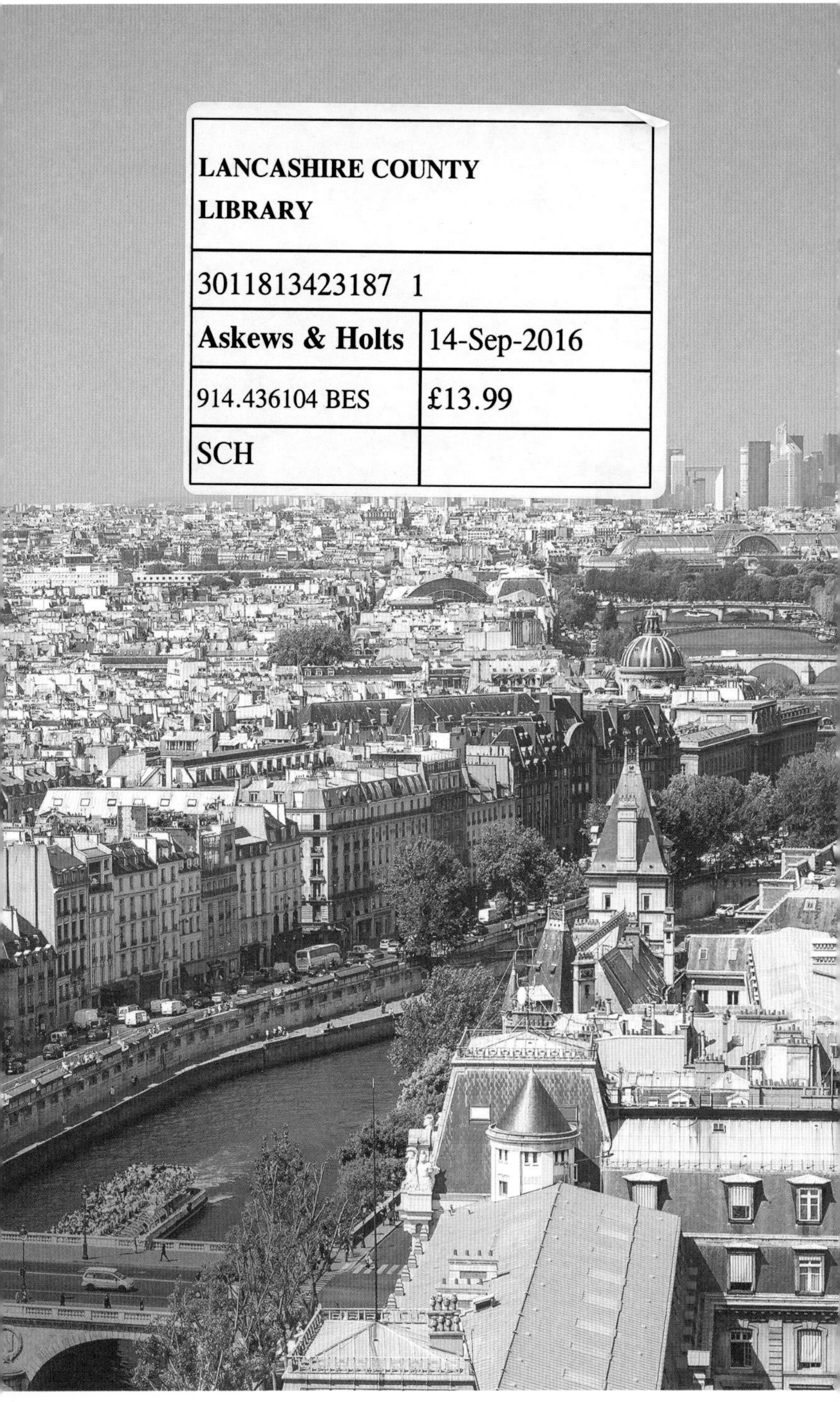

nartre &
ern Paris

nartre's en-
ng hilly streets
the red-light
district, home
Moulin Rouge.
p256)

**ilique du
ré-Cœur**
🌀

vre & Les Halles
ket streets fan out
und the mighty
vre and the
ng-edge Centre
pidou.
p p250)

⊙ **Canal
St-Martin**

**Le Marais,
Ménilmontant &
Belleville**
Hip boutiques, bars
and restaurants
squeeze alongside a
celebrity-filled ceme-
tery. *(Map p250)*

**Centre
🏛Pompidou**

⊙ **Cimetière du
Père Lachaise**

**Sainte-
Chapelle**
🌀

The Islands
Notre Dame domi-
nates the larger Île
de la Cité, while little
Île St-Louis is graced
with elegant build-
ings. *(Map p250)*

🌀
🏛 **Notre
Dame**

**Jardin des
Plantes**
⊙

🚊 **Gare de
Lyon**

🚇 **Gare
d'Austerlitz**

**Bastille &
Eastern Paris**
The Parisians' Paris,
with fabulous markets,
intimate gourmet bis-
tros and lively drinking
and dancing venues.

atin Quarter
ome to beautiful
otanic gardens and
acked with vibrant
tudent haunts.
Map p254)

🧭Ⓝ 0 ————————————— 2 km
     0 ————————————— 1 mile

Welcome to Paris

Paris is a city that transcends time, infused with the energy of generations of artists, writers and philosophers who've strolled its boulevards and cobbled lanes, debated on its cafe terraces, and shopped at its street markets.

La Ville Lumière (the City of Light) was so named because of its leading role in the Age of Enlightenment, and the name is as apt as ever today. The metropolis is awash with world-class landmarks that need no introduction – the Eiffel Tower, Arc de Triomphe and Notre Dame among them – along with a trove of specialist museums and galleries. The city's creamy-stone, grey-metal-roofed apartment buildings, lamp-lit bridges and geometrically laid-out formal parks are also an integral part of its fabric.

Yet contrary to its magnificently preserved cityscapes, Paris has never stood still, but has constantly evolved throughout the eras, leading the way in industrial, artistic, scientific and architectural endeavours. And this innovation continues today, with pioneering green transport initiatives, dazzling new architectural projects – including the glittering metallic façade encasing the Philharmonie de Paris concert hall and the translucent rainforest-inspired canopy covering the former-wholesale-markets-turned-shopping-mall Forum des Halles – and visionary creativity evident everywhere from neobistro kitchens to fashion ateliers and radical street art. Welcome to Paris.

contrary to its magnificently preserved cityscapes, Paris has never stood still

Paris skyline from the Arc de Triomphe
S.BORISOV/SHUTTERSTOCK ©

PARIS

St-Germain & Les Invalides
Literature lovers and fashionistas flock to this fabled cafe- and boutique-filled Left Bank neighbourhood.
(Map p248)

Mont... North...
Mont... chant... adjoin... Pigall... to the... *(Map...*

Bas... Sa...

Champs-Élysées & Grands Boulevards
Paris' grandest avenue, art nouveau department stores and a 19th-century opera house.
(Map p248)

Gare St-Lazare

Palais Garnier

Lou...
Ma... aro... Lou... cut... Por... *(M...*

Arc de Triomphe

Champs-Élysées

Jardin des Tuileries

Louvre

Seine

Eiffel Tower

Hôtel des Invalides

Musée d'Orsay

Musée Rodin

Musée National du Moyen Âge

Eiffel Tower & Western Paris
Stately boulevards flank the city's signature spire and major museums.
(Map p248)

Jardin du Luxembourg

Gare Montparnasse

Les Catacombes

Montparnasse & Southern Paris
Brasseries from the mid-20th-century and re-energised backstreets buzzing with local life.

L... h... b... p... s... (

This Year in Paris

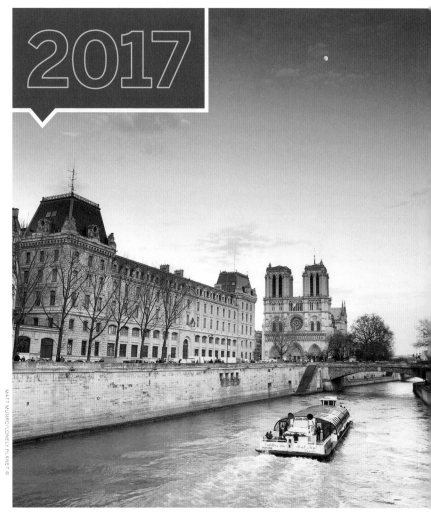

MATT MUNRO/LONELY PLANET ©

Art fairs, music festivals, open-air cinema and epicurean events are just some of the highlights of Paris' calendar in 2017, with many more in the works: check www.parisinfo.com for updates. Above: River cruise along the Seine; Top right: Maria and the Diamonds on stage, Rock en Seine; Far right: French *pâtisserie*; Right: a Parisian cafe terrace

BERTRAND GUAY/AFP/GETTY IMAGES ©

Top Festivals & Events

Paris Plages – July–August (p12)
Bastille Day – 14 July (p12)
Paris Cocktail Week – January (p6)
Rock en Seine – 25-27 August (p13)
Nuit Blanche – 7-8 October (p15)

LEFT & RIGHT MATT MUNRO/LONELY PLANET ©

Plan Your Trip
This Year in Paris

January

The frosty first month of the year isn't the most festive in Paris, but cocktails – as well as the winter soldes *(sales) – certainly brighten the mood.*

1 January

✿ Grande Parade
The New Year kicks off in style when carnival floats and brass bands make their way along the av des Champs-Élysées.

22 January

✿ Louis XVI Commemorative Mass
On the Sunday closest to 21 January, royalists and right-wingers attend a mass at the Chapelle Expiatoire (www.monuments-nationaux.fr) marking the execution by guillotine of King Louis XVI in 1793.

Late January

🍷 Paris Cocktail Week
Each of the 50-plus cocktail bars that take part in Paris Cocktail Week (www.pariscocktailweek.fr) creates two signature cocktails for the event. There are also workshops, guest bartenders, masterclasses and food pairings. Sign up for a free pass for cut-price cocktails.

From 28 January

✿ Chinese New Year
Paris welcomes the year of the rooster. The largest lantern-lit festivities and dragon parades take place in the city's main Chinatown in the 13e. Parades are also held in Belleville and Le Marais.

Grande Parade
KIEV.VICTOR/SHUTTERSTOCK ©

February

Festivities still aren't in full swing in February, but couples descend on France's romantic capital for Valentine's Day, when virtually all restaurants offer special menus.

1 February–31 March

⚡ 6 Nations Tournament

During 2017's 6 Nations rugby tournament, fixtures will take place at Paris' premier stadium, the Stade de France (www.rbs6nations.com), in St-Denis.

Until 26 February 2017

⊙ Rétrospective Bernard Buffet

February is your last chance to catch the retrospective of Parisian artist Bernard Buffet (1928–1999) at the city's modern-art museum, the Musée d'Art Moderne de la Ville de Paris (www.mam.paris.fr), in the 16e.

Late February– Early March

✗ Salon International de l'Agriculture

This appetising nine-day international agricultural fair (www.salon-agriculture.com) brings produce (and animals) from all over France, which is then turned into delectable fare at the Parc des Expositions at Porte de Versailles, 15e.

Above: Salon International de l'Agriculture; Right: Stade de France BIGMAGIC/SHUTTERSTOCK ©

XAVIER LAINE/GETTY IMAGES ©

Plan Your Trip
This Year in Paris

March

Blooms appear in Paris' parks and gardens, leaves start greening the city's avenues, festivities begin to flourish and days get longer – the last Sunday morning of the month ushers in daylight-saving time.

Mid-March

☆ Printemps du Cinéma
Cinemas across Paris offer filmgoers a unique entry fee of €4 per session over three days sometime around the middle of March (www.printempsducinema.com).

Mid-March–Mid-April

☆ Banlieues Bleues
Big-name acts perform during the Suburban Blues jazz, blues and R & B festival (www.banlieuesbleues.org) from mid-March to mid-April at venues in Paris' northern suburbs.

23–26 March

☆ Salon du Livre
France's largest international book fair (www.salondulivreparis.com) takes place over four days in late March at the Parc des Expositions at Porte de Versailles, 15e.

Above: Salon du Livre; Right: jazz club on rue des Lombards
ANADOLU AGENCY/HEINTZ JEAN/GETTY IMAGES ©

April

Sinatra sang about April in Paris, and the month sees the city's 'charm of spring' in full swing, with chestnuts blossoming and cafe terraces coming into their own.

1 April

☆ Disneyland Resort Paris 25th Anniversary

Plans for the 25th anniversary of Disneyland Resort Paris (www.disneylandparis.com) are a closel guarded secret, but you can expect grand-scale celebrations and a party atmosphere.

9 April

🏃 Marathon International de Paris

On your marks...the Paris International Marathon (www.schneiderelectricparismarathon.com), usually held on the second Sunday of April, starts on the av des Champs-Élysées, 8e, and finishes on av Foch, 16e, attracting more than 40,000 runners from over 100 countries.

Mid-April–early June

☆ Foire du Trône

Dating back some 1000 years, this huge funfair (www.foiredutrone.com) is held on the Pelouse de Reuilly of the Bois de Vincennes from around Easter to early June.

Late April

⊙ Foire de Paris

Gadgets, widgets, food and wine feature at this huge contemporary-living fair (www.foiredeparis.fr), held from late April to early May at the Parc des Expositions at Porte de Versailles, 15e.

Left: Marathon International de Paris; Above: Foire de Paris

Plan Your Trip
This Year in Paris

05

May

The temperate month of May has more public holidays than any other in France. Watch out for widespread closures, particularly on May Day (1 May).

Early May

🍷 Paris Beer Week

Craft beer's popularity in Paris peaks during Paris Beer Week (www.laparisbeerweek. com), held during the first week of May, when over 150 events take place across the city's bars, pubs, breweries, specialist beer shops and other venues.

DENNIS K JOHNSON/GETTY IMAGES ©

28 May–11 June
☆ French Open

The glitzy Internationaux de France de Tennis Grand Slam (www.roland-garros.com) hits up from late May to early June at Stade Roland Garros at the Bois de Boulogne.

Mid-May

◉ La Nuit Européenne des Musées

Key museums across Paris stay open late for the European Museums Night (www. nuitdesmusees.culturecommunication. gouv.fr), on one Saturday in mid-May. Most also offer free entry.

18–21 May

✕ Taste of Paris

Big-name chefs, such as Alain Ducasse and Guy Savoy, create dazzling dishes at the gourmet showcase Taste of Paris (www. tasteofparis.fr) inside the Grand Palais.

Late May

◉ Art St-Germain des Prés

Dozens of galleries in St-Germain des Prés come together in late May to showcase their top artists (www.artsaintgermaindespres. com). Each year has a different theme.

26–29 May

◉ Portes Ouvertes des Ateliers d'Artistes de Belleville

More than 250 painters, sculptors and other artists in Belleville open their studio doors (www.ateliers-artistes-belleville.fr) to visitors over four days (Friday to Monday) in late May.

June

Paris is positively jumping in June, thanks to warm temperatures and long daylight hours. Come evening, twilight lingering until nearly 11pm is the stuff of midsummer-night dreams.

3 June–30 July

☆ Paris Jazz Festival

Free jazz concerts swing every Saturday and Sunday afternoon in June and July in the Parc Floral de Paris during the Paris Jazz Festival (www.parisjazzfestival.fr). Park entry for adults/under 25s of €6/3 applies.

June

☆ Festival de St-Denis

Book ahead for this prestigious cycle of classical-music concerts (www.festival-saint-denis.com) at the Basilique de St-Denis and nearby venues held throughout the month.

21 June

☆ Fête de la Musique

This national music festival (www.fetedela-musique.culturecommunication.gouv.fr) on the summer solstice offers staged and impromptu live performances of jazz, reggae, classical and more all over the city.

Late June

☆ Gay Pride March

Late June's colourful Saturday-afternoon Marche des Fiertés (www.gaypride.fr) through Le Marais to Bastille celebrates Gay Pride Day with over-the-top floats and outrageous costumes.

☆ La Goutte d'Or en Fête

Raï, reggae and rap feature at this three-day world-music festival (www.goutte-dorenfete.wordpress.com) on square Léon in the 18e's Goutte d'Or neighbourhood in late June.

Gay Pride March
OLGA BESNARD/SHUTTERSTOCK ©

Plan Your Trip
This Year in Paris

July

During the Parisian summer, 'beaches' – complete with sunbeds, umbrellas, atomisers, lounge chairs and palm trees – line the banks of the Seine, while shoppers hit the summer soldes *(sales).*

14 July

✥ Bastille Day

The capital celebrates France's national day on 14 July with a morning military parade along av des Champs-Élysées accompanied by a fly-past of fighter aircraft and helicopters. By night, *feux d'artifice* (fireworks) light up the sky above the Champ de Mars.

Late July

✤ Tour de France

The last of the 21 stages of this legendary, 3500km-long cycling event (www.letour.com) finishes with a dash up av des Champs-Élysées on the third or fourth Sunday of July.

Late July–Early August

☆ Cinéma au Clair de Lune

Film screenings take place under the stars around town in late July/early August during Paris' free 'moonlight cinema', organised by the Forum des Images (www.forumdesimages.fr).

Mid-July–Mid-August
✥ Paris Plages

From mid-July to mid-August, 'Paris Beaches' (www.paris.fr) take over the Right Bank between the Louvre, 1er, and Pont de Sully, 4e; and the Rotonde de la Villette and rue de Crimée, 19e. All beaches are open from 8am to midnight.

Cinéma au Claire de Lune, Place des Vosges

2017

08

August

Parisians desert the city in droves during the summer swelter when, despite an influx of tourists, many restaurants and shops shut. It's a prime time to cycle, with far less traffic on the roads.

5 August–10 September

☆ Classique au Vert

In Paris' eastern forest, the Bois de Vincennes, the Parc Floral de Paris (www.classiqueauvert.paris.fr) hosts free classical music concerts amid the greenery. Park entry for adults/under 25s of €6/3 applies.

25 August

♣ Libération de Paris

Paris commemorates the liberation of the city from Nazi occupation in 1944 with a ceremonial drill and speeches outside the Hôtel de Ville (City Hall; www.paris.fr); in the evening the public dances to music by the Petit Orchestre de Paris.

25–27 August

☆ Rock en Seine

Headlining acts rock the Domaine National de St-Cloud, on the city's southwestern edge, at this popular three-day music festival (www.rockenseine.com).

25 August–8 October

♣ Fête à Neu-Neu

In Paris' rambling western forest, the Bois de Boulogne, exhibitions, performances, a flea market and a fair are all part of the festivities during the Fête à Neu-Neu (www.fete-a-neuneu.com).

Left: Bois de Vincennes; Above: Fête à Neu-Neu
ELENA DIJOUR/SHUTTERSTOCK ©; YVES TRENET/ALAMY STOCK PHOTO ©

Plan Your Trip
This Year in Paris

September

Tourists leave and Parisians come home: la rentrée marks residents' return to work and study after the summer break. Cultural life shifts into top gear and the weather is often at its blue-skied best.

Early–Mid-September

☆ Jazz à La Villette

This super two-week jazz festival (www.jazzalavillette.com) in the first half of September has sessions in Parc de la Villette, at the Cité de la Musique and at surrounding venues.

Mid-September–Late December

❀ Festival d'Automne

The long-running Autumn Festival of Arts (www.festival-automne.com), from mid-September to late December, incorporates painting, music, dance and theatre at venues throughout the city.

Mid-September

☆ Techno Parade

On one Saturday in mid-September, floats carrying musicians and DJs pump up the volume as they travel between place de la République and place d'Italie during the Techno Parade (www.technoparade.fr).

16 & 17 September

⊙ Journées Européennes du Patrimoine

The third weekend in September sees Paris open the doors of otherwise off-limits buildings – embassies, government ministries and so forth – during European Heritage Days (www.journeesdupatrimoine.culturecommunication.gouv.fr).

Techno Parade
FRED DUFOUR/GETTY IMAGES ©

October

October heralds an autumnal kaleidoscope in the city's parks and gardens, along with bright days, cool nights and excellent cultural offerings. Daylight saving ends on the last Sunday of the month.

7–8 October

♨ Nuit Blanche

From sundown until sunrise on the first Saturday and Sunday of October, museums and recreational facilities such as swimming pools stay open, along with bars and clubs, for one 'White Night' (ie 'All-Nighter'; www.paris.fr).

Early October

⚘ Fête des Vendanges de Montmartre

The grape harvest from the Clos Montmartre in early October is followed by five days of festivities including a parade (www.fetedesvendangesdemontmartre.com).

Late October

⊙ Foire Internationale d'Art Contemporain

Scores of galleries are represented at the contemporary-art fair known as FIAC (www.fiac.com), held over four days in late October at venues including the Grand Palais.

October–March

☆ Cirque d'Hiver Bouglione

Clowns, trapeze artists and acrobats have entertained children of all ages at the city's winter circus, Cirque d'Hiver Bouglione (www.cirquedhiver.com), inside a 20-sided polygon building in Le Marais since 1852.

Left: Nuit Blanche; Above: Cirque d'Hiver Bouglione

Plan Your Trip
This Year in Paris

November

Dark, chilly days and long, cold nights see Parisians take refuge indoors: the opera and ballet seasons are going strong and there are plenty of cosy bistros and bars.

4 November–5 January

☉ Grands Boulevards Christmas Window Displays

The Grands Boulevards' art-nouveau department stores Galeries Lafayette and Le Printemps set up enchanting themed displays in their store windows along bd Haussmann, with elevated viewing platforms for children.

Mid-November–Late December

☆ Africolor

From mid-November to late December, this six-week-long African-music festival (www.africolor.com) is primarily held in surrounding suburbs, such as St-Denis, St-Ouen and Montreuil.

15–16 November

♟ Beaujolais Nouveau

At midnight on the third Thursday (ie Wednesday night) in November – as soon as French law permits – the opening of the first bottles of cherry-bright, six-week-old Beaujolais Nouveau is celebrated in Paris wine bars, with more celebrations on the Thursday itself.

Mid-November–Early January

⌂ Champs-Élysées Christmas Market

Paris stages several Christmas markets from mid-November to early January; this one on the Champs-Élysées, with over 100 food, gift and mulled-wine 'chalets' set up along the famous avenue, is the largest.

Mid-November–Early March
⚞ Winter Ice Skating

Come winter (generally from mid-November to early March), ice-skating rinks pop up all over the city, including in some truly picturesque spots. These include the square outside the Hôtel de Ville; inside the Grand Palais beneath the art nouveau, domed glass-and-steel roof; at the Champs-Élysées Christmas Market; at the Jardins du Trocadéro; and most uniquely of all, on the 1st floor of the Eiffel Tower. Skating is usually free, but you'll need to pay for skate hire if you don't have your own. Check ahead with specific venues, as they can change from year to year.

December

Twinkling fairy lights, brightly decorated Christmas trees and shop windows, and outdoor ice-skating rinks make December a magical month to be in the City of Light.

Late November– Early December

🏇 Salon du Cheval de Paris

Sporting events and competitions including show jumping and dressage, plus a horseback parade through Paris, are all part of the Paris Horse Fair (www.salon-cheval.com) from late November to early December.

24–25 December

✿ Christmas Eve Mass

Mass is celebrated at midnight on Christmas Eve at many Paris churches, including Notre Dame – arrive early to find a place.

Late December– Early January

✿ Le Festival du Merveilleux

Normally closed to the public, the magical private museum Musée des Arts Forains (www.arts-forains.com), filled with fairground attractions of yesteryear, opens for 11 days from late December to early January, with enchanting rides, attractions and shows.

31 December

✿ New Year's Eve

Bd St-Michel, 5e; place de la Bastille, 11e; the Eiffel Tower, 7e; and especially av des Champs-Élysées, 8e – these are the Parisian hotspots to welcome in the new year, although no New Year's fireworks have taken place in recent years.

Notre Dame at Christmas
JORG GREUEL/GETTY IMAGES ©

Plan Your Trip
Need to Know

Daily Costs

Budget
Less than €100

- Dorm bed: €25–€50
- Coffee/glass of wine: from €2.50/4
- Excellent self-catering options, especially markets
- Frequent free concerts and events
- Public transport, standby theatre tickets

Midrange
€100–250

- Double room in a midrange hotel: €130–€250
- Two-course meal: €20–€40
- Museum admission: free to around €12
- Admission to clubs: free to around €20

Top End
More than €250

- Historic luxury hotel double room: from €250
- Gastronomic restaurant meal: from €40
- Designer boutiques

Advance Planning

- **Two months before**
Book accommodation; organise opera, ballet or cabaret tickets; check events calendars to find out what festivals will be on; and make reservations for high-end/popular restaurants.

- **Two weeks before**
Sign up for a local-led tour and start narrowing down your choice of museums, pre-purchasing tickets online where possible.

- **Two days before**
Pack your comfiest shoes!

Useful Websites

- **Lonely Planet** (www.lonelyplanet.com/paris) Destination information, bookings, traveller forum and more.

- **Paris Info** (www.paris-info.com) Comprehensive tourist-authority website.

- **Secrets of Paris** (www.secretsofparis.com) Loads of resources and reviews.

- **Paris by Mouth** (www.parisbymouth.com) Foodie heaven.

- **Sortiraparis** (www.sortiraparis.com) Up-to-date listings of what's on.

- **HiP Paris** (www.hipparis.com) Not only holiday rentals ('Haven in Paris'), but switched-on articles and reviews by expat locals too.

Currency
Euro (€)

Language
French

Visas
Generally no restrictions for EU citizens. Usually not required for most other nationalities for stays of up to 90 days.

Money
ATMs widely available. Visa and MasterCard accepted in most hotels, shops and restaurants; fewer accept American Express.

Mobile Phones
Check with your provider before you leave home about roaming costs and/or ensuring your phone is unlocked to use a French SIM card (available cheaply in Paris).

Time
Central European Time (GMT/UTC plus one hour).

Tourist Information
The main branch of the Paris Convention & Visitors Bureau (p232) sells tickets for tours, several attractions, museum and transport passes, and can book accommodation.

When to Go

Spring and autumn are ideal. Summer is the main tourist season but many establishments close during August. Sights are quieter and prices lower during winter.

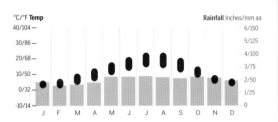

Arriving in Paris

Charles de Gaulle Airport
Trains (RER), buses and night buses to the city centre €6 to €17.50; taxi €50 to €55, 15% higher evenings and Sundays.

Orly Airport Trains (Orlyval, then RER), buses and night buses to the city centre €7.50 to €12.50; T7 tram to Villejuif-Louis Aragon then metro to centre (€3.60); taxi €30 to €35, 15% higher evenings and Sundays.

Beauvais Airport Buses (€17) to Porte Maillot then metro (€1.80); taxi at least €150.

Gare du Nord train station
Within central Paris; served by metro (€1.80).

Getting Around

Walking is a pleasure in Paris, but the city also has one of the most efficient and inexpensive public-transport systems in the world, making getting around a breeze.

○ **Metro & RER** The fastest way to get around. Runs from about 5.30am and

finishes around 12.35am or 1.15am (and to around 2.15am on Friday and Saturday nights).

○ **Bicycle** Virtually free pick-up, drop-off Vélib' bikes operate across 1800 stations citywide.

○ **Bus** Good for parents with prams/strollers and people with limited mobility.

○ **Boat** The Batobus is a handy hop-on, hop-off service stopping at nine key destinations along the Seine.

Arrondissements

Within the *périphérique* (ring road), Paris is divided into 20 *arrondissements* (city districts), which spiral clockwise like a snail shell from the centre (see p237). Each *arrondissement* has its own personality, but it's the *quartiers* (quarters, ie neighbourhoods), which often overlap *arrondissement* boundaries, that give Paris its village atmosphere.

Sleeping

Paris has a wealth of accommodation for all budgets, but it's often *complet* (full) well in advance. Reservations are recommended year-round and essential during the warmer months and all public and school holidays. Choose somewhere within Paris' 20 *arrondissements* to experience Parisian life the moment you step out the door.

Useful Websites

○ **Lonely Planet** (www.lonelyplanet.com/france/paris/hotels) Reviews of Lonely Planet's top choices.

○ **Paris Hotel Service** (www.parishotelservice.com) Boutique-hotel gems.

○ **Paris Hotel** (www.hotels-paris.fr) Well-organised hotel booking site with lots of user reviews.

○ **Room Sélection** (www.room-selection.com) Select apartment rentals centred on Le Marais.

Top Days in Paris

Central Right Bank

The central Right Bank is the ideal place to kick off your Parisian trip. As well as the ancient art and artefacts in Paris' mightiest museum, the Louvre, you'll also see ground-breaking modern and contemporary art inside the striking Centre Pompidou.

❶ Jardin des Tuileries (p96)

Start your day with a stroll through the elegant Jardin des Tuileries, stopping to view Monet's enormous *Waterlilies* at the Musée de l'Orangerie and/or photography exhibits at the Jeu de Paume.

➲ Jardin des Tuileries to Musée du Louvre

🚶 Stroll through the gardens to the Louvre.

❷ Musée du Louvre (p52)

Visiting the world's largest museum could easily consume a full day, but bear in mind that tickets are valid all day, so you can come and go as you please. Various tours (guided and self-guided) help you maximise your time.

➲ Musée du Louvre to Racines 2

🚶 Racines 2 is just northeast of the Louvre's Cour Carée.

Day 01

➌ Lunch at Racines 2 (p123)

Nip out for contemporary food at Racines 2.

⭕ Racines 2 to Jardin du Palais Royal

🕴 Walk north to rue St-Honoré then west to place du Palais Royal.

➍ Jardin du Palais Royal (p103)

Browse the colonnaded arcades of the exquisite Jardin du Palais Royal.

⭕ Jardin du Palais Royal to Église St-Eustache

🕴 Head back down rue St-Honoré, turn left into rue du Louvre and right on rue Coquillière.

➎ Église St-Eustache (p79)

One of Paris' most beautiful churches, Église St-Eustache has a magnificent organ – catch a classical concert here if you can.

⭕ Église St-Eustache to Centre Pompidou

🕴 Continue east on rue Rambuteau to place Georges-Pompidou.

➏ Centre Pompidou (p76)

Head to the late-opening Centre Pompidou for amazing modern and contemporary art.

⭕ Centre Pompidou to Café Marais

🕴 Turn right into rue Rambuteau, left on rue du Temple and right onto rue des Haudriettes.

➐ Dinner at Café Marais (p128)

Silent black-and-white Charlie Chaplin films screen on one wall of Café Marais – one of the best-value bistros in Le Marais.

⭕ Café Marais to Le Pick-Clops

🕴 Continue southeast on rue des Haudriettes, turn right into rue des Archives, left onto rue des Francs Bourgeois then right into rue Vieille du Temple.

➑ Drinks at Le Pick-Clops (p176)

Le Marais really comes into its own at night, with a cornucopia of hip clubs and bars such as Le Pick-Clops.

Left: Jardin des Tuileries; Above: Jardin du Palais Royal

Plan Your Trip
Top Days in Paris

LOIC LAGARDE/GETTY IMAGES ©

Western & Southern Paris

It's a day of Parisian icons today – from the triumphal span of the Arc de Triomphe to world-famous avenue Champs-Élysées, and, of course, the city's stunning art nouveau Eiffel Tower, with some surprises too, such as floating nightclubs.

Day
02

❶ Arc de Triomphe (p42)

Climb the mighty Arc de Triomphe for a pinch-yourself Parisian panorama. Back down on ground level, take the time to check out the intricate sculptures and historic bronze plaques, and pay your respects to the Tomb of the Unknown Soldier.

➲ Arc de Triomphe to Champs-Élysées
✦ Walk down the Champs-Élysées.

❷ Champs-Élysées (p94)

Promenade along Paris' most glamorous avenue, the Champs-Élysées, and perhaps give your credit card a workout in the adjacent Triangle d'Or (Golden Triangle), home to flagship *haute couture* fashion houses.

➲ Champs-Élysées to Musée du Quai Branly
Ⓜ Franklin D Roosevelt to Alma Marceau.

❸ Musée du Quai Branly (p40)

From Alma Marceau metro station, cross the Pont d'Alma and turn right along quai Branly to check out Musée du Quai Branly's indigenous art and awesome architecture.

○ Musée du Quai Branly to Café Branly

✈ Head to the museum's Café Branly.

❹ Lunch at Café Branly (p168)

Casual yet classy, Café Branly has ringside Eiffel Tower views.

○ Café Branly to Palais de Tokyo.

✈ Cross the Passerelle Debilly and walk up rue de la Manutention, turning right on av du Président Wilson.

❺ Palais de Tokyo (p41)

This stunning building takes on major temporary cutting-edge exhibits – the rooftop, for example, has been the setting for attention-getting projects such as the transient Hotel Everland and the see-through restaurant Nomiya.

○ Palais de Tokyo to Eiffel Tower

Ⓜ Iéna to Trocadéro.

❻ Eiffel Tower (p36)

Exiting the Trocadéro metro station, walk east through the Jardins du Trocadéro for the ultimate Eiffel Tower snapshot, and cross Pont d'Iéna to the tower itself. Sunset is the best time to ascend the Eiffel Tower, to experience both the dazzling views during daylight and then the twinkling *ville lumière* (City of Light) by night. (Pre-purchase your tickets to minimise queuing!)

○ Eiffel Tower to Firmin Le Barbier

✈ Turn left on av Gustave Eiffel, then right on av de la Bourdonnais and immediately left on rue de Monttessuy.

❼ Dinner & Drinks

Dining inside the Eiffel Tower itself is unforgettable. Alternatively, book ahead for fabulous bistro fare at Firmin Le Barbier (p120). Shadow the Seine by metro to party aboard several floating nightclubs permanently moored here, including Le Batofar (p181).

○ Firmin Le Barbier to Le Batofar

Ⓜ Bir-Hakeim to Quai de la Gare.

Left: Arc de Triomphe; Above: Musée du Quai Branly

Plan Your Trip
Top Days in Paris

ALLAN BAXTER/GETTY IMAGES ©

The Islands & Left Bank

Begin the day in the heart of Paris at the city's colossal cathedral, then venture across to Paris' elegant Left Bank to see impressionist masterpieces in the Musée d'Orsay, and to visit the city's oldest church and its loveliest gardens.

Day

03

❶ Notre Dame (p46)

Starting your day at Notre Dame gives you the best chance of beating the crowds. In addition to its stained-glass interior, allow an hour to climb up to the top to check out the gargoyles and exceptional views, and another to descend below ground to explore the crypt.

○ Notre Dame to Ste-Chapelle

🚶 Walk south along rue de la Cité, turning right on quai du Marché-Neuf, then right on bd du Palais.

❷ Sainte-Chapelle (p98)

For even more beautiful stained-glass work, don't miss the exquisite chapel Sainte-Chapelle. Consecrated in 1248, its stained glass forms a curtain of glazing on the 1st floor.

○ Sainte-Chapelle to Cuisine de Bar

Ⓜ 🚶 Catch the metro from Cité to St-Sulpice, then walk west on rue du Vieux Colombier, turning left on rue du Cherche-Midi.

CLAUDIA TOTIR/GETTY IMAGES ©

❸ Lunch at Cuisine de Bar (p137)

This stylish lunch spot serves gourmet *tartines* (open sandwiches) on sourdough made by famous bakery Poilâne next door. Pop into Poilâne afterwards to pick up some *punitions* (crispy butter biscuits).

➲ Cuisine de Bar to Musée d'Orsay

Ⓜ Sèvres-Babylone to Solférino.

❹ Musée d'Orsay (p62)

From Solférino metro station, head northwest along bd St-Germain, turning right up rue de Bellechasse to the magnificent Musée d'Orsay, filled with impressionist tours de force by masters including Renoir, Monet, Toulouse-Lautrec, Van Gogh, Degas and dozens more.

➲ Musée d'Orsay to Église St-Germain des Prés

Ⓜ Solférino to Sèvres-Babylone, then change lines for Mabillon.

Left: Sainte-Chapelle; Above: Goat's cheese and radish *tartines*

❺ Église St-Germain des Prés (p107)

Paris' oldest church sits in the heart of the buzzing St-Germain des Prés district, with chic boutiques and historic literary cafes, including Les Deux Magots (p180).

➲ Église St-Germain des Prés to Jardin de Luxembourg

🚶 Head south on rue Bonaparte to place St-Sulpice and continue on to rue Vaugirard.

❻ Jardin du Luxembourg (p68)

Enter the lovely Jardin du Luxembourg from rue Vaugirard and stroll among its chestnut groves, paths and statues.

➲ Jardin de Luxembourg to Bouillon Racine

🚶 From rue Vaugirard, turn left on rue Monsieur-le-Prince and right on rue Racine.

❼ Dinner at Bouillon Racine (p137)

Feast on French classics in this art-nouveau jewel. Afterwards, head to Shakespeare & Company (p134) for late-night book shopping.

Top Days in Paris

Northern & Eastern Paris

Montmartre's slinking streets and steep staircases lined with crooked ivy-clad buildings are especially enchanting to meander in the early morning when there are fewer tourists. Afterwards, explore charming Canal St-Martin and futuristic Parc de la Villette before drinking, dining and dancing in lively Bastille.

❶ Musée de Montmartre (p61)

Brush up on the area's fascinating history at the local museum, the Musée de Montmartre. Not only was Montmartre home to seminal artists, but Renoir and Utrillo are among those who lived in this very building.

⭘ Musée de Montmartre to Sacré-Cœur

🚶 Walk east along rue Cortot and turn right on rue du Mont Cenis then left on rue Azais.

❷ Sacré-Cœur (p58)

Head to the hilltop Sacré-Cœur basilica and, for an even more extraordinary panorama over Paris, climb up into the basilica's main dome. Regular metro tickets are valid on the funicular that shuttles up and down the steep Butte de Montmartre (Montmartre Hill).

⭘ Sacré-Cœur to Le Miroir

🚶 At the bottom of the hill, walk west along rue Tardieu and rue Yvonne le Tace, turning left on rue des Martyrs.

Day

04

❸ Lunch at Le Miroir (p126)

Dining-wise, Montmartre has more than its fair share of tourist traps, but locals' favourite Le Miroir offers lunch *menu* specials that offer superb quality and value, as do its wines from its own shop across the street. You'll also find wonderful food shops scattered nearby.

➔ Le Miroir to Canal St-Martin

M Abbesses to Marcadet-Poissonniers, then change lines for Gare de l'Est.

❹ Canal St-Martin (p90)

A postcard-perfect vision of iron footbridges, swing bridges and shaded towpaths, Canal St-Martin's banks (and the surrounding streets) are lined with a steadily growing number of offbeat cafes and boutiques. Also here is the chic Point Éphemère (p187) cultural centre.

➔ Canal St-Martin to Parc de la Villette

M Jacques Bonsergent to Porte de Pantin.

❺ Parc de la Villette (p199)

In addition to its striking geometric gardens, innovative Parc de la Villette has a slew of attractions, including the kid-friendly Cité des Sciences (p32) museum. Sailing schedules permitting, you can take a cruise to Bastille with canal-cruise operator Canauxrama (p90). Alternatively, head for the metro.

➔ Parc de la Villette to Septime

M Porte de Pantin to Oberkampf, then change lines for Charonne.

❻ Dinner at Septime (p131)

After a pre-dinner *apéro* (aperitif) at the classic, cherry-red corner cafe Le Pure Café (p177), head around the corner to enjoy modern French culinary magic at Septime. After dinner head west to rue de Lappe where you can hop between the Bastille neighbourhood's buzzing bars, starting with Bar des Ferrailleurs (p177).

Left: Canal St-Martin; Above: rue de Lappe nightlife

Plan Your Trip
Hotspots For...

ROMANCE

⊙ **Eiffel Tower** There's a reason the top platform sees up to three marriage proposals an hour. (p36)

⊙ **Musée Rodin** Swoon over Rodin's marble monument to love, *Le Baiser* (The Kiss), and stroll the museum's rose- and sculpture-filled garden. (p66)

⊙ **Le Coupe-Chou** Inside a vine-clad 17th-century townhouse, Le Coupe-Chou's maze of candlelit dining rooms is overwhelmingly romantic. (p134)

⊙ **Le Grand Véfour** Savour the romance of 18th-century Paris in one of the world's most beautiful restaurants. (p124)

⊙ **Square du Vert-Galant** This tiny, triangular park perches at the tip of the Île de la Cité. (p201)

GLITZ & GLAMOUR

⊙ **Versailles** Step inside this opulent 700-room palace and stroll its fountain-filled gardens. (pictured below; p86)

⊙ **Champs-Élysées** Stroll the world-famous, luxury-shop-lined av des Champs-Élysées. (p94)

✗ **Restaurant Guy Savoy** Access triple-Michelin-starred chef Guy Savoy's flagship in the neoclassical mint via a red-carpeted staircase. (p139)

🛍 **Galeries Lafayette** Shop beneath the magnificent century-old stained-glass dome in Paris' most lavish department store. (p148)

☆ **Palais Garnier** Catch a performance or take a backstage tour at Paris' resplendent 19th-century opera house. (p186)

BELLE ÉPOQUE PARIS

⊙ **Musée d'Orsay** View works from the 'beautiful era' at France's national impressionist, postimpressionist and art nouveau collection. (p62)

⊙ **Grand Palais** Like the Petit Palais, this beauty was designed for the 1900 Exposition Universelle (World Fair). (p94)

✕ **Le Jules Verne** Savour gastronomic cuisine and glittering views from inside the wrought-iron Eiffel Tower. (p120)

✕ **Brasserie Bofinger** Dine amid art nouveau brass, glass and mirrors in Paris' oldest brasserie. (p129)

CREATIVITY

⊙ **Canal St-Martin** Paris' picturesque canal is a hotbed of artists' galleries, studios and showrooms. (pictured above; p90)

⊙ **59 Rivoli** Some of Paris' most creative talent works at this central, now-legalised artists' squat. (p79)

✕ **La Cantine Belleville** Fab French cooking in vintage-furnished, graffitied-concrete surrounds. (p129)

⊙ **Brasserie La Parisienne** One of a new wave of craft breweries in Paris with behind-the-scenes tours. (p173)

☆ **Le 104** This former funeral parlour turned city-funded art space programs eclectic events. (p189)

REJUVENATION

⊙ **Jardin du Luxembourg** Paris' most beloved park has formal terraces, chestnut groves, lush lawns and playgrounds. (pictured above; p68)

⊙ **Les Berges de Seine** Sprint, skate, cycle or take part in activities and events along this riverside promenade. (p72)

⚶ **Piscine Joséphine Baker** Swim on (not in!) the Seine at this floating swimming pool. (p198)

✕ **Soul Kitchen** Salads, soups, savoury tarts and more grace the menu of this vegetarians' favourite. (p126)

🍷 **Wild & the Moon** Get a vitamin hit at this serious juice bar. (p176)

Plan Your Trip
What's New

Ancient Origins

Across from the Eiffel Tower, Paris' newly reopened anthropological museum, the Musée de l'Homme (p40), traces the evolution of humankind through its updated layout and revamped exhibits.

Louvre Renewal

The labyrinthine Louvre (p52) recently embarked on a 30-year renovation plan to make the museum more accessible.

Car-Free Streets

Green initiatives include closing 3.3km of Right Bank expressway between the Tuileries and Bastille and pedestrianising the Champs-Élysées (p94) on the first Sunday of each month.

Craft Breweries

Paris' *bière artisanale* (craft beer) trend sees breweries such as Brasserie La Parisienne (p173) offering behind-the-scenes tours and tastings.

Cocktail Dinners

The city's cocktail renaissance is upping the ante with restaurants, such as Dersou (p133) offering amazing food pairings, where each course comes with a custom-created cocktail.

Plan Your Trip
For Free

Free Museums

If you can, time your trip to be in Paris on the first Sunday of the month when you can visit the *musées nationaux* (national museums; www.rmn.fr) for free as well as certain monuments (some during certain months only).

European citizens under 26 get free entry to national museums and monuments.

At any time, you can visit the permanent collections of selected *musées municipaux* (municipal museums; www.paris.fr) for free.

Some museums have reduced entry at various times of the day or week.

Free Music

Concerts, DJ sets and recitals regularly take place for free (or for the cost of a drink) at venues throughout the city.

Busking musicians and performers entertain crowds on Paris' streets, squares and aboard the metro.

Free Literary Events

This literary-minded city is an inspired place to catch a reading, author signing or writing workshop. English-language bookshops such as Shakespeare & Company (p134) and Abbey Bookshop (p158) host literary events throughout the year and can point you towards others.

Free Fashion Shows

Reserve ahead to attend free weekly fashion shows at Galeries Lafayette's flagship department store (p148). While you're here, don't miss one of the best free views over the Parisian skyline from Galeries Lafayette's rooftop.

Free Festivals & Events

Loads of Paris' festivals and events are free, such as the summertime Paris Plages riverside beaches.

Best for Free

○ Jardin du Luxembourg (p68)

○ Père Lachaise (p80)

○ Galeries Lafayette Fashion Shows (p148)

○ Musée de la Sculpture en Plein Air (p111)

Above: Muséum National d'Histoire Naturelle (p109)

Plan Your Trip
Family Travel

LONELY PLANET/GETTY IMAGES ©

Sights & Activities

In addition to classic playgrounds, Paris' parks also have a host of children's activities. Among the best are the toy boats, marionettes (puppets), pony rides and carousel of the Jardin du Luxembourg (p68); the new millennium playgrounds of Parc de la Villette (p199), adjacent to the fabulous interactive science museum Cité des Sciences (☑01 56 43 20 20; www.cite-sciences.fr; 30 av Corentin Cariou, 19e, Parc de la Villette; adult/child €9/7, La Géode €12/9; ⏰10am-6pm Tue-Sat, to 7pm Sun, La Géode 10.30am-8.30pm Tue-Sun); and the Bois de Boulogne's adorable Jardin d'Acclimatation (www.jardindacclimatation.fr; av du Mahatma Gandhi; €3, per attraction €2.90; ⏰10am-7pm Apr-Sep, to 6pm Oct-Mar) amusement park.

Animal-mad kids will love the lions, cougars, white rhinos and other creatures at the Bois de Vincennes' state-of-the-art Parc Zoologique de Paris (☑08 11 22 41 22; http://parczoologiquedeparis.fr; cnr av Daumesnil & rte de Ceinture du Lac, 12e; adult/child €22/14; ⏰9.30am-7.30pm summer, shorter hours rest of year); the kid-friendly natural-history-fo-cused Muséum National d'Histoire Naturelle (p109); and the shark tank inside the Cinéaqua (www.cineaqua.com; av des Nations Unies, 16e; adult/child €20.50/13; ⏰10am-7pm) aquarium. A trip to the Louvre (p52) can be a treat, particularly following thematic trails such as hunting for lions or galloping horses.

Every kid, big and small, loves a voyage down the Seine with Bateaux-Mouches (p75) or Bateaux Parisiens (p75). But there's something extra special about the one-hour 'Paris Mystery' tours designed especially for children by Vedettes de Paris (p74).

Eating Out with Kids

Many restaurants accept little diners (confirm ahead), but they're expected to behave (bring crayons/books). Children's menus are common, but most restaurants don't have high chairs. A new wave of gourmet pizza, pasta and burger restaurants throughout the city offer kid-friendly fare. In fine weather, good options include picking up sandwiches and crêpes from a

street stall or packing a market-fresh picnic and heading to parks and gardens.

Getting Around with Kids

Paris' narrow streets and metro stairways are a trial if you have a stroller (pram or push-chair) in tow; buses offer an easier, scenic alternative. Children under four years of age travel free on public transport and generally receive free admission to sights. For older kids, discounts vary from place to place – anything from a euro off for over fours to free entry up to the age of 18.

Need to Know

○ **Baby food and nappies** The choice of baby food, formula, soy and cow's milk, nappies (diapers) and the like in French supermarkets is similar to that in any developed country, but remember that opening hours may be more limited. Pharmacies – of which a handful are open 24/7 – also sell baby paraphernalia.

Top Five for Kids

Jardin du Luxembourg (p68)

Cité des Sciences (left)

Le Grand Rex (p187)

Vedettes de Paris 'Paris Mystery' Tours (p74)

Les Berges de Seine (p72)

○ **Babysitters** Weekly listings magazine *L'Officiel des Spectacles* advertises *gardes d'enfants* (babysitting) services.

○ **Rental equipment** Rent strollers, scooters, car seats, travel beds and anything else you need from 2kids1bag (www.2kids1bag.com).

Left: Jardin d'Acclimatation;
Above: Jardin du Luxembourg (p68)

PIERRE OGERON/GETTY IMAGES ©

TOP
EXPERIENCES

The very best to see & do

Eiffel Tower

Paris today is unimaginable without its signature spire. Originally only constructed as a temporary 1889 Exposition Universelle exhibit, it went on to become the defining fixture of the city's skyline.

Great For...

❶ Need to Know

Map p248; ☎08 92 70 12 39; www.tour-eiffel. fr; Champ de Mars, 5 av Anatole France, 7e; lift to top adult/youth/child €17/14.50/8, lift to 2nd fl €11/8.50/4, stairs to 2nd fl €7/5/3, lift 2nd fl to top €6; ☉lifts & stairs 9am-12.45am mid-Jun–Aug, lifts 9.30am-11.45pm, stairs 9.30am-6.30pm Sep–mid-Jun; Ⓜ Bir Hakeim or RER Champ de Mars–Tour Eiffel)

★ **Top Tip**

Head here at dusk for the best day-time vistas and glittering night-time city views.

Named after its designer, Gustave Eiffel, the Tour Eiffel was built for the 1889 Exposition Universelle (World Fair). It took 300 workers, 2.5 million rivets and two years of nonstop labour to assemble. Upon completion the tower became the tallest human-made structure in the world (324m or 1063ft) – a record held until the completion of the Chrysler Building in New York (1930). A symbol of the modern age, it faced massive opposition from Paris' artistic and literary elite, and the 'metal asparagus', as some Parisians snidely called it, was originally slated to be torn down in 1909. It was spared only because it proved an ideal platform for the transmitting antennas needed for the newfangled science of radio-telegraphy.

Tickets & Queues

Buying tickets in advance online usually means you avoid the monumental queues at the ticket offices. Print your ticket or show it on a smartphone screen. If you can't reserve your tickets ahead of time, expect waits of well over an hour in high season.

Stair tickets can't be reserved online. They are sold at the south pillar, where the staircase can also be accessed: the climb consists of 360 steps to the 1st floor and another 360 steps to the 2nd floor.

Ascend as far as the 2nd floor (either on foot or by lift), from where it is lift-only to the top floor. Pushchairs must be folded in lifts and you are not allowed to take bags or backpacks larger than aeroplane-cabin size.

If you have reservations for either restaurant, you are granted direct access to the lifts.

View of the city from the tower

First Floor

Of the tower's three floors, the 1st (57m) has the most space, but the least impressive views. The glass-enclosed **Pavillon Ferrié** – open since summer 2014 – houses an immersion film along with a small cafe and souvenir shop, while the outer walkway features a discovery circuit to help visitors learn more about the tower's ingenious design. Check out the sections of glass flooring that proffer a dizzying view of the ant-like people walking on the ground far below.

This level also hosts the 58 Tour Eiffel restaurant.

> ### ☑ Don't Miss
> Views of the tower from the Jardins du Trocadéro outside Palais de Chaillot.

BERTRAND RIEGER/GETTY IMAGES ©

Not all lifts stop at the 1st floor (check before ascending), but it's an easy walk down from the 2nd floor should you accidentally end up one floor too high.

Second Floor

Views from the 2nd floor (115m) are the best – impressively high, but still close enough to see the details of the city below. Telescopes and panoramic maps placed around the tower pinpoint locations in Paris and beyond. Story windows give an overview of the lifts' mechanics, and the vision well allows you to gaze through glass panels to the ground. Also up here are toilets, a souvenir shop and Michelin-starred restaurant Le Jules Verne (p120).

Top Floor

Views from the wind-buffeted top floor (276m) stretch up to 60km on a clear day, though at this height the panoramas are more sweeping than detailed. Celebrate your ascent with a glass of bubbly (€12 to €21) from the Champagne bar (open noon to 10pm). Afterwards peep into Gustave Eiffel's restored top-level office where lifelike wax models of Eiffel and his daughter Claire greet Thomas Edison.

To access the top floor, take a separate lift on the 2nd floor (closed during heavy winds).

Nightly Sparkles

Every hour on the hour, the entire tower sparkles for five minutes with 20,000 6-watt lights. They were first installed for Paris' millennium celebration in 2000 – it took 25 mountain climbers five months to install the current bulbs and 40km of electrical cords. For the best view of the light show, head across the Seine to the Jardins du Trocadéro.

> ### ✕ Take a Break
> On the tower's 1st floor, 58 Tour Eiffel (p120) has panoramic views.

What's Nearby?

Parc du Champ de Mars   Park

(Map p248; Champ de Mars, 7e; MÉcole Militaire or RER Champ de Mars-Tour Eiffel) Running southeast from the Eiffel Tower, the grassy Champ de Mars – an ideal summer picnic spot – was originally used as a parade ground for the cadets of the 18th-century **École Militaire**, the vast French-classical building at the southeastern end of the park, which counts Napoleon Bonaparte among its graduates. The steel-and-etched glass **Wall for Peace** (Map p248; www.wallforpeace.com; MÉcole Militaire or RER Champ de Mars-Tour Eiffel) memorial (2000) is by Clara Halter.

Musée du Quai Branly   Museum

(Map p248; ☏01 56 61 70 00; www.quaibranly. fr; 37 quai Branly, 7e; adult/child €9/free; ☺11am-7pm Tue, Wed & Sun, 11am-9pm Thu-Sat; MAlma Marceau or RER Pont de l'Alma) No other museum in Paris so inspires travellers, armchair anthropologists and those who simply appreciate the beauty of traditional craftsmanship. A tribute to the diversity of human culture, Musée du Quai Branly presents an overview of indigenous and folk art. Its four main sections focus on Oceania, Asia, Africa and the Americas.

An impressive array of masks, carvings, weapons, jewellery and more make up the body of the rich collection, displayed in a refreshingly unique interior without rooms or high walls.

Be sure to check out the temporary exhibits and performances, both of which are generally excellent.

Palais de Chaillot   Historic Building

(Map p248; place du Trocadéro et du 11 Novembre, 16e; MTrocadéro) The two curved, colonnaded wings of this building (built for the 1937 International Expo) and the terrace in between them afford an exceptional panorama of the **Jardins du Trocadéro**, the Seine and the Eiffel Tower. The eastern wing houses the standout **Cité de l'Architecture et du Patrimoine** (Map p248; www.citechaillot.fr; adult/child €8/free; ☺11am-7pm Wed & Fri-Mon, to 9pm Thu), devoted to French architecture and heritage, as well as the Théâtre National de Chaillot (p186),staging dance and theatre. The western wing houses the **Musée de la Marine** (Maritime Museum; Map p248; ☏01 53 65 69 69; www.musee-marine.fr; adult/child €8.50/free; ☺11am-6pm Wed-Mon) and the **Musée de l'Homme** (Museum of Humankind; Map p248; ☏01 44 05 72 72; www.museedelhomme.fr; adult/

Parc du Champ de Mars

child €10/free; ⊘Thu-Mon 10am-6pm, Wed to 9pm; MPassy, Iéna).

Musée Guimet des
Arts Asiatiques   Art Museum
(Map p248; ☑01 56 52 54 33; www.guimet.fr; 6 place d'Iéna, 16e; adult/child €7.50/free; ⊘10am-6pm Wed-Mon; MIéna) France's foremost Asian art museum has a superb collection. Observe the gradual transmission of both Buddhism and artistic styles along the Silk Road in pieces ranging from 1st-century Gandhara Buddhas from Afghanistan and Pakistan, to later Central Asian, Chinese and Japanese Buddhist sculptures and art. Part of the collection is housed in the nearby **Galeries du Panthéon Bouddhique** (Map p248; 19 av d'Iéna, 16e; ⊘10am-5.45pm Wed-Mon, garden to 5pm; MIéna) FREE with a **Japanese garden**.

❶ Did You Know?

Slapping a fresh coat of paint on the tower is no easy feat. It takes a 25-person team 18 months to complete the 60-tonnes-of-paint task, redone every seven years.

Palais de Tokyo   Art Museum
(Map p248; www.palaisdetokyo.com; 13 av du Président Wilson, 16e; adult/child €10/free; ⊘noon-midnight Wed-Mon; MIéna) The Tokyo Palace, created for the 1937 Exposition Universelle, has no permanent collection. Rather its shell-like interior of concrete and steel is a stark backdrop to interactive contemporary-art exhibitions and installations. Its bookshop is fabulous for art and design magazines, and its eating and drinking options are magic.

Arc de Triomphe

If anything rivals the Eiffel Tower as the symbol of Paris, it's this magnificent 1836-built triumphal arch commemorating Napoléon's 1805 victory at Austerlitz, which he commissioned the following year.

Great For...

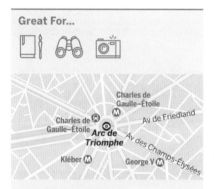

ℹ Need to Know

www.monuments-nationaux.fr; place Charles de Gaulle, 8e; adult/child €12/free; ⊙10am-11pm Apr-Sep, to 10.30pm Oct-Mar; Ⓜ Charles de Gaulle-Étoile

☑ **Don't Miss**

Some of the best vistas in Paris from the top of the arch.

History

Napoléon's armies never did march through the Arc de Triomphe showered in honour. At the time it was commissioned, his victory at Austerlitz seemed like a watershed moment that confirmed the tactical supremacy of the French army, but a mere decade later, Napoléon had already fallen from power and his empire had crumbled.

The Arc de Triomphe was never fully abandoned – simply laying the foundations had taken an entire two years – and in 1836, after a series of starts and stops under the restored monarchy, the project was finally completed. In 1840 Napoléon's remains were returned to France and passed under the arch before being interred at Invalides.

Accessing the Arch

Don't try to cross the traffic-choked round-about above ground! Stairs on the Champs Élysées' northeastern side lead beneath the Étoile to pedestrian tunnels that bring you out safely beneath the arch.

There is a lift/elevator at the arch, but it's only for visitors with limited mobility or those travelling with young children, and there are still some unavoidable steps.

Beneath the Arch

Beneath the arch at ground level lies the **Tomb of the Unknown Soldier**. Honouring the 1.3 million French soldiers who lost their lives in WWI, the Unknown Soldier was laid to rest in 1921, beneath an eternal flame that is rekindled daily at 6.30pm.

La Marseillaise by François Rude

Also here are a number of bronze plaques laid into the ground. Take the time to try and decipher some: these mark significant moments in modern French history, such as the proclamation of the Third French Republic (4 September 1870) and the return of Alsace and Lorraine to French rule (11 November 1918). The most notable plaque is the text from Charles de Gaulle's famous London broadcast on 18 June 1940, which sparked the French Resistance to life: 'Believe me, I who am speaking to you with full knowledge of the facts, and who tell you that nothing is lost for France. The same means that overcame us can bring us victory one day. For France is not alone! She is not alone!'

> ★ **Top Tip**
> Don't risk getting skittled by traffic by taking photos while crossing the Champs-Elysées.

DE AGOSTINI/C. SAPPA/GETTY IMAGES ©

Sculptures

The arch is adorned with four main sculptures, six panels in relief, and a frieze running beneath the top. Each was designed by a different artist; the most famous sculpture is the one to the right as you approach from the Champs-Élysées: *La Marseillaise* (Departure of the Volunteers of 1792). Sculpted by François Rude, it depicts soldiers of all ages gathering beneath the wings of victory, en route to drive back the invading armies of Prussia and Austria. The higher panels depict a series of important victories for the Revolutionary and imperial French armies, from Egypt to Austerlitz, while the detailed frieze is divided into two sections: the *Departure of the Armies* and the *Return of the Armies*. Don't miss the multimedia section beneath the viewing platform, which provides more detail and historical background for each of the sculptures.

Viewing Platform

Climb the 284 steps to the viewing platform at the top of the 50m-high arch and you'll be suitably rewarded with magnificent panoramas over western Paris. From here, a dozen broad avenues – many of them named after Napoléonic victories and illustrious generals – radiate towards every compass point. The Arc de Triomphe is the highest point in the line of monuments known as the *axe historique* (historic axis, also called the grand axis); it offers views that swoop east down the Champs-Élysées to the gold-tipped obelisk at place de la Concorde (and beyond to the Louvre's glass pyramid), and west to the skyscraper district of La Défense, where the colossal Grande Arche marks the western terminus of the *axe*.

> ✕ **Take a Break**
> Pair an evening visit with a traditional French dinner at Le Hide (p122).

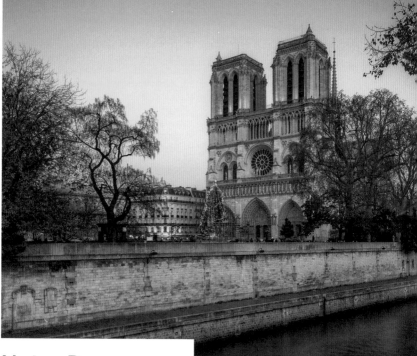

JOE DANIEL PRICE/GETTY IMAGES ©

Notre Dame

A vision of stained-glass rose windows, flying buttresses and frightening gargoyles, Paris' glorious cathedral, on the larger of the two inner-city islands, is the city's geographic and spiritual heart.

Great For...

☑ **Don't Miss**

Climbing the bell towers, which brings you face to face with the cathedral's ghoulish gargoyles.

When you enter the cathedral its grand dimensions are immediately evident: the interior alone is 127m long, 48m wide and 35m high, and can accommodate some 6000 worshippers.

Architecture

Built on a site occupied by earlier churches and, a millennium prior, a Gallo-Roman temple, Notre Dame was begun in 1163 and largely completed by the early 14th century. The cathedral was badly damaged during the Revolution, prompting architect Eugène Emmanuel Viollet-le-Duc to oversee extensive renovations between 1845 and 1864. Enter the magnificent forest of ornate flying buttresses that encircle the cathedral chancel and support its walls and roof.

Notre Dame is known for its sublime balance, though if you look closely you'll see all sorts of minor asymmetrical elements

DAVID BANK/GETTY IMAGES ©

❶ Need to Know

Map p250; 📞01 42 34 56 10; www.cathe-
draledeparis.com; 6 place du Parvis Notre
Dame, 4e; cathedral free, towers adult/child
€8.50/free, treasury €2/1; ⊙cathedral 8am-
6.45pm Mon-Fri, to 7.15pm Sat & Sun, towers
10am-6.30pm Sun-Thu, to 11pm Fri & Sat Jul &
Aug, 10am-6.30pm Apr-Jun & Sep, 10am-5pm
Oct-Mar, treasury 9.30am-6pm Apr-Sep,
10am-5.30pm Oct-Mar; Ⓜ Cité

✕ Take a Break

On hidden place Dauphine, Le Caveau
du Palais (p133) serves contemporary
French fare.

★ Top Tip

Invariably huge queues get longer
throughout the day – arrive as early
as possible.

introduced to avoid monotony, in accordance
with standard Gothic practice. These include
the slightly different shapes of each of the
three main portals, the statues of which were
once brightly coloured to make them more
effective as a *Biblia pauperum* – a 'Bible of
the poor' to help the illiterate faithful understand Old Testament stories, the Passion of
Christ and the lives of the saints.

Rose Windows & Pipe Organ

The most spectacular interior features
are three rose windows, particularly the
10m-wide window over the western façade
above the organ – one of the largest in the
world, with 7800 pipes (900 of which have
historical classification), 111 stops, five
56-key manuals and a 32-key pedal board
– and the window on the northern side of
the transept (virtually unchanged since the
13th century).

Towers

A constant queue marks the entrance to
the **Tours de Notre Dame**, the cathedral's
bell towers. Climb the 400-odd spiralling
steps to the top of the western façade of
the North Tower, where you'll find yourself
on the rooftop **Galerie des Chimères**
(Gargoyles Gallery), face to face with
frightening and fantastic gargoyles. These
grotesque statues divert rainwater from the
roof to prevent masonry damage, with the
water exiting through the elongated, open
mouth; and, purportedly, ward off evil spirits. Although they appear medieval, they
were installed by Eugène Viollet-le-Duc in
the 19th century. From the rooftop there's a
spectacular view over Paris.

In the South Tower hangs Emmanuel, the
cathedral's original 13-tonne bourdon bell (all

of the cathedral's bells are named). During the night of 24 August 1944, when the Île de la Cité was retaken by French, Allied and Resistance troops, the tolling of the Emmanuel announced Paris' approaching liberation. As part of 2013's celebrations for Notre Dame's 850th anniversary since construction began, nine new bells were installed, replicating the original medieval chimes.

Treasury

In the southeastern transept, the *trésor* (treasury) contains artwork, liturgical objects and first-class relics; pay a small fee to enter. Among its religious jewels and gems is the **Ste-Couronne** (Holy Crown), purportedly the wreath of thorns placed on Jesus' head before he was crucified. It is exhibited between 3pm and 4pm on the first Friday of each month, 3pm to 4pm every Friday during Lent, and 10am to 5pm on Good Friday.

Easier to admire is the treasury's wonderful collection, **Les Camées des Papes** (Papal Cameos). Sculpted with incredible finesse in shell and framed in silver, the 268-piece collection depicts every pope in miniature from St Pierre to the present day, ending with Pope Benedict XVI. Note the different posture, hand gestures and clothes of each pope.

The Mays

Walk past the choir, with its carved wooden stalls and statues representing the Passion of Christ, to admire the cathedral's wonderful collection of paintings in its nave side chapels. From 1449 onwards, city goldsmiths offered to the cathedral each year on 1 May a tree strung with devotional

Gargoyles adorn the Notre Dame's towers

ribbons and banners to honour the Virgin Mary, to whom Notre Dame (Our Lady) is dedicated. Fifty years later the goldsmiths' annual gift, known as a May, had become a tabernacle decorated with scenes from the Old Testament, and, from 1630, a large canvas – 3m tall – commemorating one of the Acts of the Apostles, accompanied by a poem or literary explanation. By the early 18th century, when the brotherhood of goldsmiths was dissolved, the cathedral had received 76 such monumental paintings – just 13 can be admired today.

Crypt

Under the square in front of Notre Dame lies the **Crypte Archéologique** (Archaeological Crypt; Map p250; www.crypte.paris.fr; 4e; adult/child €7/5; ⊘10am-6pm Tue-Sun), a 117m-long and 28m-wide area displaying

SYLVAIN SONNET/GETTY IMAGES ©

in situ the remains of structures built on this site during the Gallo-Roman period, a 4th-century enclosure wall, the foundations of the medieval foundlings hospice and a few of the original sewers sunk by Haussmann. Audioguides cost €5.

Audioguides & Tours

Pick up an audioguide (€5) from Notre Dame's information desk, just inside the entrance. Audioguide rental includes admission to the treasury. Free 45-minute English-language tours take place at 2pm Wednesday and Thursday and 2.30pm Saturday.

Landmark Occasions

Historic events that have taken place at Notre Dame include Henry VI of England's 1431 coronation as King of France, the 1558 marriage of Mary, Queen of Scots, to the Dauphin Francis (later Francis II of France), the 1804 coronation of Napoléon I by Pope Pius VII and the 1909 beatification and 1920 canonisation of Joan of Arc.

Music at Notre Dame

The best day to appreciate Notre Dame's musical heritage is on Sunday at a Gregorian or polyphonic Mass (10am and 6.30pm respectively) or a free organ recital (4.30pm). From October to June the cathedral stages evening concerts; find the program online at www.musique-sacree-notredamedeparis.fr.

★ The Heart of Paris

Notre Dame is very much the heart of Paris – so much so that distances from Paris to every part of metropolitan France are measured from place du Parvis Notre Dame, the vast square in front of the Cathedral of Our Lady of Paris where crowds gather in the afternoon sun to admire the cathedral façade. A bronze star across the street from the cathedral's main entrance marks the exact location of **Point Zéro des Routes de France** (Map p250; 6 place de Parvis Notre Dame, 4e; M Cité).

Notre Dame

TIMELINE

1160 Maurice de Sully becomes bishop of Paris. Mission: to grace growing Paris with a lofty new cathedral.

1182–90 The **choir with double ambulatory ❶** is finished and work starts on the nave and side chapels.

1200–50 The **west façade ❷**, with rose window, three portals and two soaring towers, goes up. Everyone is stunned.

1345 Some 180 years after the foundation stone was laid, the Cathédrale de Notre Dame is complete. It is dedicated to notre dame (our lady), the Virgin Mary.

1789 Revolutionaries smash the original **Gallery of Kings ❸**, pillage the cathedral and melt all its bells except the great bell Emmanuel. The cathedral becomes a Temple of Reason then a warehouse.

1831 Victor Hugo's novel *The Hunchback of Notre Dame* inspires new interest in the half-ruined Gothic cathedral.

1845–50 Architect Viollet-le-Duc undertakes its restoration. Twenty-eight new kings are sculpted for the west façade. The heavily decorated **portals ❹** and **spire ❺** are reconstructed. The neo-Gothic **treasury ❻** is built.

1860 The area in front of Notre Dame is cleared to create the parvis, an alfresco classroom where Parisians can learn a catechism illustrated on sculpted stone portals.

1935 A rooster bearing part of the relics of the Crown of Thorns, St Denis and St Geneviève is put on top of the cathedral spire to protect those who pray inside.

1991 The architectural masterpiece of Notre Dame and its Seine-side riverbanks become a Unesco World Heritage Site.

2013 Notre Dame celebrates 850 years since construction began with a bevy of new bells and restoration works.

Virgin & Child
Spot all 37 artworks representing the Virgin Mary. Pilgrims have revered the pearly-cream sculpture of her in the sanctuary since the 14th century. Light a devotional candle and write some words to the *Livre de Vie* (Book of Life).

North Rose Window
See prophets, judges, kings and priests venerate Mary in vivid blue and violet glass, one of three beautiful rose blooms (1225–70), each almost 10m in diameter.

Flying Buttresses

❶

Choir Screen
No part of the cathedral weaves biblical tales more evocatively than these ornate wooden panels, carved in the 14th century after the Black Death killed half the country's population. The faintly gaudy colours were restored in the 1960s.

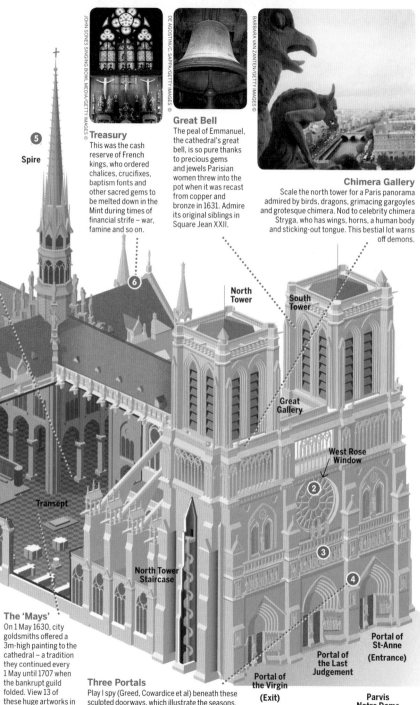

Treasury
This was the cash reserve of French kings, who ordered chalices, crucifixes, baptism fonts and other sacred gems to be melted down in the Mint during times of financial strife – war, famine and so on.

Great Bell
The peal of Emmanuel, the cathedral's great bell, is so pure thanks to precious gems and jewels Parisian women threw into the pot when it was recast from copper and bronze in 1631. Admire its original siblings in Square Jean XXII.

Chimera Gallery
Scale the north tower for a Paris panorama admired by birds, dragons, grimacing gargoyles and grotesque chimera. Nod to celebrity chimera Stryga, who has wings, horns, a human body and sticking-out tongue. This bestial lot warns off demons.

5 Spire

6

North Tower

South Tower

Great Gallery

West Rose Window

2

Transept

3

North Tower Staircase

4

The 'Mays'
On 1 May 1630, city goldsmiths offered a 3m-high painting to the cathedral – a tradition they continued every 1 May until 1707 when the bankrupt guild folded. View 13 of these huge artworks in the side chapels.

Three Portals
Play I spy (Greed, Cowardice et al) beneath these sculpted doorways, which illustrate the seasons, life and the 12 vices and virtues alongside the Bible.

Portal of the Virgin (Exit)

Portal of the Last Judgement

Portal of St-Anne (Entrance)

Parvis Notre Dame

The Louvre

The Mona Lisa and the Venus de Milo are just two of the priceless treasures resplendently housed inside the fortress turned royal palace turned France's first national museum.

Few art galleries are as prized or as daunting as the Musée du Louvre – one of the world's largest and most diverse museums. Showcasing 35,000 works of art, it would take nine months to glance at every piece, rendering advance planning essential.

Works of art from Europe form the permanent exhibition, alongside priceless collections of Mesopotamian, Egyptian, Greek, Roman and Islamic art and antiquities – a fascinating presentation of the evolution of Western art up through the mid-19th century.

Visiting

You need to queue twice to get in: once for security and then again to buy tickets. The longest queues are outside the Grande Pyramide; use the Carrousel du Louvre entrance (99 rue de Rivoli or direct from

---

Great For...

☑ **Don't Miss**

The museum's thematic trails – from the 'Art of Eating' to 'Love in the Louvre'.

MICHAEL MCQUEEN/GETTY IMAGES ©

❶ Need to Know

Map p250; 📞01 40 20 53 17; www.louvre.fr;
rue de Rivoli & quai des Tuileries, 1er; adult/
child €15/free; ⏰9am-6pm Mon, Thu, Sat
& Sun, to 9.45pm Wed & Fri; Ⓜ Palais Royal-Musée du Louvre

✕ Take a Break

The Hall Napoléon sells sandwiches,
ideal for a Jardin des Tuileries (p96)
picnic.

★ Top Tip

Tickets are valid for the whole day,
meaning you can come and go.

the metro) or the Porte de Lions entrance
(closed Wednesday and Friday).

A Paris Museum Pass or Paris City
Passport gives you priority; buying tickets
in advance (on the Louvre website) will also
help expedite the process.

Self-guided thematic trails range from
'Louvre Masterpieces' and the 'Art of Eating' to family-friendly topics. Download trail
brochures in advance from the website.

Another good option is to rent a Nin-
tendo 3DS multimedia guide (adult/child
€5/3; ID required). More formal, English-
language guided **tours** (📞01 40 20 51 77;
adult/child €12/5; ⏰11.30am & 2pm except 1st
Sun of month) depart from the Hall Napoléon.
Reserve a spot up to 14 days in advance or
sign up on arrival at the museum.

Palais du Louvre

The Louvre today rambles over four floors
and through three wings: the **Sully Wing**
creates the four sides of the Cour Carrée
(literally 'Square Courtyard') at the eastern
end of the complex; the **Denon Wing**
stretches 800m along the Seine to the
south; and the northern **Richelieu Wing**
skirts rue de Rivoli. The building started life
as a fortress built by Philippe-Auguste in
the 12th century – medieval remnants are
still visible on the lower ground floor (Sully). In the 16th century it became a royal
residence, and after the Revolution, in 1793,
it was turned into a national museum. At
the time, its booty was no more than 2500
paintings and objets d'art.

Over the centuries French governments
amassed the paintings, sculptures and
artefacts displayed today. The 'Grand
Louvre' project, inaugurated by the late
President Mitterrand in 1989, doubled the
museum's exhibition space, and both new

and renovated galleries have since opened, including the state-of-the-art **Islamic art galleries** (lower ground floor, Denon) in the stunningly restored Cour Visconti.

Priceless Antiquities

Don't rush by the Louvre's astonishing cache of treasures from antiquity: both Mesopotamia (ground floor, Richelieu) and Egypt (ground and 1st floors, Sully) are well represented, as seen in the *Code of Hammurabi* (Room 3, ground floor, Richelieu) and the *Seated Scribe* (Room 22, 1st floor, Sully). Room 12 (ground floor, Sackler Wing) holds impressive friezes and an enormous two-headed-bull column from the Darius Palace in ancient Iran, while an enormous seated statue of Pharaoh Ramesses II highlights the temple room (Room 12, Sully).

French & Italian Masterpieces

The 1st floor of the Denon Wing, where the *Mona Lisa* is found, is easily the most popular part of the Louvre – and with good reason. Rooms 75 through 77 are hung with monumental French paintings, many iconic: look for the *Consecration of the Emperor Napoleon I* (David), *The Raft of the Medusa* (Géricault) and *Grande Odalisque* (Ingres).

Rooms 1, 3, 5 and 8 are also must-visits. Filled with classic works by Renaissance masters (Raphael, Titian, Uccello, Botticini) this area culminates with the crowds around the *Mona Lisa*. But you'll find plenty else to contemplate, from Botticelli's graceful frescoes (Room 1) to the superbly detailed *Wedding Feast at Cana* (Room 6).

A crowd gathers around the *Mona Lisa*

Mona Lisa

Easily the Louvre's most admired work (and the world's most famous painting) is Leonardo da Vinci's *La Joconde* (in French; *La Gioconda* in Italian), the lady with that enigmatic smile known as *Mona Lisa* (Room 6, 1st floor, Denon).

Mona (*monna* in Italian) is a contraction of *madonna*, and Gioconda is the feminine form of the surname Giocondo. Canadian scientists used infrared technology to peer through paint layers and confirm *Mona Lisa's* identity as Lisa Gherardini (1479–1542?),

> ★ **Italian Sculptures**
>
> On the ground floor of the Denon Wing, take time for the Italian sculptures, including Michelangelo's *The Dying Slave* and Canova's *Psyche and Cupid* (Room 4).

GRAEME HARRIS/GETTY IMAGES ©

wife of Florentine merchant Francesco de Giocondo. Scientists also discovered that her dress was covered in a transparent gauze veil typically worn in early 16th-century Italy by pregnant women or new mothers; it's surmised that the work was painted to commemorate the birth of her second son around 1503, when she was aged about 24.

Louis XV's Crown

French kings wore their crowns only once – at their coronation. Lined with embroidered satin and topped with openwork arches and a fleur-de-lis, Louis XV's 1722-crafted crown (Room 66, 1st floor, Denon) was originally adorned with pearls, sapphires, rubies, topazes, emeralds and diamonds.

The Pyramid Inside & Out

Almost as stunning as the masterpieces inside is the 21m-high glass pyramid designed by Chinese-born American architect IM Pei that bedecks the main entrance to the Louvre in a dazzling crown. Beneath Pei's Grande Pyramide is the **Hall Napoléon**, the main entrance area, comprising an information booth, temporary exhibition hall, bookshop, souvenir store, cafe and auditoriums. To revel in another Pei pyramid of equally dramatic dimensions, head towards the **Carrousel du Louvre** (Map p250; www.carrouseldulouvre.com; 99 rue de Rivoli, 1er; ⊘8.30am-11pm, shops 10am-8pm; 🛜; ⓂPalais Royal-Musée du Louvre), a busy shopping mall that loops underground from the Grande Pyramide to the Arc de Triomphe du Carrousel (p97) – its centrepiece is Pei's **Pyramide Inversée** (inverted glass pyramid).

> ★ **Northern European Painting**
>
> The 2nd floor of the Richelieu Wing, directly above the gilt and crystal of the **Napoleon III Apartments** (1st floor), allows for a quieter meander through the Louvre's inspirational collection of Flemish and Dutch paintings, spearheaded by works by Peter Paul Rubens and Pieter Bruegel the Elder. Vermeer's *The Lacemaker* can be found in Room 38, while Room 31 is devoted chiefly to works by Rembrandt.

The Louvre

A HALF-DAY TOUR

Successfully visiting the Louvre is a fine art. Its complex labyrinth of galleries and staircases spiralling three wings and four floors renders discovery a snakes-and-ladders experience. Initiate yourself with this three-hour itinerary – a playful mix of Mona Lisa obvious and up-to-the-minute unexpected.

Arriving by the stunning main entrance, pick up colour-coded floor plans at the lower-ground-floor **information desk ❶** beneath IM Pei's glass pyramid, ride the escalator up to the Sully Wing and swap passport for multimedia guide (there are limited descriptions in the galleries) at the wing entrance.

The Louvre is as much about spectacular architecture as masterly art. To appreciate this zip up and down Sully's Escalier Henri II to admire **Venus de Milo ❷**, then up parallel Escalier Henri IV to the palatial displays in **Cour Khorsabad ❸**. Cross room 1 to find the escalator up to the 1st floor and staircase-as-art **L'Esprit d'Escalier ❹**. Next traverse 25 consecutive galleries (thank you, floor plan!) to flip conventional contemplation on its head with Cy Twombly's **The Ceiling ❺**, and the hypnotic **Winged Victory of Samothrace sculpture ❻** – just two rooms away – which brazenly insists on being admired from all angles. End with the impossibly famous **The Raft of Medusa ❼**, **Mona Lisa ❽** and **Virgin & Child ❾**.

TOP TIPS

» **Floor Plans** Don't even consider entering the Louvre's maze of galleries without a Plan/Information Louvre brochure, free from the information desk in the Hall Napoléon

» **Crowd dodgers** The Denon Wing is always packed; visit on late nights Wednesday or Friday or trade Denon in for the notably quieter Richelieu Wing

» **2nd floor** Not for first-timers: save its more specialist works for subsequent visits

MISSION MONA LISA

If you just want to venerate the Louvre's most famous lady, use the Porte des Lions entrance (closed Tuesday and Friday), from where it's a five-minute walk. Go up one flight of stairs and through rooms 26, 14 and 13 to the Grande Galerie and adjoining room 6.

Mona Lisa
Room 6, 1st Floor, Denon
No smile is as enigmatic or bewitching as hers. Da Vinci's diminutive *La Joconde* hangs opposite the largest painting in the Louvre – sumptuous, fellow Italian Renaissance artwork *The Wedding at Cana.*

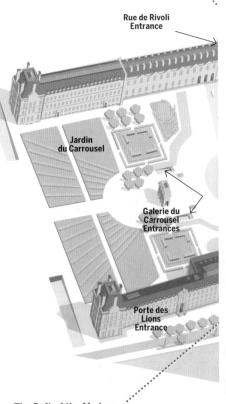

Rue de Rivoli Entrance

Jardin du Carrousel

Galerie du Carrousel Entrances

Porte des Lions Entrance

The Raft of the Medusa
Room 77, 1st Floor, Denon
Decipher the politics behind French romanticism in Théodore Géricault's *Raft of the Medusa.*

DEA/G DAGLI ORTI/GETTY IMAGES ©

L'Esprit d'Escalier
Escalier Lefuel, Richelieu
Discover the 'Spirit of the Staircase' through François Morellet's contemporary stained glass, which casts new light on old stone. **DETOUR»** Napoleon III's gorgeous gilt apartments.

Cour Khorsabad
Ground Floor, Richelieu
Time travel with a pair of winged human-headed bulls to view some of the world's oldest Mesopotamian art. **DETOUR»** Night-lit statues in Cour Puget.

The Ceiling
Room 32, 1st Floor, Sully
Admire the blue shock of Cy Twombly's 400-sq-metre contemporary ceiling fresco – the Louvre's latest, daring commission. **DETOUR»** *The Braque Ceiling*, room 33.

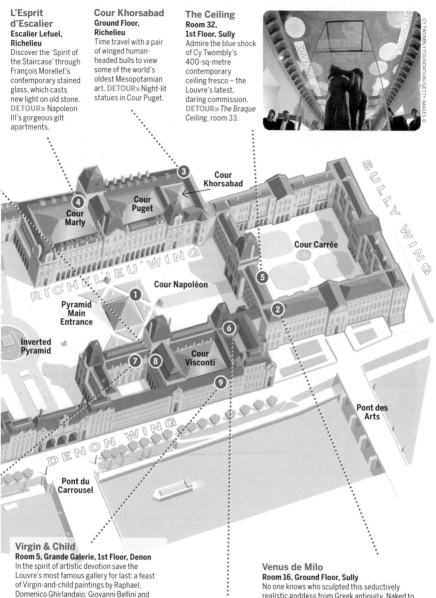

Cour Khorsabad

③ Cour Puget

④ Cour Marly

Cour Carrée

⑤

SULLY WING

Cour Napoléon

① RICHELIEU WING

②

Pyramid Main Entrance

Inverted Pyramid

⑥

⑦ ⑧ Cour Visconti

⑨

Pont des Arts

DENON WING

Pont du Carrousel

Virgin & Child
Room 5, Grande Galerie, 1st Floor, Denon
In the spirit of artistic devotion save the Louvre's most famous gallery for last: a feast of Virgin-and-child paintings by Raphael, Domenico Ghirlandaio, Giovanni Bellini and Francesco Botticini.

Winged Victory of Samothrace
Escalier Daru, 1st Floor, Sully
Draw breath at the aggressive dynamism of this headless, handless Hellenistic goddess. **DETOUR»** The razzle-dazzle of the Apollo Gallery's crown jewels.

Venus de Milo
Room 16, Ground Floor, Sully
No one knows who sculpted this seductively realistic goddess from Greek antiquity. Naked to the hips, she is a Hellenistic masterpiece.

GIUSEPPE TORRE/GETTY IMAGES ©

Sacré-Cœur

Staircased, ivy-clad streets slink up the hill of the fabled artists' neighbourhood of Montmartre to a funicular that glides up to the dove-white domes of Paris' landmark basilica, Sacré-Cœur.

Great For...

☑ Don't Miss

Dizzying vistas across Paris, especially from up inside the basilica's main dome.

More than just a basilica, Sacré-Cœur is a veritable experience, from the musicians performing on the steps to the groups of friends picnicking on the hillside park.

History

It may appear to be a place of peacefulness and worship today, but in truth Sacré-Cœur's foundations were laid amid bloodshed and controversy. Its construction began in 1875, in the wake of France's humiliating defeat by Prussia and the subsequent chaos of the Paris Commune. Following Napoléon III's surrender to von Bismarck in September 1870, angry Parisians, with the help of the National Guard, continued to hold out against Prussian forces – a harrowing siege that lasted four long winter months. By the time a ceasefire was negotiated in early 1871, the split between the radical working-class Parisians

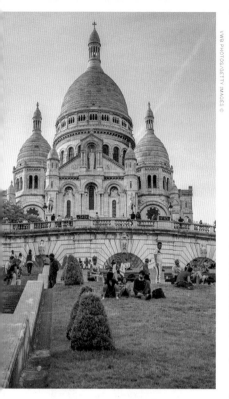

VWB PHOTOS/GETTY IMAGES ©

ℹ Need to Know

Map p256; ☎01 53 41 89 00; www.sacre-coeur-montmartre.com; place du Parvis du Sacré-Cœur; dome adult/child €6/4, cash only; ⏱6am-10.30pm, dome 8.30am-8pm May-Sep, to 5pm Oct-Apr; Ⓜ Anvers

✖ Take a Break

Head to the terrace of L'Été en Pente Douce (p125) for French classics.

★ Top Tip

To skip walking up the hill, use a regular metro ticket aboard the funicular.

The Basilica

In this context, the construction of an enormous basilica to expiate the city's sins seemed like a gesture of peace and forgiveness – indeed, the seven million French francs needed to construct the church's foundations came solely from the contributions of local Catholics. However, the Montmartre location was certainly no coincidence: the conservative old guard desperately wanted to assert its power in what was then a hotbed of revolution. The battle between the two camps – Catholic versus secular, royalists versus republican – raged on, and in 1882 the construction of the basilica was even voted down by the city council (on the grounds that it would continue to fan the flames of civil war), only to be overturned in the end by a technicality.

Six successive architects oversaw construction of the Romano-Byzantine-style basilica, and it wasn't until 1919 that Sacré-Cœur was finally consecrated, even then standing in

(supported by the National Guard) and the conservative national government (supported by the French army) had become insurmountable.

Over the next several months, the rebels, known as Communards, managed to overthrow the reactionary government and take over the city. It was a particularly chaotic and bloody moment in Parisian history, with mass executions on both sides and a wave of rampant destruction that spread throughout Paris. Montmartre was a key Communard stronghold – it was on the future site of Sacré-Cœur that the rebels won their first victory – and it was consequently the first neighbourhood to be targeted when the French army returned in full force in May 1871. Ultimately, many Communards were buried alive in the gypsum mines beneath the Butte.

utter contrast to the bohemian lifestyle that surrounded it. While criticism of its design and white travertine stone has continued throughout the decades (one poet called it a giant baby's bottle for angels), the interior is enlivened by the glittering apse mosaic *Christ in Majesty*, designed by Luc-Olivier Merson in 1922 and one of the largest in the world.

In 1944, 13 Allied bombs were dropped on Montmartre, falling just next to Sacré-Cœur. Although the stained-glass windows all shattered from the force of the explosions, miraculously no one died and the basilica sustained no other damage.

The Dome & Crypt

Outside, some 234 spiralling steps lead you to the basilica's dome, which affords one of Paris' most spectacular panoramas; it's said you can see for 30km on a clear day. Weighing in at 19 tonnes, the bell called La Savoyarde in the tower above is the largest in France. The chapel-lined crypt, visited in conjunction with the dome (for an additional €2), is huge, but not very interesting.

What's Nearby?

Place du Tertre   Square

(Map p256; place du Tertre, 18e; Ⓜ Abbesses)
It would be hard to miss this busy square, one of the most touristy spots in all of Paris. Although today it's filled with visitors, buskers and portrait artists, place du Tertre was originally the main square of the village of Montmartre before it was incorporated into the city proper.

Place du Tertre

Dalí Espace Montmartre
Art Museum

(Map p256; ☎01 42 64 40 10; www.daliparis. com; 11 rue Poulbot, 18e; adult/child €11.50/6.50; ⏱10am-6pm, to 8pm Jul & Aug; Ⓜ Abbesses) More than 300 works by Salvador Dalí (1904–89), the flamboyant Catalan surrealist printmaker, painter, sculptor and self-promoter, are on display at this surrealist-style basement museum located just west of place du Tertre. The collection includes Dalí's strange sculptures (most in reproduction), lithographs, and many of his illustrations and furniture, including the famous Mae West lips sofa.

Clos Montmartre
Vineyard

(Map p256; 18 rue des Saules, 18e; Ⓜ Lamarck-Caulaincourt) No, it is not a hallucination. If only to confirm Montmartre's enchanting village-like atmosphere the *quartier* even has its own small vineyard. Planted in 1933, its 2000 vines produce an average of 800 bottles of wine a year. Each October the grapes are pressed, fermented and bottled in Montmartre's town hall, then sold by auction to raise funds for local community projects.

Musée de Montmartre
Museum

(Map p256; ☎01 49 25 89 39; www. museedemontmartre.fr; 12 rue Cortot, 18e; adult/child €9.50/5.50; ⏱10am-6pm; Ⓜ Lamarck-Caulaincourt) One of Paris' most romantic spots, this enchanting 'village' museum showcases paintings, lithographs and documents illustrating Montmartre's bohemian, artistic and hedonistic past – one room is dedicated entirely to the French cancan! The museum is in a 17th-century manor where several artists, including Renoir and Raoul Dufy, had their studios in the 19th century. The studio of pioneering female painter Suzanne Valadon, who lived and worked here with her son Maurice Utrillo and partner André Utter between 1912 and 1926, can also be visited.

Moulin Blute Fin
Windmill

(Moulin de la Galette; Map p256; rue Lepic, 18e; Ⓜ Abbesses) Sister windmill to surviving Moulin Radet on the same street, this abandoned 18th-century windmill ground flour on its hillock perch. It later became known as Moulin de la Galette after the *guinguette* (dance hall) – immortalised in Renoir's painting, *Bal du Moulin de la Galette* (1876), now in the Musée d'Orsay – that sprung up around its feet in the 1930s.

ⓘ Did You Know?
On Christmas Eve 1898, Louis Renault's first car was driven up the Montmartre Butte to the place du Tertre, igniting the start of the French auto industry.

STUART DEE / ROBERTHARDING/GETTY IMAGES ©

Musée d'Orsay

The grand former railway station in which the Musée d'Orsay is located is an art nouveau marvel, but the masterpieces from 1848 to 1914 are the stara of the show.

Great For...

ℹ️ Need to Know

Map p248; www.musee-orsay.fr; 62 rue de Lille, 7e; adult/child €12/free; ⏱9.30am-6pm Tue, Wed & Fri-Sun, to 9.45pm Thu; MAssemblée Nationale or RER Musée d'Orsay

★ **Top Tip**
Musée d'Orsay admission drops to €9 after 4.30pm (after 6pm on Thursday).

History

The Gare d'Orsay railway station was designed by competition-winning architect Victor Laloux. Even on its completion, just in time for the 1900 Exposition Universelle, painter Edouard Detaille declared that the new station looked like a Palais des Beaux Arts. But although it had all the modcons of the day – including luggage lifts and passenger elevators – by 1939 the increasing electrification of the rail network meant the platforms were too short for mainline trains, and within a few years all rail services ceased.

The station was used as a mailing centre during WWII, and in 1962 Orson Welles filmed Kafka's *The Trial* in the then-abandoned building. Fortunately, it was saved from being demolished and replaced with a hotel complex by a Historical Monument listing in 1973, before the government set about establishing the palatial museum.

Transforming the languishing building into the country's premier showcase for art from 1848 to 1914 was the grand project of President Valéry Giscard d'Estaing, who signed off on it in 1977. The museum opened its doors in 1986.

Far from resting on its laurels, the Musée d'Orsay's recent renovations incorporated a re-energised layout and increased exhibition space. Prized paintings now gleam from richly coloured walls that create an intimate, stately-home-like atmosphere, with high-tech illumination literally casting the masterpieces in a new light.

Paintings & Graphic Arts

On the top of every visitor's must-see list is the world's largest collection of impression-

ist and post-impressionist art. Just some of its highlights include Manet's *On the Beach* and *Woman with Fans;* Monet's gardens at Giverny and *Rue Montorgueil, Paris, Celebration of June 30, 1878;* Cézanne's card players, *Green Apples* and *Blue Vase;* Renoir's *Ball at the Moulin de la Galette* and *Young Girls at the Piano;* Degas' ballerinas; Toulouse-Lautrec's cabaret dancers; Pissarro's *The Seine and the Louvre;* Sisley's *View of the Canal St-Martin;* and Van Gogh's self-portraits, *Bedroom in Arles* and *Starry Night over the Rhône.* One of the museum's newer acquisitions is James Tissot's 1868 painting *The Circle of the Rue Royale,* classified a National Treasure.

☑ **Don't Miss**

The Parisian panorama through the railway station's giant glass clockface and from the adjacent terrace.

HIROSHI HIGUCHI/GETTY IMAGES ©

Drawings, pastels and sketches from major artists are another of the d'Orsay's lesser-known highlights. Look for Georges Seurat's *The Black Bow* (c 1882), and Paul Gaugin's poignant self-portrait (c 1902–03), drawn near the end of his life.

Decorative Arts & Sculpture

Household items such as hat and coat stands, candlesticks, chairs, vases and wall mirrors become works of art in the hands of their creators from the era, incorporating exquisite design elements.

The cavernous former station is also a magnificent setting for sculptures, including works by Degas, Gaugin, Camille Claudel, Renoir and Rodin.

Visiting

Combined tickets with the Musée de l'Orangerie (p96) cost €14, while combined tickets with the Musée Rodin (p39) are €18; both combination tickets are valid for a single visit to the museums within three months.

The museum is busiest Tuesday and Sunday, followed by Thursday and Saturday. Save time by buying tickets online and head directly to entrance C.

For a thorough introduction to the museum, 90-minute 'Masterpieces of the Musée d'Orsay' guided tours (€6) in English run at 11.30am and 2.30pm on Tuesday and 11.30am from Wednesday to Saturday; 90-minute 'Nineteenth-Century Art' tours (€6) are also available at the same hours. Kids under 13 aren't permitted on tours. An audioguide costs €5.

Photography of all kinds (including from mobile phones) is forbidden to avoid crowd bottlenecks. If you want something more tangible than memories to take away, there's an excellent book and gift shop.

✕ **Take a Break**

Time has scarcely changed the museum's (originally the station's) **Restaurant Musée d'Orsay** (☎01 45 49 47 03; 2-/3-course lunch menus €22/32, mains €16-23; ⊙11.45am-5.30pm Tue, Wed & Fri-Sun, 11.45am-2.45pm & 7-9.30pm Thu).

JAMES WHITESMITH/GETTY IMAGES ©

Musée Rodin

Paris' most romantic museum displays Auguste Rodin's sculptural masterpieces in his former workshop and showroom, the 1730-built, beautifully restored Hôtel Biron, as well as in its rambling, rose-scented gardens.

Sculptor, painter, sketcher, engraver and collector Auguste Rodin donated his entire collection to the French state in 1908 on the proviso they dedicate his former workshop and showroom to displaying his works. They're now installed not only in the mansion itself, but also in its rose-filled garden – one of the most peaceful places in central Paris.

Sculptures

The first large-scale cast of Rodin's famous sculpture *Le Penseur* (The Thinker), made in 1902, resides in the garden – the perfect place to contemplate this heroic naked figure conceived by Rodin to represent intellect and poetry (it was originally titled 'The Poet').

Great For...

☑ Don't Miss

Rodin's collection of works by artists including Van Gogh, Renoir and Camille Claudel.

Le Penseur (The Thinker)

HARALD SUND/GETTY IMAGES ©

ℹ️ Need to Know

Map p248; www.musee-rodin.fr; 79 rue de
Varenne, 7e; adult/child museum incl garden
€10/7, garden only €4/2; 🕙10am-5.45pm Tue
& Thu-Sun, to 8.45pm Wed; Ⓜ️Varenne

✕ Take a Break

Paris' oldest restaurant, À la Petite
Chaise (p138), still serves excellent
traditional fare.

★ Top Tip

Cheaper garden-only entry is available.

La Porte de l'Enfer (The Gates of Hell)
was commissioned in 1880 as the entrance
for a never-built museum, and Rodin
worked on his sculptural masterwork up
until his death in 1917. Standing 6m high
by 4m wide, its 180 figures comprise an
intricate scene from Dante's *Inferno*.

Marble monument to love, *Le Baiser*
(The Kiss) was originally part of The Gates
of Hell. The sculpture's entwined lovers
caused controversy on its completion due
to Rodin's then-radical approach of depicting women as equal partners in ardour.

The museum also features many sculptures by Camille Claudel, Rodin's protégé.

Rodin at the Hôtel Biron

Magnificent recent renovations to the
museum – the first since Rodin worked
here until his death in 1917 – included the

creation of a new paint colour, Biron Grey,
by British company Farrow & Ball, which
now provides a backdrop to the sculptures.

The Rodin at the Hôtel Biron room incorporates original furniture to re-create the
space as it was when he lived and worked
here.

Visiting

Prepurchase tickets online to avoid queuing.
Audioguides cost €6. A combined ticket with
the Musée d'Orsay costs €18; combination
tickets are valid for a single visit to each of the
museums within three months.

What's Nearby?

Hôtel Matignon   Landmark
(Map p248; 57 rue de Varenne, 7e; Ⓜ️Solférino)
Hôtel Matignon has been the official residence of the French prime minister since
the start of the Fifth Republic (1958). It's
closed to the public.

Jardin du Luxembourg

The city's most beautiful park, the Jardin du Luxembourg is an inner-city oasis encompassing 23 gracefully laid-out hectares of formal terraces, chestnut groves and lush lawns.

Great For...

❶ Need to Know

Map p254; www.senat.fr/visite/jardin; numerous entrances; ⊘vary; Ⓜ Mabillon, St-Sulpice, Rennes, Notre Dame des Champs or RER Luxembourg

★ **Top Tip**
For a quick snack or drink, kiosks and cafes are dotted throughout the park.

The Jardin du Luxembourg has a special place in Parisians' hearts. Napoléon dedicated the gardens to the children of Paris, and many residents spent their childhood prodding little wooden sailboats with long sticks on the octagonal pond, watching puppet shows, and riding the carousel or ponies.

All those activities are still here today, as are modern playgrounds and sporting and games venues.

History

The Jardin du Luxembourg's history stretches further back than Napoléon's dedication. The gardens are a backdrop to the Palais du Luxembourg, built in the 1620s for Marie de Médici, Henri IV's consort, to assuage her longing for the Pitti Palace in Florence. The Palais is now home to the French Senate, which, in addition to parliamentary-assembly activities like voting on legislation, is charged with promoting the palace and its gardens.

Numerous overhauls over the centuries have given the Jardin du Luxembourg a blend of traditional French- and English-style gardens that is unique in Paris.

Grand Bassin

All ages love the octagonal Grand Bassin, a serene ornamental pond where adults can lounge and kids can play with 1920s **toy sailboats** (per 30min/hr €2/3.30; ⊗Apr-Oct). Nearby, littlies can take **pony rides** (pony rides €3.50; ⊗3-6pm Wed, Sat, Sun & school holidays) or romp around the **playgrounds** (adult/child €1.20/2.50; ⊗vary) – the green half is for kids aged seven to 12 years, the blue half for under-sevens.

Grand Bassin

Puppet Shows

You don't have to be a kid or speak French to be delighted by marionette shows, which have entertained audiences in France since the Middle Ages. The lively puppets perform in the Jardin du Luxembourg's little **Théâtre du Luxembourg** (www.marionnettesduluxembourg.fr; Jardin du Luxembourg; tickets €6; ⊙usually 2pm Wed, Sat & Sun, plus 4pm daily during school holidays). Show times can vary; check the program online and arrive half an hour ahead.

Orchards

Dozens of apple varieties grow in the orchards in the gardens' south. Bees have

> ☑ **Don't Miss**
>
> Discovering the park's many sculptures, which include statues of Stendhal, Chopin, Baudelaire and Delacroix.

LAPAS77/SHUTTERSTOCK ©

produced honey in the nearby apiary, the **Rucher du Luxembourg** (Map p254), since the 19th century. The annual Fête du Miel (Honey Festival) offers two days of tasting and buying its sweet harvest around late September in the ornate **Pavillon Davioud** (Map p254; 55bis rue d'Assas, 6e).

Palais du Luxembourg

The **Palais du Luxembourg** (Map p254; www.senat.fr; rue de Vaugirard, 6e; Ⓜ Mabillon or RER Luxembourg) was built in the 1620s and has been home to the Sénat (French Senate) since 1958. It's occasionally open for visits by guided tour.

East of the palace is the ornate, Italianate **Fontaine des Médici** (Map p254; Jardin du Luxembourg; Ⓜ Mabillon or RER Luxembourg), built in 1630. During Baron Haussmann's 19th-century reshaping of the roads, the fountain was moved 30m, and the pond and dramatic statues of the giant bronze Polyphemus discovering the white-marble lovers Acis and Galatea were added.

Musée du Luxembourg

Prestigious temporary art exhibitions, such as 'Cézanne et Paris', take place in the beautiful **Musée du Luxembourg** (Map p254; http://museeduluxembourg.fr; 19 rue de Vaugirard, 6e; most exhibitions adult/child €13.50/9; ⊙10am-7pm Tue-Thu, Sat & Sun, to 9.30pm Fri & Mon; Ⓜ St-Sulpice or RER Luxembourg).

Around the back of the museum, lemon and orange trees, palms, grenadiers and oleanders shelter from the cold in the palace's **orangery** (Map p254; Jardin du Luxembourg; Ⓜ St-Sulpice or RER Luxembourg). Nearby, the heavily guarded **Hôtel du Petit Luxembourg** was where Marie de Médici lived while the Palais du Luxembourg was being built. The president of the Senate has called it home since 1825.

> ✗ **Take a Break**
>
> Park picnics aside, nearby options include family-style French cuisine at historic Polidor (p139).

FLAVIA MORLACHETTI/GETTY IMAGES ©

The Seine

The lifeline of Paris, the Seine sluices through the city, spanned by 37 bridges. Its Unesco World Heritage–listed riverbanks offer picturesque promenades, parks, activities and events, including summertime beaches.

Great For...

☑ Don't Miss

A river cruise, floating past Parisian landmarks such as the Louvre and Notre Dame.

Riverbank Rejuvenation

Paris' riverbanks have been reborn with the creation of **Les Berges de Seine** (Map p248; btwn Musée d'Orsay & Pont de l'Alma, 7e; ☺information point noon-7pm Sun-Thu, 10am-10pm Fri & Sat May-Sep, shorter hours Oct-Apr; MSolférino, Assemblée Nationale, Invalides). On the Right Bank, east of the Hôtel de Ville, 1.5km of former expressway now incorporates walkways and cycleways. Even more revolutionary is the completely car-free 2.3km stretch of the Left Bank from the Pont de l'Alma to the Musée d'Orsay (linked to the water's edge by a grand staircase that doubles as amphitheatre seating). A further 3.3km of Right Bank expressway between the Tuileries and Bastille is also set to close to cars.

A resounding success since it opened in 2013, this innovative promenade is dotted

ⓘ Need to Know

There are no barriers at the water's edge; keep a close eye on young children.

✕ Take a Break

For an idyllic picnic spot, stop by the Musée de la Sculpture en Plein Air (p111).

★ Top Tip

While the main islands are enchanting, the Île aux Cygnes is a little-known gem.

with restaurants and bars (some aboard boats), chessboard tables, hopscotch and ball-game courts, a skate ramp, kids' climbing wall, a 100m running track and floating gardens on 1800 sq metres of artificial islands (complete with knotted-rope hammocks where you can lie back and soak up the river's reclaimed serenity).

Les Berges de Seine also offers temporary events and activities as diverse as film screenings and knitting workshops, and even wintertime curling on ice.

Promenading & Pausing

The Seine's riverbanks are where Parisians come to cycle, jog, inline skate and stroll – staircases along the banks lead down to the water's edge.

Particularly picturesque spots for a riverside promenade include the areas around Paris' two elegant inner-city islands, the Île de la Cité and Île Saint-Louis. Up at street level, the banks are lined with the distinctive green-metal *bouquiniste* stalls selling antiquarian books, sheet music and old advertising posters. A lesser-known island stroll is the artificial **Île aux Cygnes** (Isle of Swans; Map p248; btwn Pont de Grenelle & Pont de Bir Hakeim, 15e; Ⓜ Javel-André Citroën, Bir Hakeim) via its tree-shaded walkway, the Allée des Cygnes (walking from west to east gives you a stunning view of the Eiffel Tower).

The river also acts as a giant backyard for apartment-dwelling Parisians. All along its banks you'll find locals reading, picnicking, canoodling or just basking in the sunshine. Among the best-loved spots is the tiny, triangular park Square du Vert-Galant (p201) beneath the Pont Neuf.

River Cruises & Tours

The best way, of course, to become acquainted with the Seine is to take a cruise along its waters. A plethora of companies run day- and night-time boat tours (usually lasting around an hour) with commentary in multiple languages. Many cruise companies also offer brunch, lunch and dinner cruises, and the standard of cuisine is generally high (this *is* Paris, after all).

An alternative to traditional boat tours is the Batobus (p239), a handy hop-on, hop-off service that stops at quintessentially Parisian attractions: the Eiffel Tower, Champs-Élysées, Musée d'Orsay, Musée du Louvre, St-Germain des Prés, Hôtel de Ville, Notre Dame and Jardin des Plantes. Single- and multiday tickets allow you to spend as long as you like sightseeing between stops.

Vedettes de Paris   Boat Trips

(Map p248; 01 44 18 19 50; www.vedettesde-paris.fr; Port de Suffren, 7e; adult/child €14/6; MBir Hakeim or RER Pont de l'Alma) It might

be a small company, but its one-hour sightseeing cruises on smaller boats are second to none. It runs themed cruises too, including imaginative 'Mysteries of Paris' tours for kids (adult/child €14/8).

Vedettes du Pont Neuf   Boat Trips

(Map p250; ☑01 46 33 98 38, classical-music cruises 01 42 77 65 65; www.vedettesdupontneuf. com; Square du Vert Galant, 1er; adult/child €14/7; MPont Neuf) One-hour cruises depart year-round from Vedettes' centrally located dock at the western tip of Île de la Cité; commentary is in French and English. Tickets are cheaper if you buy in advance online (adult/child morning cruises €9/5, afternoon cruises €11/5). Check the website for details of its wonderful 'Concerts en Seine' – classical music afloat after dusk (tickets €30 to €40).

Notre Dame by the Seine

Bateaux Parisiens   Boat Trips

(Map p248; www.bateauxparisiens.com; Port de la Bourdonnais, 7e; adult/child €14/6; Ⓜ Bir Hakeim or RER Pont de l'Alma) This vast operation runs 1½-hour river circuits with recorded commentary in 13 languages (every 30 minutes 10am to 10.30pm April to September, hourly 10am to 10pm October to March), and a host of themed lunch and dinner cruises. It has two locations: one by the Eiffel Tower, the other south of Notre Dame.

Bateaux-Mouches   Boat Trips

(Map p248; ☎ 01 42 25 96 10; www.bateaux-mouches.com; Port de la Conférence, 8e; adult/child €13.50/6; Ⓜ Alma Marceau) The largest river-cruise company in Paris and a favourite with tour groups. Cruises (70 minutes) run regularly from 10.15am to 10.30pm April to September and 13 times a day between 11am and 9.20pm the rest of the year. Commentary is in French and English. It's located on the Right Bank, just east of the Pont de l'Alma.

Seine-Side Entertainment

In addition to Les Berges de Seine, entertainment options include floating nightclubs aboard boats moored in southern Paris, such as the red-metal tugboat Le Batofar (p181), and even a floating swimming pool, Piscine Joséphine Baker (p198).

On the banks, riverside venues include the Docks en Seine (p111), which incorporates the French fashion institute, vast outdoor terraces, uber-hip bars, clubs and restaurants, an entertainment-themed contemporary-art museum, and more.

Summertime Beaches

Presaging the anti-auto revolution that ushered in Les Berges de Seine were the Paris Plages (Paris Beaches), with traffic supplanted by *pétanque* (boules) courts, pop-up bars and cafes, sun lounges, parasols, water fountains and sprays, and sand brought in by barges lining the river from mid-July to mid-August.

The Paris Plages were established in 2002 for Parisians who couldn't escape to the coast to cool off in the summer months. They now cover the square in front of the Hôtel de Ville, 1km along the Right Bank (from the Pont des Arts to the Pont de Sully) and the quays by the Bassin de la Villette in the 19e.

★ **Need to Know**

Swimming is strictly forbidden, even during Paris Plages, due to boat traffic and the health hazards posed by the water quality.

MATTEO COLOMBO/GETTY IMAGES ©

☑ **Top Tip**

Stairs leading to the water can be especially slippery after rain – beware!

Centre Pompidou

The primary-coloured, inside-out Centre Pompidou building houses France's national modern- and contemporary-art museum, the Musée National d'Art Moderne (MNAM), showcasing creations from 1905 to the present day.

Great For...

☑ **Don't Miss**

The sweeping panorama of Paris from the rooftop.

Galleries and exhibitions, hands-on workshops, dance performances, a bookshop, a design boutique, cinemas and other entertainment venues here are an irresistible cocktail.

Architecture & Views

Former French President Georges Pompidou wanted an ultracontemporary artistic hub and he got it: competition-winning architects Renzo Piano and Richard Rogers designed the building inside out, with utilitarian features like plumbing, pipes, air vents and electrical cables forming part of the external façade. The building was completed in 1977.

Viewed from a distance (such as from Sacré-Cœur), the Centre Pompidou's primary-coloured, boxlike form amid a sea of muted grey Parisian rooftops makes it look like a child's Meccano set abandoned on

Rooftop walkway

❶ Need to Know

Map p250; 📞01 44 78 12 33; www.centrepompidou.fr; place Georges Pompidou, 4e; museum, exhibitions & panorama adult/child €14/free; ⏱11am-10pm Wed-Mon; Ⓜ Rambuteau

✕ Take a Break

For a meal or a casual drink, head to nearby Café La Fusée (p171).

★ Top Tip

The Centre Pompidou opens late; head here around 5pm to avoid daytime crowds.

someone's elegant living-room rug. Although the Centre Pompidou is just six storeys high, the city's low-rise cityscape means stupendous views extend from its roof (reached by external escalators enclosed in tubes). Rooftop admission is included in museum and exhibition admission – or buy a panorama ticket (€3; 11am to 10pm Wednesday to Monday) just for the roof.

Musée National d'Art Moderne

Europe's largest collection of modern art fills the bright and airy, well-lit galleries of the National Museum of Modern Art, covering two complete floors of the Pompidou. For art lovers, this is one of the jewels of Paris. On a par with the permanent collection are the two temporary exhibition halls (on the ground floor/basement and the top floor), which showcase some memorable

blockbuster exhibits. Also of note is the fabulous children's gallery on the 1st floor.

The permanent collection changes every two years, but the basic layout generally stays the same. The 5th floor showcases artists active between 1905 and 1970 (give or take a decade); the 4th floor focuses on more contemporary creations, roughly from the 1990s onward.

The dynamic presentation of the 5th floor mixes up works by Picasso, Matisse, Chagall and Kandinsky with lesser-known contemporaries from as far afield as Argentina and Japan, as well as more famous cross-Atlantic names such as Arbus, Warhol, Pollock and Rothko.

One floor down on the 4th, you'll find monumental paintings, installation pieces, sculpture and video taking centre stage. The focus here is on contemporary art, architecture and design. The 4th floor also has an Espace des Collections Nouveaux Médias et Film, where visitors can discover 40 years of image and sound experimentation.

Tours & Guides

Guided tours are only in French (the information desk in the central hall on the ground floor has details), but the gap is easily filled by the excellent multimedia guide (adult/child under 13 years €5/3), which explains selected works in the museum in detail on a 1½-hour trail. There is also a guide for each temporary exhibit, another covering the unique architecture of the Centre Pompidou, and one created with kids (ages eight to 12) in mind.

Atelier Brancusi

West of the Centre Pompidou main building, this reconstruction of the **studio** (Map p250; 55 rue Rambuteau, 4e; ⊗2-6pm Wed-Mon; MRambuteau) FREE of Romanian-born sculptor Constantin Brancusi (1876–1957) –

known for works such as *The Kiss* and *Bird in Space* – contains over 100 sculptures in stone and wood. You'll also find drawings, pedestals and photographic plates from his original Paris studio.

Street Fun

The full-monty Pompidou experience is as much about hanging out in the busy streets and squares around it, packed with souvenir shops and people, as absorbing the centre's contents. West of the Centre Pompidou, fun-packed place Georges Pompidou and its nearby pedestrian streets attract bags of buskers, musicians, jugglers and mime artists.

Église St-Eustache

What's Nearby?

Église St-Eustache   Church

(Map p250; www.st-eustache.org; 2 impasse St-Eustache, 1er; ⊙9.30am-7pm Mon-Fri, 9am-7pm Sat & Sun; MLes Halles) Just north of the gardens snuggling up to the city's old marketplace, now the bustling Forum des Halles, is one of the most beautiful churches in Paris. Majestic, architecturally magnificent and musically outstanding, St-Eustache has made spirits soar for centuries.

Constructed between 1532 and 1637, St-Eustache is primarily Gothic, though a

---

★ **Don't Miss**
Nearby place Igor Stravinsky with its fanciful mechanical fountains of skeletons, hearts, treble clefs, and a big pair of ruby-red lips by Jean Tinguely and Niki de St-Phalle.

GARDEL BERTRAND/GETTY IMAGES ©

neoclassical façade was added on the western side in the mid-18th century. Highlights include a work by Rubens, Raymond Mason's colourful bas-relief of market vendors (1969) and Keith Haring's bronze triptych (1990) in the side chapels. Outside the church is a gigantic sculpture of a head and hand entitled *L'Écoute* (Listen; 1986) by Henri de Miller.

One of France's largest organs, above the church's western entrance, has 101 stops and 8000 pipes dating from 1854. Free organ recitals at 5.30pm on Sunday are a must for music lovers. Audioguides are available for €3.

Forum des Halles   Shopping Mall

(Map p250; www.forumdeshalles.com; 1 rue Pierre Lescot, 1er; ⊙shops 10am-8pm Mon-Sat; MChâtelet–Les Halles) Paris' main wholesale food market stood here for nearly 800 years before being replaced by this underground shopping mall in 1971. Long considered an eyesore by many Parisians, the mall's exterior was finally demolished in 2011 to make way for the new golden-hued translucent canopy, unveiled in 2016. Below, four floors of stores, cafes and a cinema extend down to the city's busiest metro hub.

Spilling out from the curvilinear, leaflike rooftop are new gardens, with *pétanque* and chess tables, a central patio and pedestrian walkways.

59 Rivoli   Gallery

(Map p250; http://59rivoli-eng.org; 59 rue de Rivoli, 1er; ⊙1-8pm; MLouvre-Rivoli) FREE In such a classical part of Paris crammed with elegant historic architecture, 59 Rivoli is quite the bohemian breath of fresh air. Take time out to watch artists at work in the 30 ateliers (studios) strung on six floors of the long-abandoned bank building, now a legalised squat where some of Paris' most creative talent works (but doesn't live).

The ground-floor gallery hosts a new exhibition every fortnight and free gigs, concerts and shows pack the place out most weekends. Look for the sculpted façade festooned with catchy drapes, banners and unconventional recycled piping above the shop fronts.

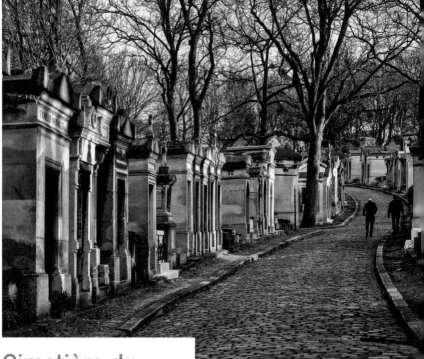

BRUNO DE HOGUES/GETTY IMAGES ©

Cimetière du Père Lachaise

Paris is a collection of villages, and this sprawling cemetery of cobbled lanes and elaborate tombs, with a 'population' of close to one million, qualifies as one in its own right.

Great For...

☑ Don't Miss

Oscar Wilde, Jim Morrison, Édith Piaf and countless other famous names.

The world's most visited cemetery was founded in 1804, and initially attracted few funerals because of its distance from the city centre. The authorities responded by exhuming famous remains and resettling them here. Their marketing ploy worked and Cimetière du Père Lachaise has been Paris' most fashionable final address ever since.

Famous Occupants

Paris residency was the only criterion needed to be buried in Père Lachaise, hence the cemetery's cosmopolitan population. Among the million-odd people buried here are the composer Chopin; the playwright Molière; the poet Apollinaire; writers Balzac, Proust, Gertrude Stein and Colette; the actors Simone Signoret, Sarah Bernhardt and Yves Montand; the painters Pissarro, Seurat, Modigliani and Delacroix; the *chanteuse* Édith Piaf and the dancer Isadora Duncan.

BRUNO DE HOGUES/GETTY IMAGES ©

ℹ Need to Know

☎ 01 55 25 82 10; www.pere-lachaise.com; 16 rue du Repos & 8 bd de Ménilmontant, 20e; ⊙ 8am-6pm Mon-Fri, 8.30am-6pm Sat, 9am-6pm Sun, shorter hrs winter; Ⓜ Père Lachaise, Gambetta, Philippe Auguste **FREE**

✕ Take a Break

Stroll to nearby Yard (p130) for modern French fare in a trendy neobistro.

★ Top Tip

Arriving at Gambetta metro station allows you to walk through the cemetery downhill.

The grave of Irish playwright and humorist **Oscar Wilde** (1854–1900), in division 89, is among the most visited (as the unfortunate glass barrier erected around his sculpted tomb, designed to prevent fans impregnating the stone with red lipstick imprints, attests). The other big hitter, likewise barricaded from over-zealous fans, is 1960s rock star **Jim Morrison** (1943–71; he died in Le Marais), in division 6.

Up in division 92, protests saw the removal of a fence around the grave of **Monsieur Noir**, aka journalist Yvan Salman (1848–70), shot aged 22 by Pierre Bonaparte, great-nephew of Napoléon. Legend says women who stroke the amply filled crotch of Monsieur Noir's prostrate bronze effigy will enjoy a better sex life and fertility.

Commemorative memorials to victims of almost every war in modern history form a poignant alley alongside the **Mur des Fédérés**, an unmemorable plain brick wall against which Communard insurgents were lined up, shot and buried in a mass grave in 1871.

Art & Architecture

For those visiting Paris for its exceptional art and architecture, this vast cemetery – the city's largest – is not a bad starting point. It's one of central Paris' biggest green spaces, with 5300 trees and a treasure trove of magnificent 19th-century sculptures by artists such as David d'Angers, Hector Guimard, Visconti and Chapu.

Visiting

The cemetery has five entrances, two of which are on bd de Ménilmontant. To save time searching for famous graves, pick up cemetery maps at the **conservation office** (rue du Repos, 20e; ⊙ 8.30am-12.30pm & 2-5pm Mon-Fri; Ⓜ Père Lachaise) near the main bd de Ménilmontant entrance.

Cimetière du Père Lachaise

A HALF-DAY TOUR

There is a certain romance to getting lost in Cimetière du Père Lachaise, a grave jungle spun from centuries of tales. But to search for one grave among one million in this 44-hectare land of the dead is no joke – narrow the search with this itinerary.

From the main bd de Ménilmontant entrance (metro Père Lachaise or Philippe Auguste), head up av Principale, turn right onto av du Puits and collect a map from the **Bureaux de la Conservation** ❶.

Backtrack along av du Puits, turn right onto av Latérale du Sud, scale the stairs and bear right along chemin Denon to New Realist artist **Arman** ❷, film director **Claude Chabrol** ❸ and **Chopin** ❹.

Follow chemin Méhul downhill, cross av Casimir Périer and bear right onto chemin Serré. Take the second left (chemin Lebrun – unsigned), head uphill and near the top leave the footpath to weave through graves on your right to rock star **Jim Morrison** ❺. Back on chemin Lauriston, continue uphill to roundabout **Rond-Point Casimir Périer** ❻.

Admire the funerary art of contemporary photographer **André Chabot** ❼, av de la Chapelle. Continue uphill for energising city views from the **chapel** ❽ steps, then zig-zag to **Molière & La Fontaine** ❾, on chemin Molière.

Cut between graves onto av Tranversale No 1 – spot potatoes atop **Parmentier's** ❿ headstone. Continue straight onto av Greffülhe and left onto av Tranversale No 2 to rub **Monsieur Noir's** ⓫ shiny crotch.

Navigation to **Édith Piaf** ⓬ and the **Mur des Fédérés** ⓭ is straightforward. End with lipstick-kissed Oscar Wilde ⓮ near the Porte Gambetta entrance.

TOP TIPS

→ **Say 'Cheese!'** Père Lachaise is photography paradise any time of day/year, but best are sunny autumn mornings after the rain.

→ **Guided Tours** Cemetery lovers will appreciate themed guided tours (two hours) led by entertaining cemetery historian Thierry Le Roi (www.necro-romantiques.com).

BRUNO DE HOGUES / GETTY IMAGES ©

Chopin, Division 11
Add a devotional note to the handwritten letters and flowers brightening the marble tomb of Polish composer/pianist Frédéric Chopin (1810–49), who spent his short adult life in Paris. His heart is buried in Warsaw.

Monuments aux Morts

Main Entrance

av du Puits

av Latérale du Sud

chemin Denon

chemin Méhul

av Principale

Bureaux de la Conservation

Porte du Repos

av Casimir Périer

chemin Maison

chemin Serré

Jim Morrison, Division 6
The original bust adorning the disgracefully dishevelled grave of Jim Morrison (1943–71), lead singer of The Doors, was stolen. Pay your respects to rock's greatest legend – no chewing gum or padlocks please.

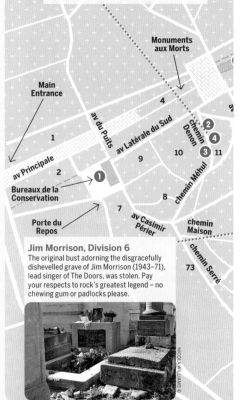

NICOLA WILLIAMS ©

André Chabot, Division 20

Contemporary photographer André Chabot (b 1941) shoots funerary art, hence the bijou 19th-century chapel he's equipped with monumental granite camera in preparation for the day he departs – and a QR code.

Molière & La Fontaine, Division 25

Parisians refused to leave their local *quartier* for Père Lachaise so in 1817 the authorities moved in popular playwright Molière (1622–73) and poet Jean de la Fontaine (1621–95). The marketing strategy worked.

Oscar Wilde, Division 89

Homosexual Irish writer Oscar Wilde (1854–1900) was forever scandalous: check the enormous packet of the sphinx on his tomb, sculpted by British-American sculptor Jacob Epstein 11 years after he died.

Monsieur Noir, Division 92

Cemetery sex stud Mr Black, alias 21-year-old journalist Victor Noir (1848–70), was shot by Napolèon III's nephew in a botched duel. Urban myth means women rub his crotch to boost fertility.

Édith Piaf, Division 97

The archbishop of Paris might have refused Parisian diva Édith Piaf (1915–63) the Catholic rite of burial, but that didn't stop more than 100,000 mourners attending her internment at Père Lachaise.

Mur des Fédérés, Division 76

This plain brick wall was where 147 Communard insurgents were lined up and shot in 1871. Equally emotive is the sculpted walkway of commemorative war memorials surrounding the mass grave.

Map labels:

av des Combattants Étrangers morts pour la France

Porte Gambetta Entrance

Crematorium

av Circulaire

av Tranversale No 3

Chapel

av de Saint Morys

av Tranversale No 1

av Tranversale No 2

chemin Berthollé

chemin Molière

rue de la Chapelle

Rond-Point Casimir Périer

av Greffülhe

chemin Lauriston

av Pacthod

Commemorative war memorials

chemin Lebrun

av Circulaire

Porte de la Réunion

Marché Bastille

Street Markets

Not simply places to shop, the city's street markets are social gatherings for the entire neighbourhood, and visiting one will give you a true appreciation for Parisian life.

Stall after stall of cheeses, stacked baguettes, sun-ripened tomatoes, freshly lopped pigs' trotters, spit-roasted chickens, glass bottles of olives and olive oils, quail eggs, boxes of chanterelle mushrooms and knobbly truffles, and prickly sea urchins on beds of crushed ice – along with belts, boots, wallets, cheap socks, chic hats, colourful scarves, striped t-shirts, wicker baskets, wind-up toys, buckets of flowers...Paris' street markets are a feast for the senses.

Great For...

☑ Don't Miss

The city is also home to some wonderful covered food markets.

Top Choices

Marché Bastille   Market
(Map p250; bd Richard Lenoir, 11e; ⊙7am-2.30pm Thu, to 3pm Sun; Ⓜ Bastille, Richard Lenoir) If you only get to one open-air street market in Paris, this one – stretching between the Bastille and Richard Lenoir metro stations – is among the city's very best.

Fresh market produce

LYDIA EVANS/GETTY IMAGES ©

The website www.paris.fr lists every market by *arrondissement* (city district), including speciality markets.

✕ **Take a Break**

Paris' markets have aromatic snacks and meals cooked on-site.

★ **Top Tip**

Neighbourhood street markets take place at least once a week, but never Mondays.

Marché d'Aligre   Market

(rue d'Aligre, 12e; ⊙9am-1pm & 4-7.30pm Tue-Fri, 9am-1pm & 3.30-7.30pm Sat, 9am-1.30pm Sun; Ⓜ Ledru-Rollin) All the staples of French cuisine can be found in this chaotic street market, a real favourite with Parisians. At weekends follow locals into the historic covered market hall, signposted **Marché Beauvau** (place d'Aligre, 12e; ⊙9am-1pm & 4-7.30pm Tue-Fri, 9am-1pm & 3.30-7.30pm Sat, 9am-1.30pm Sun; Ⓜ Ledru-Rollin), on place d'Aligre for a glass of white wine and platter of freshly shucked oysters.

The morning flea market Marché aux Puces d'Aligre (p156) takes place on the square.

Marché Raspail   Market

(bd Raspail btwn rue de Rennes & rue du Cherche Midi, 6e; ⊙regular market 7am-2.30pm Tue & Fri, organic market 9am-2pm Sun; Ⓜ Rennes) A traditional open-air market on Tuesday and Friday, Marché Raspail is especially popular on Sunday, when it's filled with *biologique* (organic) produce.

Marché Biologique des Batignolles   Market

(34 bd des Batignolles, 17e; ⊙9am-3pm Sat; Ⓜ Place de Clichy) Abuzz with market stalls, this busy boulevard in northern Paris had its own covered market from 1846 until 1867 (when it shut and moved to its current location on nearby rue Lemercier). These days it's the organic produce that pulls in the punters. Dozens of the 50 or so stalls offer tastings and everything is super fresh.

Marché Edgar Quinet   Market

(bd Edgar Quinet, 14e; ⊙7am-2.30pm Wed, to 3pm Sat; Ⓜ Edgar Quinet, Montparnasse Bienvenüe) Opposite Tour Montparnasse, this open-air street market teems with neighbourhood shoppers. There's always a great range of cheeses, as well as stalls sizzling up snacks to eat on the run, from crêpes to spicy felafels.

Avenue leading to Château de Versailles

VW PICS/GETTY IMAGES ©

Day Trip: Versailles

This monumental, 700-room palace and sprawling estate – with its gardens, fountains, ponds and canals – is a Unesco World Heritage–listed wonder situated an easy 40-minute train ride from central Paris.

Great For...

☑ **Don't Miss**
Summertime 'dancing water' displays set to music by baroque- and classical-era composers.

Amid magnificently landscaped formal gardens, this splendid and enormous palace was built in the mid-17th century during the reign of Louis XIV – the Roi Soleil (Sun King) – to project the absolute power of the French monarchy, which was then at the height of its glory. The château has undergone relatively few alterations since its construction, though almost all the interior furnishings disappeared during the Revolution and many of the rooms were rebuilt by Louis-Philippe (r 1830–48).

Some 30,000 workers and soldiers toiled on the structure, the bills for which all but emptied the kingdom's coffers.

Work began in 1661 under the guidance of architect Louis Le Vau (Jules Hardouin-Mansart took over from Le Vau in the mid-1670s); painter and interior designer Charles Le Brun; and landscape artist

An opulent entrance to the palace

Versailles 🚇 Av de St-Cloud

Versailles-Château
–Rive Gauche 🚉 Av de Paris

Versailles-
Chantier 🚉

❶ Need to Know

📞01 30 83 78 00; www.chateauversailles.
fr; place d'Armes; passport ticket incl
estate-wide access adult/child €18/free, with
musical events €25/free, palace €15/free;
🕑9am-6.30pm Tue-Sun Apr-Oct, to 5.30pm
Tue-Sun Nov-Mar; Ⓜ RER Versailles-Château–
Rive Gauche

✕ Take a Break

Nearby rue de Satory is lined with restaurants and cafes.

★ Top Tip

Arrive early morning and avoid Tuesday, Saturday and Sunday, Versailles'
busiest days.

André Le Nôtre, whose workers flattened
hills, drained marshes and relocated forests
as they laid out the seemingly endless
gardens (free except during musical events;
🕑gardens 8am-8.30pm Apr-Oct, to 6pm Nov-Mar,
park 7am-8.30pm Apr-Oct, 8am-6pm Nov-Mar),
ponds and fountains.

Le Brun and his hundreds of artisans
decorated every moulding, cornice, ceiling
and door of the interior with the most lux-
urious and ostentatious of appointments:
frescos, marble, gilt and woodcarvings,
many with themes and symbols drawn
from Greek and Roman mythology. The
King's Suite of the Grands Appartements
du Roi et de la Reine (King's and Queen's
State Apartments), for example, includes
rooms dedicated to Hercules, Venus, Diana,
Mars and Mercury. The opulence reaches

its peak in the Galerie des Glaces (Hall of
Mirrors), a 75m-long ballroom with 17 huge
mirrors on one side and, on the other, an
equal number of windows looking out over
the gardens and the setting sun.

To access areas that are otherwise off
limits and to learn more about Versailles'
history, prebook a 90-minute guided **tour**
(📞01 30 83 77 88; tours €7, plus palace entry;
🕑English-language tours 9.30pm Tue-Sun) of
the Private Apartments of Louis XV and
Louis XVI and the Opera House or Royal
Chapel. Tours also cover the most famous
parts of the palace.

The château is situated in the leafy,
bourgeois suburb of Versailles, about
22km southwest of central Paris. Take the
frequent RER C5 (€4.20) from Paris' Left
Bank RER stations to Versailles-Château–
Rive Gauche station.

Versailles

A DAY IN COURT

Visiting Versailles – even just the State Apartments – may seem overwhelming at first, but think of it as a house where people ate, drank, worked, slept and conspired and you'll be on the right path.

Some two decades into his long reign, Louis XIV began turning his father's hunting lodge into a palace large enough to house his entire court (to keep closer tabs on the 6000-strong army of courtiers). Sparing no expense, the Sun King employed the greatest artists and craftspeople of the day and by 1682 he'd created the most extravagant dormitory in history.

The royal schedule was as accurate and predictable as a Swiss watch. By following this itinerary of rooms you can recreate the king's day, starting with the **King's Bedchamber ❶** and the **Queen's Bedchamber ❷**, where the royal couple was roused at about the same time. The royal procession then leads through the **Hall of Mirrors ❸** to the **Royal Chapel ❹** for morning Mass and returns to the **Council Chamber ❺** for late-morning meetings with ministers. After lunch the king might ride or hunt or visit the **King's Library ❻**. Later he could join courtesans for an 'apartment evening' starting from the **Hercules Drawing Room ❼** or play billiards in the **Diana Drawing Room ❽** before supping at 10pm.

VERSAILLES BY NUMBERS

➡ **Rooms** 700 (11 hectares of roof)
➡ **Windows** 2153
➡ **Staircases** 67
➡ **Gardens and parks** 800 hectares
➡ **Trees** 200,000
➡ **Fountains** 50 (with 620 nozzles)
➡ **Paintings** 6300 (measuring 11km laid end to end)
➡ **Statues and sculptures** 2100
➡ **Objets d'art and furnishings** 5000
➡ **Visitors** 5.3 million per year

Queen's Bedchamber
Chambre de la Reine
The queen's life was on constant public display and even the births of her children were watched by crowds of spectators in her own bedchamber. **DETOUR »** The Guardroom, with a dozen armed men at the ready.

LUNCH BREAK

Diner-style food at Sister's Café, crêpes at Le Phare St-Louis or picnic in the park.

Guardroom

South Wing

King's Library
Bibliothèque du Roi
The last resident, bibliophile Louis XVI, loved geography and his copy of *The Travels of James Cook* (in English, which he read fluently) is still on the shelf here.

SAVVY SIGHTSEEING

Avoid Versailles on Monday (closed), Tuesday (Paris' museums close, so visitors flock here) and Sunday, the busiest day. Also, book tickets online so you don't have to queue.

Hall of Mirrors
Galerie des Glaces
The solid-silver candelabra and furnishings in this extravagant hall, devoted to Louis XIV's successes in war, were melted down in 1689 to pay for yet another conflict. **DETOUR»** The antithetical Peace Drawing Room, adjacent.

King's Bedchamber
Chambre du Roi
The king's daily life was anything but private and even his *lever* (rising) at 8am and *coucher* (retiring) at 11.30pm would be witnessed by up to 150 sycophantic courtiers.

Council Chamber
Cabinet du Conseil
This chamber, with carved medallions evoking the king's work, is where the monarch met his various ministers (state, finance, religion etc) depending on the days of the week.

Peace Drawing Room

Hall of Mirrors

Apollo Drawing Room

Marble Courtyard

Entrance

Entrance

North Wing

To Royal Opera

Diana Drawing Room
Salon de Diane
With walls and ceiling covered in frescos devoted to the mythical huntress, this room contained a large billiard table reserved for Louis XIV, a keen player.

Hercules Drawing Room
Salon d'Hercule
This salon, with its stunning ceiling fresco of the strong man, gave way to the State Apartments, which were open to courtiers three nights a week. **DETOUR»** Apollo Drawing Room, used for formal audiences and as a throne room.

Royal Chapel
Chapelle Royale
This two-storey chapel (with gallery for the royals and important courtiers, and the ground floor for the B-list) was dedicated to St Louis, patron of French monarchs. **DETOUR»** The sumptuous Royal Opera.

LOIC LAGARDE/GETTY IMAGES ©

Exploring Canal St-Martin

Bordered by shaded towpaths and traversed by iron footbridges, Canal St-Martin's quaint setting lured artists, designers and students, who set up artists' collectives, offbeat boutiques and neoretro cafes.

Great For...

☑ Don't Miss

A canal cruise – it's the best way to experience Paris' lesser-known waterway.

The charming, 4.5km-long canal was originally slated to be concreted over when barge transportation declined, but local residents rallied to save it. Enduring maritime legacies include old swing bridges that still pivot 90 degrees when boats pass through the canal's double locks.

Canal Cruises

Two companies, **Canauxrama** (www. canauxrama.com; 13 quai de la Loire, 19e; adult/ child €12/8; ⓂJaurès) and **Paris Canal Croisières** (☎01 42 40 96 97; www.pariscanal. com; Parc de la Villette, 19e; ☺mid-Mar–mid-Nov; ⓂPorte de Pantin), run leisurely trips along the Canal St-Martin, chugging back and forth between central Paris and Parc de la Villette. Boats pass through an under-ground section (livened up somewhat by an art installation).

ⓘ Need to Know

Map p251; MRépublique, Jaurès, Jacques Bonsergent

✕ Take a Break

The canal's banks are perfect picnicking territory; fantastic eateries hereabouts include Holybelly (p126).

★ Top Tip

Have a drink at Chez Prune (p172) and catch a gig at Point Éphémère (p187).

Art & Fashion

One of the first designers to open on bou-tique-lined rue Beaurepaire was **Liza Korn** (Map p250; www.liza-korn.com; 19 rue Beaurepaire, 10e; ⊘11am-2pm & 3-7.30pm Mon-Sat; MJacques Bonsergent), whose collections range from rock and roll fashion to a children's line. Vintage boutique **Frivoli** (Map p250; 26 rue Beaurepaire, 10e; ⊘11am-7pm Wed-Fri, 2-7pm Sat; MJacques Bonsergent) is across the street.

Local artwork is often on display at **Espace Beaurepaire** (Map p250; ☑01 42 45 59 64; www.espacebeaurepaire.com; 28 rue Beaurepaire, 10e; ⊘variable; MJacques Bonsergent) **FREE**, a gallery and cultural centre that also hosts events such as book signings, pop-up concept stores and dance performances.

Around the corner is rue de Marseille, another great shopping street. You'll find a trio of famous Parisian brands here – Maje,

Agnès B and APC – along with **Medecine Douce** (Map p250; www.bijouxmedecinedouce. com; 14 rue de Marseille, 10e; ⊘11am-7pm Tue-Sat; MRépublique, Jacques Bonsergent), a studio-showroom displaying gorgeous jewellery handmade on-site.

Artazart (www.artazart.com; 83 quai de Valmy, 10e; ⊘10.30am-7.30pm Mon-Fri, 11am-7.30pm Sat, 1-7.30pm Sun; MRépublique, Jacques Bonsergent) is the leading design bookshop in Paris.

Delivery Service

Once the weather warms up, **Pink Flamingo Pizza** (☑01 42 02 31 70; www.pinkflamingo pizza.com; 67 rue Bichat, 10e; pizzas €11.50-17; ⊘7-11.30pm Mon-Thu, noon-3pm & 7-11.30pm Fri-Sun; MJacques Bonsergent) unveils its secret weapon – pink helium balloons that the delivery guy uses to locate you and your perfect canalside picnic spot (GPS not needed). Order a Poulidor (duck, apple and chèvre) or a Basquiat (gorgonzola, figs and cured ham), pop into Le Verre Volé (p126) across the canal for the perfect bottle of vino and you're set.

Hôtel de Cluny

BRIAN KINNEY/SHUTTERSTOCK ©

Musée National du Moyen Âge

An enormous Roman-era bathhouse (c AD 200) and the ornate 15th-century mansion, the Hôtel de Cluny, house France's fascinating National Museum of the Middle Ages, famed for its medieval tapestries.

Great For...

☑ **Don't Miss**

The extraordinary Gallo-Roman remains.

The Hôtel de Cluny

Initially the residential quarters of the Cluny abbots, the Hôtel de Cluny was later occupied by Alexandre du Sommerard, who moved here in 1833 with his collection of medieval and Renaissance objects. Bought by the state after his death, the museum opened a decade later, retaining the Hôtel de Cluny's original layout and features.

Today it holds some fascinating relics, not least of which is an entire room (No 8) dedicated to statuary from Notre Dame's façade, removed during the Revolution and later used to support the foundations of a private mansion.

The restored 1st-floor late-Gothic chapel, La Chapelle de l'Hôtel de Cluny, with rich carvings of Christ on the cross, 13 angels, and floral and foliage ornaments, has direct access to the garden.

A stained-glass window of the museum

MAZIARZ/SHUTTERSTOCK ©

❶ Need to Know

Map p254; www.musee-moyenage.fr; 6 place
Paul Painlevé, 5e; adult/child €8/free, during
temporary exhibitions €9/free; ⊙9.15am-
5.45pm Wed-Mon; ⓜCluny-La Sorbonne

✕ Take a Break

Treat yourself to *choux* (pastry), tea and
champagne at the charming tearoom
and patisserie, Odette (p134).

★ Top Tip

Arrive after 3.30pm on Mondays,
Thursdays and Fridays to bypass
school groups.

Gallo-Roman Bathhouse

The museum's northwestern corner is where
you'll find the remains of the Gallo-Roman
bathhouse, built around AD 200. Look for the
display of the fragment of mosaic *Love Riding
a Dolphin*, as well as a gorgeous marble
bathtub from Rome. Outside the museum,
remnants of the other rooms – a *palestra*
(exercise room), *tepidarium* (warm bath) and
calidarium (hot bath) – are visible.

Tapestries

Upstairs on the 1st floor (room 13) are the
unicorn tapestries, representing the five
senses and an enigmatic sixth, perhaps the
heart. It's believed that they were originally
commissioned around 1500 by the Le Viste
family in Paris. Discovered in 1814 in the
Chateau de Boussac, they were acquired by
the museum in 1882.

Gardens

Small gardens to the museum's northeast,
including the Jardin Céleste (Celestial
Garden) and the Jardin d'Amour (Garden
of Love), have inspired works hanging
throughout the museum.

What's Nearby?

Panthéon   Mausoleum

(Map p254; www.monum.fr; place du Panthéon,
5e; adult/child €8.50/free; ⊙10am-6.30pm
Apr-Sep, to 6pm Oct-Mar; ⓜMaubert-Mutualité or
RER Luxembourg) Overlooking the city from
its Left Bank perch, the Panthéon's stately
neoclassical dome stands out as one of the
most recognisable icons on the Parisian
skyline. An architectural masterpiece, the
interior is impressively vast. Originally a
church and now a mausoleum, it has served
since 1791 as the resting place of some of
France's greatest thinkers, including Voltaire,
Rousseau, Braille and Hugo.

FAVILHA/GETTY IMAGES ©

Strolling the Champs-Élysées

No trip to Paris is complete without strolling this broad, tree-shaded avenue named for the Elysian Fields ('heaven' in Greek mythology), where Paris turns out for organised and impromptu celebrations.

Great For...

☑ Don't Miss

The mighty Arc de Triomphe (p42), which stands sentinel at the avenue's western end.

Landmark Sights

Grand Palais   Art Museum

(Map p248; ☎01 44 13 17 17; www.grandpalais.fr; 3 av du Général Eisenhower, 8e; adult/child €15/1; ⏱10am-8pm Sun, Mon & Thu, to 10pm Wed, Fri & Sat; Ⓜ Champs-Élysées–Clemenceau) Erected for the 1900 Exposition Universelle, the Grand Palais today houses several exhibition spaces beneath its huge 8.5-tonne art nouveau glass roof. Some of Paris' biggest shows (Renoir, Chagall, Turner) are held in the Galeries Nationales. Hours, prices and exhibition dates vary significantly for all galleries. Those listed here generally apply to the Galeries Nationales, but always check the website for exact details. Reserving a ticket online for any show is strongly advised.

Other exhibit spaces include the imaginative Nef – which plays host to concerts, art installations, a seasonal amusement

Grand Palais glass roof

ℹ Need to Know

Map p248; 8e; Ⓜ Charles de Gaulle-Étoile, George V, Franklin D Roosevelt, Champs-Élysées–Clemenceau

✕ Take a Break

Stop by historic tearoom Ladurée (p121), original creator of delectable macarons.

★ Top Tip

Cars are banished from the Champs-Élysées on the first Sunday of each month.

---

park and horse shows – and several other minor galleries, entered from av Winston-Churchill. There's also an MK2 cinema and fabulous restaurant, **Mini Palais** (Map p248; ☎ 01 42 56 42 42; www.minipalais. com; av Winston Churchill, 8e; lunch menu €29, mains €17-39; ⊙ 10am-2am, kitchen to midnight; Ⓜ Champs-Élysées–Clemenceau, Invalides).

Petit Palais   Art Museum

(Map p248; ☎ 01 53 43 40 00; www.petitpalais.par-is.fr; av Winston-Churchill, 8e; permanent collections free; ⊙ 10am-6pm Tue-Sun; Ⓜ Champs-Élysées–Clemenceau) This architectural stunner was built for the 1900 Exposition Universelle, and is home to the Paris municipality's Museum of Fine Arts, the Musée des Beaux-Arts de la Ville de Paris. It specialises in medieval and Renaissance objets d'art, such as porce-lain and clocks, tapestries, drawings, and 19th-century French painting and sculpture;

and also has paintings by such artists as Rembrandt, Colbert, Cézanne, Monet, Gaugin and Delacroix. The cafe here has lovely garden seating.

Place de la Concorde   Square

(Map p248; 8e; Ⓜ Concorde) Paris spreads around you, with views of the Eiffel Tower, the Seine and along the Champs-Élysées, when you stand in the city's largest square. Its 3300-year-old pink granite obelisk was a gift from Egypt in 1831. The square was first laid out in 1755 and originally named after King Louis XV, but its royal associations meant that it took centre stage during the Revolution – Louis XVI was the first to be guillotined here in 1793.

During the next two years, 1343 more people, including Marie Antoinette, Danton and Robespierre, also lost their heads here. The square was given its present name after the Reign of Terror in the hope that it would become a place of peace and harmony. The corners of the square are marked by eight statues representing what were once the largest cities in France.

Jardin des Tuileries

Filled with fountains, classical sculptures and magnificent panoramas at every turn, this quintessentially Parisian 28-hectare formal park constitutes part of the Banks of the Seine Unesco World Heritage Site.

Great For...

☑ **Don't Miss**

Combining a park visit with a stroll along the Champs-Élysées (p94).

Museums & Galleries

Musée de l'Orangerie Museum

(Map p248; ☎01 44 77 80 07; www.musee-orang-erie.fr; adult/child €9/free; ⊙9am-6pm Wed-Mon) Located in the southwestern corner of the Jardin des Tuileries, this museum, with the Jeu de Paume, is all that remains of the former Palais des Tuileries, which was razed during the Paris Commune in 1871. It exhibits important impressionist works, including a series of Monet's *Decorations des Nymphéas* (Water Lilies), as well as works by Cézanne, Matisse, Picasso, Renoir, Sisley, Soutine and Utrillo. An audioguide costs €5.

Jeu de Paume Gallery

(Map p248; ☎01 47 03 12 50; www.jeudepaume. org; 1 place de la Concorde, 8e; adult/child €10/ free; ⊙11am-9pm Tue, to 7pm Wed-Sun; Ⓜ Concorde) The Galerie du Jeu de Paume, which

ℹ Need to Know

Map p248; ⏱7am-11pm Jun-Aug, shorter hours rest of year; 🎫; ⓂTuileries, Concorde)

✕ Take a Break

Famed hot chocolate at Angelina (p170) comes with a pot of whipped cream.

★ Top Tip

Kids will love the the Fête des Tuileries funfair in July and August.

stages innovative photography exhibitions, is housed in an erstwhile *jeu de paume* (royal tennis court) in the northwestern corner of the Jardin des Tuileries.

What's Nearby?

Arc de Triomphe
du Carrousel   Monument

(Map p250; place du Carrousel, 1er; ⓂPalais Royal-Musée du Louvre) This triumphal arch, erected by Napoléon to celebrate his battlefield successes of 1805, sits with aplomb in the **Jardin du Carrousel**, the gardens immediately next to the Louvre. The eastern counterpoint to the other Arc de Triomphe (the more famous one), it is one of several monuments that comprise the *axe historique*, which terminates with the statue of Louis XIV next to the Pyramide du Louvre.

Colonne Vendôme   Monument

(Map p248; place Vendôme; ⓂTuileries, Opéra) In the centre of place Vendôme, this column consists of a stone core wrapped in a 160m-long bronze spiral made from hundreds of Austrian and Russian cannons captured by Napoléon at the Battle of Austerlitz in 1805. The statue on top depicts Napoléon in classical Roman dress.

Musée Maxim's   Museum

(Map p248; ☎01 42 65 30 47; www.maxims-musee-artnouveau.com; 3 rue Royale, 8e; adult/child €20/free; ⏱English tours 2pm Wed-Sun, closed Jul & Aug; ⓂConcorde) During the belle époque, Maxim's bistro was the most glamorous place to be in the capital. The restaurant has lost much of its cachet (though the food is actually excellent), but for art nouveau buffs, the real treasure is the upstairs museum. Opened by Maxim's owner, fashion designer Pierre Cardin, it's filled with some 550 pieces of art nouveau artworks, objets d'art and furniture detailed during one-hour guided tours.

BOTOND HORVATH/SHUTTERSTOCK ©

Sainte-Chapelle

This gemlike Holy Chapel is Paris'
most exquisite Gothic monument.
Try to save it for a sunny day, when
Paris' oldest, finest stained glass is
at its dazzling best.

Great For...

☑ Don't Miss

The ethereal experience of classical-
and sacred-music concerts amid the
stained glass.

Sainte-Chapelle was built in just six years
(compared with nearly 200 years for Notre
Dame) and consecrated in 1248. The chapel
was conceived by Louis IX to house his personal collection of holy relics, including the famous Ste-Couronne (Holy Crown), acquired
by the French king in 1239 from the emperors
of Constantinople for a sum of money easily
exceeding the amount it cost to build the
chapel. The wreath of thorns is safeguarded
today in the treasury at Notre Dame.

Statues, foliage-decorated capitals and
angels decorate this sumptuous, bijou
chapel. But it is the 1113 scenes depicted in
its 15 floor-to-ceiling stained-glass windows –
15.5m high in the nave, 13.5m in the apse –
that stun visitors. From the bookshop in the
former ground-floor chapel reserved for palace staff, spiral up the staircase to the upper

SIRAANAMWONG/GETTY IMAGES ©

❶ Need to Know

Map p250; ☎01 53 40 60 80, concerts 01 42 77 65 65; http://sainte-chapelle.monuments-nationaux.fr; 4 bd du Palais, 1er; adult/child €8.50/free, joint ticket with Conciergerie €15; ☺9.30am-6pm Thu-Tue, to 9pm Wed mid-May–mid-Sep, 9.30am-6pm Mar–mid-May & mid-Sep–Oct, 9am-5pm Nov-Feb; Ⓜ Cité

✕ Take a Break

Savour simple yet inspired fare at delightful little bistro Ma Salle à Manger (p133).

★ Top Tip

Combination tickets pre-purchased at the Conciergerie allow you to skip the ticket queues.

chapel, where only the king and his close friends were allowed.

Before arriving, download a free storyboard in English from the website to 'read' the 15-window biblical story – from Genesis through to the resurrection of Christ. Once here, rent an audioguide (€4.50/6 for one/two people) or join a free 1½-hour guided tour in English at 11am, 3pm or 4pm.

Sainte-Chapelle's location within the Palais de Justice (Law Courts) means security is tight; be sure to leave pocket knives, scissors etc at your accommodation. Even combination ticket-holders still need to go through the security queue.

You can peek at Sainte-Chapelle's exterior from across the street (albeit not a patch on its interior), by the law courts' magnificently gilded 18th-century gate facing rue de Lutèce.

What's Nearby?

Conciergerie   Monument

(Map p250; www.monuments-nationaux.fr; 2 bd du Palais, 1er; adult/child €8.50/free, joint ticket with Sainte-Chapelle €15; ☺9.30am-6pm; Ⓜ Cité) A royal palace in the 14th century, the Conciergerie later became a prison. During the Reign of Terror (1793–94) alleged enemies of the Revolution were incarcerated here before being brought before the Revolutionary Tribunal next door in the **Palais de Justice**. Top-billing exhibitions take place in the beautiful, Rayonnant Gothic **Salle des Gens d'Armes**, Europe's largest surviving medieval hall.

Of the almost 2800 prisoners held in the dungeons during the Reign of Terror (in various 'classes' of cells, no less) before being sent in tumbrils to the guillotine, the star prisoner was Queen Marie-Antoinette – see a reproduction of her cell.

STEFANO EMBER/SHUTTERSTOCK ©

Les Catacombes

*Paris' most macabre sight is its
series of subterranean passages
lined with skulls and bones. It's
a 2km walk through the creepy
ossuary and definitely not for the
faint-hearted.*

Great For...

☑ **Don't Miss**

Combining a visit to Les Catacombes
with a wander through Cimetière du
Montparnasse.

In 1785 it was decided to rectify the hygiene
problems of Paris' overflowing cemeteries
by exhuming the bones and storing them
in disused quarry tunnels; the Catacombes
were created in 1810.

The route through Les Catacombes
begins at a small, dark-green belle époque
building in the centre of a grassy area of
av Colonel Henri Roi-Tanguy, adjacent to
place Denfert Rochereau. After descending
20m (via 130 narrow, dizzying spiral steps)
below street level, you follow the dark,
subterranean passages to reach the ossuary itself, with a mind-boggling number of
bones and skulls of millions of Parisians
neatly packed along the walls.

The exit is back up 83 steps onto rue
Rémy Dumoncel, 14e (metro Mouton-
Duvernet), 700m southwest of av Colonel
Henri Roi-Tanguy. Bag searches are carried

OBSERVE.CO/SHUTTERSTOCK ©

❶ Need to Know

www.catacombes.paris.fr; 1 av Colonel Henri Roi-Tanguy, 14e; adult/child €12/free; ⏰10am-8pm Tue-Sun; Ⓜ Denfert Rochereau

✕ Take a Break

Book ahead for brilliant bistro dining at Jeu de Quilles (p141).

★ Top Tip

Wear sturdy shoes for the uneven, often-muddy surface and loose stones.

Bear in mind that the Catacombes are not suitable for young children. Also be aware there are no toilets, flash photography isn't permitted and the temperature is a cool 14°C below ground.

out to prevent visitors 'souveniring' bones. A **gift shop** (www.compoirdescatacombes.com; 31 rue Rémy Dumoncel, 14e; ⏰10.30am-8.30pm Tue-Sun; Ⓜ Alésia) selling quirky skull-and-bone-themed items (Jenga, candles, shot glasses) is across the street from the exit.

Visiting

A maximum of 200 people are allowed in the tunnels at a time and queues can be huge – when the queue extends beyond a 20-minute wait, you'll be handed a coupon with a return entry time later that day. Last entry is at 7pm.

Renting an audioguide (€5) greatly enhances the experience; 90-minute guided tours in English (€4.50) take place at 10am and noon on Tuesday.

What's Nearby?

Cimetière du Montparnasse
Cemetery

(www.paris.fr; 3 bd Edgar Quinet, 14e; ⏰8am-6pm Mon-Fri, 8.30am-6pm Sat, 9am-6pm Sun; Ⓜ Edgar Quinet) FREE Opened in 1824, Montparnasse Cemetery, Paris' second largest after Père Lachaise, sprawls over 19 hectares shaded by 1200 trees, including maples, ash, lime trees and conifers. Among its illustrious 'residents' are poet Charles Baudelaire, writer Guy de Maupassant, playwright Samuel Beckett, sculptor Constantin Brancusi, painter Chaim Soutine, photographer Man Ray, industrialist André Citroën, Captain Alfred Dreyfus of the infamous Dreyfus Affair, actress Jean Seberg, and philosopher-writer couple Jean-Paul Sartre and Simone de Beauvoir, as well as legendary singer Serge Gainsbourg.

RIEGER BERTRAND/HEMIS.FR/GETTY IMAGES ©

Palais Garnier

The fabled 'phantom of the opera' lurked in this opulent opera house designed in 1860 by Charles Garnier (then an unknown 35-year-old architect). It offers behind-the-scenes tours.

Reserve a spot on an English-language guided tour or take an unguided tour of the attached museum, with posters, costumes, backdrops, original scores and other memorabilia, which includes a behind-the scenes peek (except during matinées and rehearsals). Highlights include the Grand Staircase and horseshoe-shaped, gilded auditorium with red velvet seats, a massive chandelier and Chagall's gorgeous ceiling mural.

Interestingly, a prop man at the opera set up beehives on the roof some 20 years ago – the honey is now sold at the gift shop when available.

What's Nearby

Église de la Madeleine   Church
(Church of St Mary Magdalene; Map p248; www.
eglise-lamadeleine.com; place de la Madeleine,
8e; ⊙9.30am-7pm; MMadeleine) Place de la
Madeleine is named after the 19th-century

Great For...

☑ **Don't Miss**

Taking a stroll through the beautiful Jardin des Tuileries (p96) nearby.

neoclassical church at its centre, the Église de la Madeleine. Constructed in the style of a massive Greek temple, 'La Madeleine' was consecrated in 1842 after almost a century of design changes and construction delays.

The church is a popular venue for classical-music concerts (some free).

On the south side, the monumental staircase affords one of the city's most quintessential Parisian panoramas. From here, you can see down rue Royale to place de la Concorde and its obelisk and across the Seine to the Assemblée Nationale. The Invalides' gold dome appears in the background.

Jardin du Palais Royal Gardens
(Map p250; 2 place Colette, 1er; ☺7am-10.15pm Apr & May, to 11pm Jun-Aug, shorter hours rest of year; ⓂPalais Royal-Musée du Louvre) **FREE**
The Jardin du Palais Royal is a perfect spot to sit, contemplate and picnic between

boxed hedges, or shop in the arcades that frame the garden: the Galerie de Valois (east), Galerie de Montpensier (west) and Galerie Beaujolais. However, it's the southern end of the complex, polka-dotted with sculptor Daniel Buren's 260 black-and-white striped columns, that has become the garden's signature feature.

This elegant urban space is fronted by the neoclassical **Palais Royal** (closed to the public), constructed in 1633 by Cardinal Richelieu but mostly dating to the late 18th century. Louis XIV hung out here in the 1640s; today it is home to the **Conseil d'État** (State Council; Map p250).

The **Galerie de Valois** is the most up-market arcade, with designer boutiques like Stella McCartney and Pierre Hardy. Across the garden, in the **Galerie de Montpensier**, the Revolution broke out on a warm mid-July day just three years after the galleries opened in the Café du Foy. The third arcade, tiny **Galerie Beaujolais**, is crossed by **Passage du Perron**, a passageway above which the writer Colette (1873–1954) lived out the last dozen years of her life.

Seine-Side Romantic Meander

The world's most romantic city has no shortage of beguiling spots, but the Seine and its surrounds are Paris at its most seductive. Descend the steps along the quays wherever possible to stroll along the water's edge.

Start: Place de la Concorde
Distance: 7km
Duration: 3 hours

3 Take the steps to **Square du Vert Galant**, before ascending to place du Pont Neuf and place Dauphine.

Classic Photo: The 360-degree Parisian panorama from place de la Concorde.

1 After taking in the panorama at place de la Concorde, stroll through the **Jardin des Tuileries**.

JEAN-PIERRE LESCOURRET/GETTY IMAGES ©

2 Walk through the Jardin de l'Oratoire to the **Cour Carrée** and exit at the Jardin de l'Infante.

PAVEL L PHOTO AND VIDEO/SHUTTERSTOCK ©

7 End your romantic meander at the tranquil **Jardin des Plantes**. Cruise back along the Seine by Batobus.

CHICUREL ARNAUD/HEMIS.FR/GETTY IMAGES ©

N
0 — 500 m
0 — 0.25 miles

Jardin du Palais Royal

M Palais-Royal – Musée du Louvre

2

R du Louvre

M Louvre Rivoli

Pont Neuf **M**

Q du Louvre

3

Pont Neuf

Q des Grands Augustins

M Châtelet

M Cité

Île de la Cité

Bd du Palais

M St-Michel

St-Michel– Notre Dame

Bd St-Germain

4

Sq Jean XXIII

Pont St-Louis

Hôtel de Ville

4E

Q de l'Hôtel de Ville

Pont Marie

Île St-Louis

5

Pont de Sully

6

Bd St-Germain

Jardin du Luxembourg

Place Monge **M**

Jardin des Plantes

R Cuvier

Q Henri IV

Q St-Bernard

Seine

7 FINISH

R Buffon

M Place Monge

Gare d'Austerlitz **A**

4 Curl up with a volume of poetry in the magical **Shakespeare & Company** bookshop.

DENNIS K. JOHNSON/GETTY IMAGES ©

Take a Break...
Morning or night, try hip **Café Saint Régis** (6 rue Jean du Bellay, 4e; ⊙8am-2am)

5 Cross to Île St-Louis and share an ice cream from glacier (ice-cream maker) **Berthillon**.

6 Wander among late-20th-century unfenced sculptures at the **Musée de la Sculpture en Plein Air** (Open-Air Sculpture Museum).

PHOTO BY BENJAWAN SITTIDECH/GETTY IMAGES ©

Hôtel des Invalides

Flanked by the 500m-long Esplanade des Invalides lawns, this massive military complex built in the 1670s by Louis XIV to house 4000 invalides (disabled war veterans) contains Napoléon's tomb.

Great For...

☑ **Don't Miss**

France's largest military museum, the Musée de l'Armée.

On 14 July 1789, a mob broke into the Hôtel des Invalides and seized 32,000 rifles before heading on to the prison at Bastille and the start of the French Revolution.

In the **Cour d'Honneur**, the nation's largest collection on the history of the French military is displayed at the **Musée de l'Armée** (Army Museum; Map p248; www.musee-armee.fr; 129 rue de Grenelle, 7e; incl in Hôtel des Invalides entry; ⊗10am-6pm Apr-Oct, to 5pm Nov-Mar; MVarenne). South is **Église St-Louis des Invalides**, once used by soldiers, and **Église du Dôme** (Map p248; www.musee-armee.fr; 129 rue de Grenelle, 7e; incl in Hôtel des Invalides entry; ⊗10am-6pm Apr-Oct, to 5pm Nov-Mar; MVarenne) which, with its sparkling golden dome (1677–1735), is one of the finest religious edifices erected under Louis XIV and was the inspiration for the US Capitol building. It received the

NEIL FARRIN/GETTY IMAGES ©

ℹ **Need to Know**

Map p248; www.musee-armee.fr; 129 rue de Grenelle, 7e; adult/child €11/free; ☺10am-6pm Apr-Oct, to 5pm Nov-Mar, hours can vary; Ⓜ Varenne

✕ **Take a Break**

Coutume (p181) brews up some of Paris' best coffee from its own-roasted beans.

★ **Top Tip**

Atmospheric classical concerts (ranging from €5 to €30) take place regularly here year-round.

---

remains of Napoléon in 1840. The extravagant **Tombeau de Napoléon 1er**, in the centre of the church, comprises six coffins fitting into one another like a Russian doll. Scale models of towns, fortresses and châteaux across France fill the esoteric **Musée des Plans-Reliefs**.

Admission includes entry to all Hôtel des Invalides sights. Hours for individual sites often vary – check the website for updates.

What's Nearby?
Église St-Germain des Prés   Church
(Map p250; www.eglise-stgermaindespres.fr; 3 place St-Germain des Prés, 6e; ☺8am-7.45pm; Ⓜ St-Germain des Prés) Paris' oldest standing church, the Romanesque St Germanus of the Fields was built in the 11th century on the

site of a 6th-century abbey and was the main place of worship in Paris until the arrival of Notre Dame. It's since been altered many times, but the **Chapelle de St-Symphorien** (to the right as you enter) was part of the original abbey and is believed to be the resting place of St Germanus (496–576), the first bishop of Paris.

The Merovingian kings were buried here during the 6th and 7th centuries, but their tombs disappeared during the Revolution. Over the western entrance, the **bell tower** has changed little since 990, although the spire dates only from the 19th century.

An English brochure (€10) is available. Free organ concerts are held on the last Sunday of the month; check the website's calendar for times. Other concerts take place on Thursdays and Fridays at 8.30pm; details including prices are listed online.

CHICUREL ARNAUD/HEMIS.FR/GETTY IMAGES ©

Jardin des Plantes

Founded in 1626 as a medicinal herb garden for Louis XIII, Paris' 24-hectare botanic gardens are an idyllic spot to stroll or visit its museums or zoo.

Great For...

☑ Don't Miss

The gardens' beautiful glass-and-metal Grandes Serres (greenhouses).

Visually defined by the double alley of plane trees that run the length of the park, these sprawling gardens allow you to escape the city concrete for a spell.

Highlights here include peony and rose gardens, an alpine garden, and the gardens of the École de Botanique, used by students of the school and green-fingered Parisians. The gorgeous glass-and-metal **Grandes Serres** (Map p254; www.mnhn.fr; adult/child €6/4; ⏰10am-6pm; Ⓜ Jussieu) – a series of four greenhouses – have been in use since 1714, and several of Henri Rousseau's jungle paintings, sometimes on display in the Musée d'Orsay, were inspired by his frequent visits here.

CHRISTIAN RIVIERE/GETTY IMAGES ©

❶ Need to Know

Map p254; www.jardindesplantes.net; place Valhubert & 36 rue Geoffroy-St-Hilaire, 5e; ⏱7.30am-8pm Apr-Oct, 8am-5.30pm Nov-Mar; Ⓜ Gare d'Austerlitz, Censier Daubenton, Jussieu; FREE

✕ Take a Break

Bring a picnic with you (but watch out for the automatic sprinklers!).

★ Top Tip

A tranquil way to travel to/from here is by Batobus (p239) along the Seine.

Museums & Zoo

Muséum National d'Histoire Naturelle
Museum

(Map p254; www.mnhn.fr; place Valhubert & 36 rue Geoffroy-St-Hilaire, 5e; Ⓜ Gare d'Austerlitz, Censier Daubenton, Jussieu) Despite the name, the Natural History Museum is not a single building, but a collection of sites throughout France. Its historic home is in the Jardin des Plantes, and it's here you'll find the greatest number of branches: taxidermied animals in the excellent **Grande Galerie de l'Évolution** (Map p254; www.mnhn.fr; 36 rue Geoffroy-St-Hilaire, 5e; adult/child €9/free; ⏱10am-6pm Wed-Mon; Ⓜ Censier Daubenton), fossils and dinosaur skeletons in the **Galeries d'Anatomie Comparée et de Paléontologie** (Map p254; www.mnhn.fr; 2 rue Buffon, 5e; adult/child €7/free; ⏱10am-5pm Mon & Wed-Fri, to 6pm Sat & Sun Apr-Sep, 10am-5pm

Wed-Mon Oct-Mar; Ⓜ Gare d'Austerlitz) and meteorites and crystals in the **Galerie de Minéralogie et de Géologie** (Map p254; www.mnhn.fr; 36 rue Geoffroy-St-Hilaire, 5e; adult/child €6/free; ⏱10am-5pm Mon & Wed-Fri, to 6pm Sat & Sun Apr-Sep, 10am-5pm Wed-Mon Oct-Mar; Ⓜ Censier Daubenton).

Created in 1793, the National Museum of Natural History became a site of significant scientific research in the 19th century. Of the three museums here, the four-floor Grande Galerie de l'Évolution is a particular winner if you're travelling with kids: life-sized elephants, tigers and rhinos play safari, and imaginative exhibits on evolution, extinction and global warming fill 6000 sq metres. The temporary exhibits are generally excellent. Within this building is a separate attraction, the **Galerie des Enfants** (Map p254; www.mnhn.fr; 36 rue Geoffroy-St-Hilaire, 5e; adult/child €11/9; ⏱10am-6pm, last entry 5pm; Ⓜ Censier Daubenton) – a hands-on science museum tailored to children from ages six to 12.

Ménagerie du Jardin
des Plantes   Zoo

(Map p254; www.mnhn.fr; 57 rue Cuvier, 5e; adult/child €13/9; ☉9am-6pm Mon-Fri, to 6.30pm Sat & Sun Easter-Oct, to 5pm Nov-Easter; Ⓜ Gare d'Austerlitz) Like the Jardin des Plantes in which it's located, this 1000-animal zoo is more than a tourist attraction, also doubling as a research centre for the reproduction of rare and endangered species. During the Prussian siege of 1870, the animals of the day were themselves endangered, when almost all were eaten by starving Parisians.

Do note that the recently renovated zoo (p32) in Vincennes is considerably larger.

What's Nearby?

Mosquée de Paris   Mosque

(Map p254; ☏01 45 35 97 33; www.la-mosquee.com; 2bis place du Puits de l'Ermite, 5e; adult/child €3/2; ☉mosque 9am-noon & 2-7pm Sat-Thu Apr-Sep, 9am-noon & 2-6pm Sat-Thu Oct-Mar; Ⓜ Place Monge) Paris' central mosque, with a striking 26m-high minaret, was completed in 1926 in an ornate art deco Moorish style. You can visit the interior to admire the intricate tilework and calligraphy. A separate entrance leads to the wonderful North African–style **hammam** (Map p254; ☏01 43 31 14 32; 39 rue Geoffroy-St-Hilaire, 5e; admission/spa package €18/from €43; ☉10am-9pm Mon, Wed, Thu & Sat, 2-9pm Fri;), **restaurant** (Map p254; ☏01 43 31 14 32; 39 rue Geoffroy-

Mosquée de Paris

St-Hilaire, 5e; mains €15-26; ⊙kitchen noon-2.30pm & 7.30-10.30pm) and **tearoom** (p179), and a small souk (actually more of a gift shop). Visitors must be modestly dressed.

Musée de la Sculpture en Plein Air
Museum

(Map p254; quai St-Bernard, 5e; Ⓜ Gare d'Austerlitz) FREE Along quai St-Bernard, this open-air sculpture museum (also known as the Jardin Tino Rossi) has more than 50 late 20th-century unfenced sculptures, and makes a great picnic spot. A salad beneath a César or a baguette beside a Brancusi is a pretty classy way to see the Seine up close.

> ★ **Don't Miss**
> The incredible views from the top (9th) floor observation terrace of the Institut du Monde Arabe.

ERIC SCHAEFFER/GETTY IMAGES ©

Institut du Monde Arabe
Architecture, Museum

(Arab World Institute; Map p254; www.imarabe. org; 1 place Mohammed V, 5e; adult/child €8/4; ⊙10am-6pm Tue-Thu, to 9.30pm Fri, to 7pm Sat & Sun; Ⓜ Jussieu) The Arab World Institute was jointly founded by France and 18 Middle Eastern and North African nations in 1980, with the aim of promoting cross-cultural dialogue. In addition to hosting concerts, film screenings and a research centre, the stunning landmark is also home to a museum and temporary exhibition space.

You certainly can't miss the building: architect Jean Nouvel took his inspiration from traditional latticed-wood windows, creating thousands of modern *mashrabiya*, photo-electrically sensitive apertures built into the glass walls that regulate the amount of light that enters the interior.

Docks en Seine
Cultural Centre

(Cité de la Mode et du Design; www.cite-modedesign.fr; 34 quai d'Austerlitz, 13e; ⊙10am-midnight; Ⓜ Gare d'Austerlitz) Framed by a lurid-lime wave-like glass façade, a transformed Seine-side warehouse now houses the French fashion institute, the Institut Français de la Mode (hence the docks' alternative name, Cité de la Mode et du Design), mounting fashion and design exhibitions and events throughout the year. Other draws include an entertainment-themed contemporary-art museum **Art Ludique-Le Musée** (www.artludique.com; Docks en Seine, 34 quai d'Austerlitz, 13e; adult/child €16.50/11; ⊙11am-7pm Mon, 11am-10pm Wed-Fri, 10am-10pm Sat & Sun; Ⓜ Gare d'Austerlitz), along with ultra-hip bars, clubs and restaurants and huge riverside terraces.

For the best view of the water-facing façade, cross the Seine over Pont Charles de Gaulle.

> ✕ **Take a Break**
> Sip a sweet mint tea and nibble on a *pâtisserie orientale* at the Mosquée de Paris' tearoom.

HEMIS.FR/RM/GETTY IMAGES ©

Day Trip: Maison et Jardins de Claude Monet

Monet lived in Giverny from 1883 until his death in 1926, in a rambling house – surrounded by flower-filled gardens – that's now the immensely popular Maison et Jardins de Claude Monet.

Great For...

☑ Don't Miss

Monet's trademark lily pond, immortalised in his *Nymphéas* (Water Lilies) series.

Monet's home for the last 43 years of his life is now a delightful house-museum. His pastel-pink house and Water Lily studio stand on the periphery of the Clos Normand, with its symmetrically laid-out gardens bursting with flowers. Monet bought the Jardin d'Eau (Water Garden) in 1895 and set about creating his trademark lily pond, as well as the famous Japanese bridge (since rebuilt).

The charmingly preserved house and beautiful bloom-filled gardens (rather than Monet's works) are the draws here.

Draped with purple wisteria, the Japanese bridge blends into the asymmetrical foreground and background, creating the intimate atmosphere for which the 'painter of light' was renowned.

Seasons have an enormous effect on Giverny. From early to late spring, daffodils,

PASCAL PRETI/GETTY IMAGES ©

Vernon

Maison et Jardins de Claude Monet

Giverny

Vétheuil

Seine

Pacy-sur-Eure

Mantes-la-Jolie

❶ Need to Know

☏02 32 51 28 21; http://fondation-monet.com; 84 rue Claude Monet; adult/child €9.50/5.50, incl Musée des Impressionnismes Giverny €16.50/8.50; ☉9.30am-6pm Easter-Oct

✗ Take a Break

Michelin-starred dishes are exquisite at country estate **Le Jardin des Plumes** (1 rue du Milieu; 3-course/tasting menu €48/75, mains €32-48; ☉12.15-1.45pm & 7.15-9pm Wed-Sun, hotel closed Mon & Tue Nov-Mar).

★ Top Tip

Note the sight closes from November to Easter, along with most accommodation and restaurants.

tulips, rhododendrons, wisteria and irises appear, followed by poppies and lilies. By June, nasturtiums, roses and sweet peas are in flower. Around September, there are dahlias, sunflowers and hollyhocks.

Combined tickets with Paris' **Musée Marmottan Monet** (☏01 44 96 50 33; www.marmottan.fr; 2 rue Louis Boilly, 16e; adult/child €11/6.50; ☉10am-6pm Tue-Sun, to 9pm Thu; Ⓜ La Muette) cost €20.50/12 per adult/child, and combined adult tickets with Paris' Musée de l'Orangerie cost €18.50.

Visiting

The tiny country village of Giverny is 74km northwest of Paris. From Paris' Gare St-Lazare there are up to 15 daily trains to Vernon (€14.70, 45 minutes to one hour), 7km to the west of Giverny, from where buses, taxis and cycle/walking tracks run to Giverny.

Shuttle buses (€8 return, 20 minutes, four daily Easter to October) meet most trains from Paris at Vernon. There are limited seats, so arrive early for the return trip from Giverny.

Rent bikes (cash only) at the **Café L'Arrivée de Giverny** (☏02 32 21 16 01; 1 place de la Gare, Vernon; per day €15; ☉7am-11pm), opposite the train station in Vernon, from where Giverny is a signposted 5km along a direct (and flat) cycle/walking track.

Taxis (☏02 32 51 10 24) usually wait outside the train station in Vernon and charge around €15 for the one-way trip to Giverny. There's no taxi rank in Giverny, however, so you'll need to phone one for the return trip to Vernon.

A 10-minute stroll from the museum, Le Jardin des Plumes has beautiful rooms and suites (€180 to €350) and exquisite cuisine.

Be aware that the village has no public toilets, ATMs or bureaux de change.

DINING OUT

Produce-laden markets, intimate bistros, gastronomic temples and more

Dining Out

The inhabitants of some cities rally around local sports teams, but in Paris, they rally around la table – and everything on it. Pistachio macarons, shots of tomato consommé, decadent bœuf bourguignon, a gooey wedge of Camembert running onto the cheese plate...food is not fuel here, it's the reason you get up in the morning.

Paris doesn't have its own 'local' cuisine, but is the crossroads for the regional flavours of France. Dishes from the hot south favour olive oil, garlic and tomatoes; the cooler, pastoral northern regions turn to cream and butter; and coastal areas concentrate on seafood. The freshness of ingredients and reliance on natural flavours combined with refined, often very complex cooking methods – and, of course, wine – means you're in a gourmet's paradise.

In This Section

Price Ranges

The following price ranges apply to a two-course meal:

€	less than €20
€€	€20–€40
€€€	more than €40

Tipping

A *pourboire* (tip) isn't necessary, as service is always included in the bill, but it's not uncommon to round up if you were pleased with your waiter.

**Montmartre &
Northern Paris**
Neobistros, wine bars
and world cuisine
(p125)

**Champs-Élysées &
Grands Boulevards**
Big-name chefs,
backstreet bistros
(p121)

**Louvre &
Les Halles**
Trendy restaurants
on the rise (p122)

**Le Marais,
Ménilmontant &
Belleville**
Premier foodie
destination
(p127)

**Eiffel Tower &
Western Paris**
Gastronomic palaces
and museum restaurants
(p120)

Seine

*Eiffel
Tower*

**St-Germain &
Les Invalides**
Chic cafes,
haute cuisine (p136)

The Islands
Romantic setting
but limited
options (p133)

Latin Quarter
Cheap eats and
Left Bank treasures
(p134)

**Bastille &
Eastern Paris**
Balances tradition
and innovation
(p130)

Seine

**Montparnasse
& Southern Paris**
Historic brasseries,
neighbourhood favourites
(p140)

Useful Phrases

I'd like to reserve a table for...
Je voudrais réserver une table pour...

... (eight) o'clock *(vingt) heures*

...one/two/three people *...une/deux/
trois...personnes*

I don't eat... *Je ne mange pas...*

Please bring the bill. *Apportez-moi
l'addition, s'il vous plaît.*

Must-Try/Classic Dishes

Bœuf bourguignon Beef marinated
and cooked in young red wine with
mushrooms, onions, carrots and bacon.

Confit de canard Duck cooked slowly
in its own fat.

Entrecôte Steak.

Macarons Two light-as-air ground-
almond biscuits sandwiched with
ganache filling, in a rainbow of colours
and flavours.

Tarte Tatin Upside-down apple tart.

The Best...

Experience Paris' top
restaurants & cafes

Traditional French

À la Biche au Bois (p131) Game, especially *la biche*, is the speciality of the countrified 'doe in the woods'.

Le Miroir (p126) Excellent French standards at this Montmartre favourite.

Bouillon Racine (p137) Art nouveau jewel with traditional fare inspired by age-old recipes.

Le Bon Georges (p122) For those who thrive on nostalgia.

Wine-Bar Dining

Le Verre Volé (p126) Excellent wines, expert advice and hearty *plats du jour*.

Vivant (p127) Where else will you get to wine and dine in a century-old exotic bird shop?

Floquifil (p122) The backstreet Parisian wine-bar dining experience of your imagination.

Frenchie Bar à Vins (p123) Can't get a reservation at Frenchie? Try the wine bar instead.

Neobistros

Richer (p121) Smart setting and genius flavour combinations, but no reservations, so arrive early.

Mamou (p122) For *haute cuisine* sans *haute* attitude.

Abri (p126) Unassuming temple to gastronomic wizardry.

Semilla (p138) Edgy, modern dishes in factory-style premises.

Le Beurre Noisette (p140) Creative, locally loved cooking.

Clover (p138) Watch the chefs at work in the combined dining space/kitchen.

Classic Bistros

Le Petit Rétro (p120) Zinc bar and art nouveau tiling.

La Tour de Montlhéry – Chez Denise (p122) Red-chequered tablecloths, and snails on the menu.

Le Bistrot Paul Bert (p131) Legendary address with timeless vintage decor and perfectly executed classic dishes.

Chez Paul (p131) Paris as your grandmother knew it.

Chez Dumonet (p137) The quintessential Parisian bistro experience, lace curtains and all.

Terraces

L'Été en Pente Douce (p125) The finest terrace in Montmartre.

Le Caveau du Palais (p133) Contemporary French fare on the Île de la Cité's pretty place Dauphine.

Shakespeare & Company Café (p134) Live the Left Bank literary dream.

La Salle à Manger (p134) Tree-shaded terrace at the foot of foodie rue Mouffetard.

Views

Le Jules Verne (p120) A magical, Michelin-starred address perched in the Eiffel Tower.

Le Comptoir du Panthéon (p134) Cafe right by the Panthéon, with Eiffel Tower views.

La Tour d'Argent (p136) Gastronomic dining overlooking Notre Dame.

Le Ciel de Paris (p141) City panoramas from 'the Sky of Paris' atop Tour Montparnasse.

Les Ombres (p121) In the patterned shadows of the Eiffel Tower.

By Budget

€

Fric-Frac (p125) Wildly creative croques monsieurs by Canal St-Martin.

Au Pied de Fouet (p137) Bistro classics are astonishingly good value at this 150-year-old charmer.

€€

Le Casse Noix (p140) Cosy retro interior, affordable prices and exceptional cuisine.

Le Clos Y (p141) Utterly original daily changing menus.

€€€

Restaurant David Toutain (p140) Mystery degustation courses showcasing creative high-end cooking.

Septime (p131) A beacon of modern cuisine.

★ Lonely Planet's Top Choices

Restaurant AT (p135) Abstract-art-like masterpieces made from rare ingredients.

Restaurant Guy Savoy (p139) Resplendent triple-Michelin-starred flagship rehoused in the neoclassical mint.

Le Pantruche (p126) Superb modern French cuisine at fantastic value.

Hugo Desnoyer (p120) Feast for meat lovers courtesy of Paris' most famous butcher.

✕ Eiffel Tower & Western Paris

Firmin Le Barbier   French €€

(Map p248; 📞01 45 51 21 55; www.firminlebarbier.fr; 20 rue de Monttessuy, 7e; mains €26-35; 🕙noon-2pm Wed-Fri & Sun, 7-10.30pm Wed-Sat; Ⓜ Pont de l'Alma) This brick-walled bistro was opened by a retired surgeon turned gourmet, and his passion is apparent in everything from the personable service to the wine list. The menu is traditional French (sirloin steak with polenta, decadent boeuf bourguignon), while the modern interior is bright and cheery with an open kitchen. Find it a five-minute walk from the Eiffel Tower. Reserve.

Le Petit Rétro   Bistro €€

(Map p248; 📞01 44 05 06 05; www.petitretro.fr; 5 rue Mesnil, 16e; 2-/3-course menus lunch €26/31, dinner €30/36; 🕙noon-2.30pm & 7-10.30pm Mon-Wed, to 11pm Thu-Sat; Ⓜ Victor Hugo) From the gorgeous 'Petit Rétro' emblazoned on the zinc bar to the ceramic, art nouveau folk tiles on the wall, this is a handsome old-style bistro. Its fare is French classic: for example, blood sausage, *blanquette de veau* (veal in a butter and cream sauce) and *oreilles de cochon* (pig's ears). Delicious.

Omelet and *frites*

58 Tour Eiffel   Brasserie €€

(Map p248; 📞01 45 55 20 04; www.restaurants-toureiffel.com; 1st fl, Eiffel Tower, Champ de Mars, 7e; 2-/3-course lunch menus €22.50/27, dinner menus €70/80; 🕙11.30am-4.30pm & 6.30-11pm; Ⓜ Bir Hakeim or RER Champ de Mars-Tour Eiffel) While the food is nothing to write home about, you'll certainly remember the meal – after all, a table on the 1st floor of the Eiffel Tower is only bested by the Michelin-starred Jules Verne, one floor up. Make reservations at the kiosk between the north and east pillars and you can skip the queue. Avoid online bookings; it's considerably more expensive.

Hugo Desnoyer   Modern French €€€

(📞01 46 47 83 00; www.hugodesnoyer.fr; 28 rue du Docteur Blanche, 16e; mains from €28; 🕙restaurant 11.30am-3.30pm Tue-Sat, 8-11pm Wed; Ⓜ Jasmin) Hugo Desnoyer is Paris' most famous butcher and the trip to his shop in the 16e is well worth it. Arrive by noon or reserve to snag a table and settle down to a *table d'hôte* (set menu at fixed price) feast of homemade terrines, quiches, foie gras and cold cuts followed by the finest meat in Paris – cooked to perfection *naturellement*.

A more convenient branch, **Steak Point** (Lafayette Gourmet, bd Haussmann, 9e; mains €14-26; 🕙noon-7.30pm Mon-Sat; Ⓜ Havre Caumartin or RER Auber), is located in the basement of Galeries Lafayette Gourmet.

L'Astrance   Gastronomic €€€

(Map p248; 📞01 40 50 84 40; 4 rue Beethoven, 16e; lunch menus €70-150, dinner €230; 🕙12.15-1.15pm & 8.15-9.15pm Tue-Fri; Ⓜ Passy) It's been over 15 years since Pascal Barbot's dazzling cuisine at the three-star L'Astrance made its debut, but it has shown no signs of losing its cutting edge. Look beyond the complicated descriptions on the menu – what you should expect are teasers of taste that you never even knew existed. Reserve one to two months in advance.

Le Jules Verne   Gastronomic €€€

(Map p248; 📞01 45 55 61 44; www.julesverne-paris.com; 2nd fl, Eiffel Tower, Champ de Mars, 7e; menus lunch €105, dinner €190-230;

⏰noon-1.30pm & 7-9.30pm; Ⓜ Bir Hakeim or RER Champ de Mars–Tour Eiffel) Book way ahead (online only) to feast on Michelin-starred cuisine and the most beautiful view of Paris at this magical address, on the Eiffel Tower's 2nd floor. Cuisine is contemporary, with a five- or six-course 'experience' menu allowing you to taste the best of chef Pascal Féraud's stunning gastronomic repertoire.

Les Ombres   Modern French €€€

(Map p248; 📞 01 47 53 68 00; www.lesombres-restaurant.com; 27 quai Branly, 7e; 2-/3-course weekday lunch menus €35/42, dinner menu €71; ⏰noon-2.15pm & 7-10.20pm; Ⓜ Iéna or RER Pont de l'Alma) This glass-enclosed rooftop restaurant on the 5th floor of the Musée du Quai Branly is named the 'Shadows' after the patterns cast by the Eiffel Tower's webbed ironwork. Dramatic Eiffel views are complemented by kitchen creations such as scampi with spicy mango coulis, or beef tenderloin in watercress sauce. Reserve.

✖ Champs-Élysées & Grands Boulevards

Ladurée   Patisserie €

(Map p248; www.laduree.com; 75 av des Champs-Élysées, 8e; pastries from €1.50; ⏰7.30am-11.30pm Mon-Fri, 8.30am-12.30am Sat, 8.30am-11.30pm Sun; Ⓜ George V) One of the oldest patisseries in Paris, Ladurée has been around since 1862 and was the original creator of the lighter-than-air macaron. Its tearoom is the classiest spot to indulge on the Champs. Alternatively, pick up some pastries to go – from croissants to its trademark macarons, it's all quite heavenly.

Richer   Neobistro €€

(www.lericher.com; 2 rue Richer, 9e; mains €19-20; ⏰8am-midnight; Ⓜ Poissonière, Bonne Nouvelle) Run by the same team as across-the-street neighbour **L'Office** (📞 01 47 70 67 31; 3 rue Richer, 9e; 2-/3-course lunch menus €22/28, dinner menus €27/34; ⏰noon-2.30pm & 7.30-10.30pm Mon-Fri; Ⓜ Poissonière, Bonne Nouvelle), Richer's pared-back, exposed-brick decor is a smart setting for

♚ When to Eat

Petit déjeuner (breakfast) The French kick-start the day with a *tartine* (slice of baguette smeared with unsalted butter and jam) and *un café* (espresso) or – for kids – hot chocolate. Parisians might grab a coffee and croissant on the way to work, but otherwise croissants (eaten straight, never with butter or jam) are more of a weekend or 4pm treat along with *pains au chocolat* (chocolate-filled croissants) and other *viennoiseries* (sweet pastries).

Déjeuner (lunch) The traditional main meal of the day, lunch translates to a starter and main course with wine, followed by a short sharp *café*. During the work week this is less likely to be the case – many busy Parisians now grab a sandwich to go and pop off to run errands – but the standard hour-long lunch break, special *prix-fixe* menus and *tickets restaurant* (company-funded meal vouchers) ensure that many restaurants fill up at lunch.

Apéritif Otherwise known as an *apéro*, the pre-meal drink is sacred. Cafes and bars get packed out from around 5pm onwards as Parisians wrap up work for the day and relax over a chit-chat-fuelled glass of wine or beer.

Diner (dinner) Traditionally lighter than lunch, but a meal that is increasingly being treated as the main meal of the day. In restaurants the head chef will almost certainly be in the kitchen, which is not always the case during lunch.

Pains au chocolat

genius creations like trout tartare with cauliflower and tomato and citrus mousse, and quince and lime cheesecake for dessert. It doesn't take reservations, but it serves up snacks, Chinese tea and has a full bar outside meal times. Fantastic value.

Le Hide   French €€

(☑01 45 74 15 81; www.lehide.fr; 10 rue du Général Lanrezac, 17e; 2-/3-course menus €27/35; ⏰6-10.30pm Mon-Sat; Ⓜ Charles de Gaulle-Étoile) A perpetual favourite, Le Hide is a tiny neighbourhood bistro serving scrumptious traditional French fare: snails, baked shoulder of lamb with pumpkin purée or monkfish in lemon butter. Unsurprisingly, this place fills up faster than you can scamper down the steps of the nearby Arc de Triomphe. Reserve well in advance.

Floquifil   Traditional French €€

(☑01 42 46 11 19; www.floquifil.fr; 17 rue de Montyon, 9e; mains €14-20; ⏰11am-midnight Mon-Fri, from 6pm Sat; Ⓜ Grands Boulevards) If you were to envision the ultimate backstreet Parisian wine bar, it would probably look a lot like Floquifil: table-strewn terrace, dark timber furniture, aquamarine-painted walls and bottles galore. But while the by-the-glass wines are superb, you're missing out if you don't dine here (on rosemary-roasted lamb with ratatouille or at the very least a charcuterie platter).

Mamou   Neobistro €€

(☑01 44 63 09 25; www.restaurantmamou.fr; 42 rue Taitbout, 9e; 2-course lunch €19, mains €20-26; ⏰noon-2.30pm Mon-Fri, 7.30-10.30pm Wed-Sat; Ⓜ Chaussée d'Antin) Fans of *haute cuisine* minus the attitude should seek out this casual bistro by the Palais Garnier. Romain Lalu, who previously worked at the Parisian icon **Lasserre** (Map p248; ☑01 43 59 53 43; www.restaurant-lasserre.com; 17 av Franklin Roosevelt, 8e; lunch menu €90, tasting menu €195, mains €85-120; ⏰noon-2pm Thu & Fri, 7-10pm Tue-Sat; Ⓜ Franklin D Roosevelt), runs the kitchen, and diners can expect all the playful flavour combos of a chef free to follow his whims. Excellent natural wine selection. Reserve ahead.

Le Bon Georges   Bistro €€

(☑01 48 78 40 30; http://lebongeorges.com; 45 rue Saint-Georges, 9e; 2-course lunch menu €19, mains €24-29; ⏰noon-2.30pm Mon-Fri, 7.30-10.30pm Tue-Fri; Ⓜ St-Georges) For a classic French meal, look no further. Le Bon Georges thrives on nostalgia, focusing on personable service (the proprietor works the room himself) and a hearty bistro menu consisting of standards like cheesy onion soup, shoulder of lamb and a delicious steak tartare. Beef from the Polmard butchers (who raise their own cattle) and seasonal produce are guaranteed.

✖ Louvre & Les Halles

Stohrer   Patisserie €

(Map p250; www.stohrer.fr; 51 rue Montorgueil, 2e; ⏰7.30am-8.30pm; Ⓜ Les Halles) This bakery was opened in 1730 by the Polish pastry chef of queen consort Marie Leczinska (wife of Louis XV). Specialities include its very own *baba au rhum* (sponge cake soaked in rum-flavoured syrup) and *puits d'amour* (puff pasty with vanilla cream and caramel).

Le Camion Qui Fume   Fast Food €

(Map p250; http://lecamionquifume.com; 168 rue Montmartre, 2e; burgers €9-11; ⏰11am-11pm Sun-Thu, to midnight Fri & Sat; Ⓜ Grands Boulevards) The sedentary outpost of the famous food truck, Le Camion Qui Fume has staked a claim on burger-happy rue Montmartre, and judging by the late-night crowds, business is good. The Camion's claim to fame are gourmet burgers made with high-grade French beef and freshly baked buns, but you'll also appreciate the draught beer, friendly service and smothered chilli cheese fries.

La Tour de Montlhéry –
Chez Denise   Traditional French €€

(Map p250; ☑01 42 36 21 82; 5 rue des Prouvaires, 1er; mains €23-28; ⏰noon-2.30pm & 7.30pm-5am Mon-Fri; Ⓜ Châtelet) The most traditional eatery near the former Les Halles marketplace, this boisterous old bistro with red-chequered tablecloths has

been run by the same team for 30-some years. If you've just arrived and are ready to feast on all the French classics – snails in garlic sauce, veal liver, steak tartare, braised beef cheeks and housemade pâtés – reservations are in order. Open till dawn.

Le Cochon à l'Oreille   Cafe €€
(Map p250; ☏01 42 36 07 56; 15 rue Montmartre, 1er; 2-course lunch €17, 3-course dinner €32; ◷10am-2am Tue-Sat; Ⓜ Les Halles) A Parisian jewel, the heritage-listed hole-in-the-wall Le Cochon à l'Oreille retains 1890-laid tiles depicting vibrant market scenes of the old *halles* (halls). Hours can vary.

Racines 2   Modern French €€
(Map p250; ☏01 42 60 77 34; www.racinesparis. com; 39 rue de l'Arbre Sec, 1er; 2-/3-course lunch menus €28/32, mains €24-31; ◷noon-2.30pm Mon-Fri, 7.30-10.30pm Mon-Sat; Ⓜ Louvre Rivoli) R2 is a cousin of **Racines** in Passage des Panoramas, but that is about the extent of the family resemblance. No 2 is a thoroughly modern, urban bistro with a contemporary, Philippe Starck interior and an open stainless-steel kitchen where you can watch the

hip, young, black-dressed chefs, tattoos and all, at work.

Frenchie   Bistro €€€
(Map p250; ☏01 40 39 96 19; www.frenchie-restaurant.com; 5-6 rue du Nil, 2e; prix-fixe menu €68; ◷7-11pm Mon-Fri; Ⓜ Sentier) Tucked down an alley you wouldn't venture down otherwise, this bijou bistro with wooden tables and old stone walls is iconic. Frenchie is always packed and for good reason: excellent-value dishes are modern, market-driven and prepared with just the right dose of unpretentious creative flair by French chef Gregory Marchand.

The only hiccup is snagging a table: reserve well in advance; arrive at 6.30pm; pray for a cancellation (it does happen); or – failing that – share tapas-style small plates with friends across the street at **Frenchie Bar à Vins** (Map p250; 6 rue du Nil, 2e; dishes €9-23; ◷7-11pm Mon-Fri; Ⓜ Sentier) No reservations at the latter – write your name on the sheet of paper strung outside, loiter in the alley and wait for your name to be called.

🍽 Dining Tips

Bread Order a meal and within seconds a basket of fresh bread will be brought to the table. Butter is rarely an accompaniment. Except in the most upmarket of places, don't expect a side plate – simply put it on the table.

Water Asking for *une carafe d'eau* (jug of tap water) is perfectly acceptable, although some waiters will presume you don't know this and only offer mineral water, which you have to pay for. Should bubbles be more your cup of tea, ask for *de l'eau gazeuze* (fizzy mineral water). Ice (*glaçons*) can be hard to come by.

Service Acknowledge the expertise of your *serveur* by asking for advice (even if you don't really want it) and don't be afraid to flirt. In France flirtation is not the same as picking someone up, it is both a game that makes the mundane more enjoyable and a vital life skill to help you get what you want (such as the bill).

Dress Smart casual is best. How you look is very important, and Parisians favour personal style above all else. But if you're going some place dressy, don't assume this means suit and tie – that's more business-meal attire. At the other end of the spectrum, running shoes may be too casual, unless, of course, they are more hip than functional, in which case you may fit right in.

MINT IMAGES/GETTY IMAGES ©

Verjus American €€€

(Map p250; ☎01 42 97 54 40; www.verjusparis. com; 52 rue de Richelieu, 1er; prixe-fixe menu €68; ⏰7-11pm Mon-Fri; MᴮBourse, Palais Royal–Musée du Louvre) Opened by American duo Braden Perkins and Laura Adrian, Verjus was born out of a wildly successful clandestine supper club known as the Hidden Kitchen. The restaurant builds on that tradition, offering a chance to sample some excellent, creative cuisine in a casual space. The tasting menu is a series of small plates, using ingredients sourced straight from producers.

If you're just after an aperitif or a prelude to dinner, the downstairs **Verjus Bar à Vins** (Map p250; 47 rue de Montpensier, 1er; ⏰6-11pm Mon-Fri; MᴮBourse, Palais Royal–Musée du Louvre) serves a handful of charcuterie and cheese plates. For lunch or a more casual dinner, don't miss nearby **Ellsworth** (Map p250; ☎01 42 60 59 66; www.ellsworthparis.com; 34 rue de Richelieu, 1er; 2-/3-course lunch menus €20/26, mains €11-15; ⏰12.30-2.30pm Tue-Sat, 7-10.30pm Mon-Sat, 11.30am-3pm Sun; MᴮPyramides). Reserve well in advance for Verjus.

Yam'Tcha Fusion €€€

(Map p250; ☎01 40 26 08 07; www.yamtcha. com; 121 rue St Honoré, 1er; prix-fixe lunch/dinner menus €65/135; ⏰noon-2.30pm Wed-Fri, 7.30-10.30pm Tue-Sat; MᴮLouvre Rivoli) Adeline Grattard's ingeniously fused French and Cantonese flavours (fried squid with sweet-potato noodles) has earned the female chef no shortage of critical praise. Pair dishes on the frequently changing menu with wine or tea, or indulge in the famous steamed buns (*bāozi*) over a pot of oolong at the **Boutique Yam'Tcha** (Map p250; ☎01 40 26 06 06; 4 rue Sauval, 1er; steamed buns from €3; ⏰11.30am-10pm Wed-Sat; MᴮLouvre Rivoli). Reserve up to two months in advance.

Le Grand Véfour Traditional French €€€

(Map p250; ☎01 42 96 56 27; www.grand-vefour. com; 17 rue de Beaujolais, 1er; lunch/dinner menus €115/315; ⏰noon-2.30pm & 7.30-10.30pm Mon-Fri; MᴮPyramides) This 18th-century jewel on the

Macarons and other traditional French sweets

northern edge of the Jardin du Palais Royal has been a dining favourite of the Parisian elite since 1784; just look at who gets their names ascribed to each table – from Napoleon and Victor Hugo to Colette (who lived next door). The food is tip-top; expect a voyage of discovery in one of the most beautiful restaurants in the world.

Pirouette Neobistro €€€

(Map p250; ☎01 40 26 47 81; 5 rue Mondétour, 1er; lunch menus €20, 3-/6-course dinner menu €42/62; ☺noon-2.30pm & 7.30-10.30pm Mon-Sat; ⓂLes Halles) In one of the best restaurants in the vicinity of the old 'belly of Paris', chef Tomy Gousset's kitchen crew works wonders at this cool loftlike space, serving tantalising creations that range from seared duck, asparagus and Buddha's hand fruit to *baba au rhum* with chantilly and lime. Some unique ingredients and a new spin for French cuisine.

✖ Montmartre & Northern Paris

L'Été en Pente Douce Cafe €

(Map p256; ☎01 42 64 02 67; 23 rue Muller, 18e; mains €10.30-18.30; ☺noon-midnight; ⓂAnvers) Parisian terraces don't get much better than Summer on a Gentle Slope, named after the 1987 French film. It's a secret square wedged in between two flights of steep staircases on the backside of Montmartre, in a neighbourhood that's very much the real thing. Quiches, giant salads and classic dishes like Niçois-style stuffed veggies make up the menu.

Fric-Frac Sandwiches €

(http://fricfrac.fr; 79 quai de Valmy, 10e; sandwiches €11.50-14.50; ☺noon-3pm & 8-11pm Tue-Fri, noon-11pm Sat, noon-7pm Sun; ⓂJacques Bonsergent) Traditional snack croque monsieur (a toasted cheese and ham sandwich) gets a contemporary makeover at this quayside space. Grab a toasted sarnie to munch on along the canal banks, or eat in: gourmet Winnie (Crottin de Chavignol cheese, dried fruit, chestnut honey, chives and rosemary) and exotic Shaolin (king prawns and Thai chutney) are among the creative combos served with salad and fries.

Holybelly   International €

(http://holybel.ly; 19 Rue Lucien Sampaix, 10e; breakfast €5-11.50, lunch mains €13.50-16.50; ⊙9am-6pm Thu, Fri, Mon, from 10am Sat & Sun; MJacques Bonsergent) This outstanding barista-run coffee shop and kitchen is always crammed with a buoyant crowd, who never tire of Holybelly's exceptional service, Belleville-roasted coffee and cuisine. Sarah's breakfast pancakes served with egg, bacon, homemade bourbon butter and maple syrup are legendary, while her lunch menu features everything from traditional braised veal shank to squid à la plancha (grilled).

Soul Kitchen   Vegetarian €

(Map p256; www.soulkitchenparis.fr; 33 rue Lamarck, 18e; lunch menu €13.50; ⊙8.30am-6pm Tue-Fri, 10am-6.30pm Sat & Sun; 🛜🏃🏼‍♂️🚻; MLamarck-Caulaincourt) This vegetarian eatery with shabby-chic vintage interior and tiny open kitchen is as soulful as its name suggests. Market-driven dishes include feisty bowls of creative salads, homemade soups, savoury tarts, burritos and wraps – all gargantuan in size and packed with seasonal veggies. Round off lunch or snack between meals on muffins, cakes and the finest mint-laced citronnade maison (homemade lemonade) in town.

Le Verre Volé   Bistro €€

(☏01 48 03 17 34; http://leverrevole.fr; 67 rue de Lancry, 10e; mains €15-25; ⊙bistro 12.30-2pm & 7.30-10.30pm, wine cellar 9am-1am; MJacques Bonsergent) The tiny 'Stolen Glass' – a wine shop with a few tables – is just about the most perfect wine-bar-restaurant in Paris, with top wines and expert advice. Unpretentious and hearty plats du jour (dishes of the day) are excellent. Reserve well in advance for meals, or stop by to pick up a bottle.

Abri   Neobistro €€

(☏01 83 97 00 00; 92 rue du Faubourg Poissonnière, 9e; lunch/dinner menus €26/46; ⊙12.30-2pm Mon, 12.30-2pm & 8-10pm Tue-Sat; MPoissonnière) It's no bigger than a shoebox and the decor is borderline non-existent, but that's all part of the charm. Katsuaki Okiyama is a seriously talented chef with an artistic flair, and his surprise tasting menus (three courses at lunch, six at dinner) are exceptional. On Monday and Saturday, a giant gourmet sandwich is all that's served for lunch. Reserve well in advance.

La Bulle   Modern French €€

(☏01 40 37 34 51; www.restolabulle.fr; 48 rue Louis Blanc, 10e; 2-/3-course lunch menu €18.50/24, dinner menus €43 & €55; ⊙noon-2.30pm & 7.30-10.30pm Mon-Sat; MLouis Blanc) It's worth the short detour to this contemporary corner bistro with oyster-grey façade, lime-green seating on a sunny pavement terrrace, and talented young chef Romain Perrollaz in the kitchen. His cuisine is creative and strictly fait maison (homemade), with lots of tempting combos like beef with dill-spiked spelt risotto or pork pot au feu (beef stew) with old-time veg, watercress and peanut vinaigrette.

Le Miroir   Bistro €€

(Map p256; ☏01 46 06 50 73; http://restaurant-miroir.com; 94 rue des Martyrs, 18e; lunch menu €19.50, dinner menus €35-46; ⊙noon-2pm & 7.30-10pm; MAbbesses) This modern bistro is a local favourite, smack in the middle of the Montmartre tourist trail. There are lots of delightful pâtés and rillettes to start off with – guinea hen with dates, duck with mushrooms, haddock and lemon – followed by well-prepared standards like stuffed veal shoulder. Excellent wine list, sourced from the Mirror's wine shop across the street.

Le Pantruche   Bistro €€

(Map p256; ☏01 48 78 55 60; www.lepantruche.com; 3 rue Victor Massé, 9e; menus €19 & €36; ⊙12.30-2.30pm & 7.30-10.30pm Mon-Fri; MPigalle) Named after a nearby 19th-century theatre, classy Pantruche woos foodies in the dining hot spot of south Pigalle with seasonal bistro fare, reasonable prices and an intimate setting. The menu runs from classics (steak with Béarnaise sauce) to more daring creations (scallops served in a parmesan broth with cauliflower mousse-line). Reserve well in advance.

Matière à.　Modern French €€

(Map p250; ☎09 83 07 37 85; 15 rue Marie et Louise, 10e; 2-/3-course lunch menus €19/23, dinner menu €44; ☺noon-2.30pm & 7.30pm-1am Mon-Fri, 7pm-1am Sat; Ⓜ République) The short but stunning, seasonal menu changes daily at this unique space. *Table d'hôte*–style memorable dining for no more than 14 is around a shared oak table lit by dozens of naked light bulbs. In the kitchen is young chef Anthony Courteille, who prides himself on doing everything *fait maison* (home-made), including bread and butter to die for. Reservations essential.

Vivant　Modern French €€

(☎01 42 46 43 55; http://vivantparis.com; 43 rue des Petites Écuries, 10e; mains €23-29; ☺noon-2pm & 7-10.30pm Mon-Sat; Ⓜ Poisson-nière, Bonne Nouvelle) Simple but elegant dishes – creamy *burrata*, crispy duck leg with mashed potatoes, foie gras and roasted onion – showcase the carefully sourced ingredients used at this small but chic restaurant, inside a century-old exot-ic-bird shop with a stunning ceramic wall and ceiling. Swiss-born Pierre Jancou is a natural-wine activist and at least one glass of *vin* is an essential part of the meal here. Reserve ahead.

✕ Le Marais, Ménilmontant & Belleville

Breizh Café　Crêperie €

(Map p250; www.breizhcafe.com; 109 rue Vieille du Temple, 3e; crêpes & galettes €6.50-17.80; ☺11.30am-11pm Wed-Sat, to 10pm Sun; Ⓜ St-Sébastien-Froissart) It is a well-known fact among Parisians: everything at the Breton Café (*breizh* is 'Breton' in Breton) is 100% authentic, rendering it the top spot in the city for authentic crêpes. Be it the

🍴 Menu Advice

À la carte Order whatever you fancy from the menu (as opposed to opting for a *prix-fixe* menu).

Carte Menu, as in the written list of what's cooking, listed in the order you'd eat it: starter, main course, cheese, then dessert. Note that an *entrée* is a starter, not the main course (as in the US).

Menu Not at all what it means in English, *le menu* in French is a *prix-fixe* menu: a multicourse meal at a fixed price. It's by far the best-value dining there is, and most restaurants chalk one on the board. In some cases, particular-ly at neobistros, there is no *carte* – only a stripped-down *menu* with one or two choices.

Formule Similar to a *menu, une formule* is a cheaper lunchtime option compris-ing a main plus starter or dessert. Wine or coffee is sometimes included.

Plat du jour Dish of the day, invariably good value.

Menu enfant Two- or three-course kids' meal (generally up to the age of 12) at a fixed price; usually includes a drink.

Menu dégustation Fixed-price tasting menu served in many top-end restaurants, consisting of five to seven modestly sized courses.

Cancale oysters, 20 types of cider or the buttery organic-flour crêpes, everything here is cooked to perfection. If you fail to snag a table, try **L'Épicerie** (Map p250;

MAISANT LUDOVIC/GETTY IMAGES ©

Terrace dining in the Marais

http://breizhcafe.com; 111 rue Vieille du Temple, 3e; crêpes & galettes €6.50-17.80; ☾11.30am-9pm; Ⓜ St-Sébastien-Froissart) next door.

Jacques Genin   Patisserie €
(Map p250; ☎ 01 45 77 29 01; 133 rue de Turenne, 3e; pastries €9; ☾11am-7pm Tue-Sun; Ⓜ Oberkampf) Wildly creative chocolatier Jacques Genin is famed for his flavoured caramels, *pâtes de fruits* (fruit jellies) and exquisitely embossed *bonbons de chocolat* (chocolate sweets). But what completely steals the show at his elegant chocolate showroom is the *salon de dégustation* (aka tearoom), where you can order a pot of outrageously thick hot chocolate and legendary Genin millefeuille, assembled to order.

Candelaria   Mexican €
(Map p250; ☎ 01 42 74 41 28; www.candelaria-paris.com; 52 rue de Saintonge, 3e; tacos €3-5; ☾12.30pm-11pm Sun-Wed, to midnight Thu-Sat, bar 6pm-2am; Ⓜ Filles du Calvaire) You need to know about this terribly cool *taqueria* to find it. Made of pure, unadulterated hipness in that brazenly nonchalant manner Paris does so well, clandestine Candelaria serves delicious homemade tacos, quesadillas

and tostadas in a laid-back setting – squat at the bar in the front or lounge out back around a shared table with bar stools or at low coffee tables.

Café Marais   Modern French €
(Map p250; ☎ 01 42 71 61 46; 10 rue des Haudriettes, 3e; lunch/dinner menus €16.50/18.50; ☾noon-3.30pm Mon & Tue, noon-3.30pm & 7-11pm Wed-Fri, 7-11pm Sat; Ⓜ Arts et Métiers) Exposed stone, a beamed ceiling and silent B&W Charlie Chaplin movies screened on one wall create an appealing vintage feel in this small and excellent bistro – one of the best-value spots for dining in Le Marais. The round of Camembert roasted with honey, homemade courgette gratin and parmesan crème brûlée are all excellent.

L'As du Fallafel   Jewish €
(Map p250; 34 rue des Rosiers, 4e; takeaway €6-8.50; ☾noon-midnight Sun-Thu, to 5pm Fri; Ⓜ St-Paul) The lunchtime queue stretching halfway down the street from this place says it all. This Parisian favourite, 100% worth the inevitable wait, is *the* address for kosher, perfectly deep-fried felafel (chickpea balls; €6) and turkey or lamb shawarma sandwiches (€8.50). Do as every Parisian does and get takeaway.

Chatomat   Modern French €
(☎ 01 47 97 25 77; 6 rue Victor Letalle, 20e; mains €15-20; ☾7.30-10.30pm Tue-Sat & 1st Sun of month; Ⓜ Ménilmontant, Couronnes, Père Lachaise) No dinner address is worth the trek to Belleville more than this contemporary bistro with plain white walls, post-industrial flavour and bags of foodie buzz. In the kitchen of the old shop-turned-restaurant, Alice and Victor cook up just three starters, three mains and three desserts each night – and none disappoint. Book in advance.

Café Pinson   Cafe €
(Map p250; ☎ 09 83 82 53 53; www.cafepinson.fr; 6 rue du Forez, 3e; mains €14; ☾9am-10pm Mon-Fri, 10am-10pm Sat, noon-6pm Sun; 🛜 ✐; Ⓜ Filles du Calvaire) ✐ This small lifestyle cafe, with an interior by celebrity designer Dorothée Meilichzon, is tucked down an

alley in the fashionable Haut Marais. A trendy lunchtime crowd flocks here for sweet-potato felafel, pumpkin-spiked couscous, creative salads and an organic, market-driven menu that changes daily. Its freshly squeezed juices are predictably excellent, and vegetarians and vegans are well catered for. Superb weekend brunch.

La Cantine Belleville   French €

(01 43 15 99 29; http://lacantinebelleville.fr; 108 bd de Belleville, 20e; 2-/3-course lunch €12/14, dinner €14/18; ☺8am-2am; ☎; MBelleville) For a taste of how trendy the edgy Belleville neighbourhood is becoming, hit its local 'canteen', a vibrant one-stop shop for dining, drinking and dancing after dark. Old school chairs, vintage lighting and a mix of red brick and graffitied concrete give the place an appealing garage vibe. Cuisine is classic French, with particularly excellent steaks – two meat lovers can share the *côte de boeuf*.

Derrière   Modern French €€

(Map p250; 01 44 61 91 95; www.derriere-resto. com; 69 rue des Gravilliers, 3e; 2-/3-course lunch menus €25/30, mains €19-30; ☺noon-2.30pm & 8-11.30pm Mon-Sat, noon-4.30pm & 8-11pm Sun; MArts et Métiers) Play table tennis, sit on the side of the bed, glass of champers in hand, or lounge between bookcases – such is the nature of this restaurant. Chilled vibe in a trendy 'shoes-off' style aside, Derrière (literally 'behind') is deadly serious in the kitchen. Classic French bistro dishes and more inventive creations are excellent, as is Sunday brunch.

Brasserie Bofinger   Brasserie €€

(Map p250; 01 42 72 87 82; www.bofingerparis. com; 5-7 rue de la Bastille, 4e; menus €31 & €56; ☺noon-2pm & 6.30pm-midnight Mon-Sat, noon-11pm Sun; ▮; MBastille) Founded in 1864, Bofinger is reputedly Paris' oldest brasserie, though its polished art nouveau brass, glass and mirrors indicates redecoration a few decades later. Specialties include Alsatian-inspired dishes like *choucroute* (sauerkraut), oysters (from €27.90 for a dozen) and magnificent seafood platters (€29.90 to €122). Ask for a seat down-

¶O¶ A Culinary Renaissance

A new generation of chefs has emerged in the past several years, re-emphasising France's time-honoured market-driven cuisine and displaying a willingness to push the boundaries of traditional tastes, while at the same time downplaying the importance of Michelin stars and the formal, chandelier-studded dining rooms of yesteryear.

Even more significantly, the real change that is taking place in Paris today is that more and more of these chefs – and, just as importantly, more and more diners – are open to culinary traditions originating outside of France. Some have trained abroad (in what is surely one of the greatest examples of Gallic pride-swallowing, French chef Gregory Marchand went to the UK to work for Jamie Oliver), while others aren't even French, originally hailing from Japan, the US or elsewhere. The latter group has come to Paris specifically because they love French cooking, but none are so beholden to its traditions that they are afraid to introduce new concepts or techniques from back home.

French cuisine has finally come to the realisation that a global future doesn't necessarily mean a loss of identity – decadent work-of-art pastries and the divine selection of pungent cheeses aren't going anywhere. Instead, there is an opportunity to once again create something new.

stairs beneath the *coupole* (stained-glass dome). Kids are catered for with a €14.50 children's *menu*.

Le Clown Bar   Modern French €€
(Map p250; 📞01 43 55 87 35; www.clown-bar-paris.fr; 114 rue Amelot, 11e; mains €25-30; 🕑noon-2.30pm & 7-10.30pm Wed-Sun; Ⓜ Filles du Calvaire) A historic monument next to the 1852 Cirque d'Hiver, the city's winter circus, this unique address is practically a museum with its ceramics, mosaics, original zinc bar and purist art deco style. A restaurant for decades, this mythical address now serves up fabulous modern French cuisine and excellent natural wines for a jovial crowd. Its pavement terrace gets packed out on sunny days.

✖ Bastille & Eastern Paris

CheZaline   Sandwiches €
(85 rue de la Roquette, 11e; sandwiches €5.50-8; 🕑11am-5.30pm Mon-Fri; Ⓜ Voltaire) A former horse-meat butcher's shop (*chevaline*, hence the spin on the name) is now a

fabulous deli creating seasonally changing baguettes filled with ingredients like ham and house-made pesto. Other delicacies include salads and homemade terrines. There's a handful of seats (and plenty of parks nearby). Prepare to queue.

Yard   Modern French €
(📞01 40 09 70 30; www.yardparis.com; 6 rue de Mont Louis, 11e; 2-/3-course lunch menus €16/19, mains €15-18; 🕑noon-2.30pm & 8-10.30pm Mon-Fri, tapas 6pm-midnight Mon-Fri; Ⓜ Philippe Auguste) This modern bistro near the Père Lachaise cemetery is squirreled away in a former construction yard, hence its name. The short but inventive menu changes daily, incorporating seasonal dishes such as spring lamb with leeks or a wintery wild boar *mijoté* (stew) with olives and polenta. To watch the chefs cook in the tiny open kitchen, sit at the bar.

Come dusk Yard cooks up tapas dishes over drinks in its neighbouring wine bar; for a lunchtime sandwich to go (unusual fillings are always a reflection of what's cooking that day in the bistro), nip into its next-door sandwich bar.

Charcuterie

Le Bistrot Paul Bert   Bistro €€

(01 43 72 24 01; 18 rue Paul Bert, 11e; 2-/3-course lunch/dinner menus €19/41; noon-2pm & 7.30-11pm Tue-Sat; Faidherbe-Chaligny) When food writers list Paris' best bistros, one name that consistently pops up is Paul Bert. The timeless vintage decor and perfectly executed classic dishes like *steak-frites* and hazelnut-cream Paris-Brest pastry merit booking ahead. In the same street, look out for its siblings **L'Écailler du Bistrot** (01 43 72 76 77; 22 rue Paul Bert, 11e; weekday lunch menu €19, mains €17-34; noon-2.30pm & 7.30-11pm Tue-Sat; Faidherbe-Chaligny), featuring seafood; **La Cave Paul Bert** (01 58 53 30 92; 16 rue Paul Bert, 11e; noon-midnight, kitchen noon-2pm & 7.30-11.30pm; Faidherbe-Chaligny), a wine bar with small plates; and **Le 6 Paul Bert** (01 43 79 14 32; 6 rue Paul Bert, 12e; 2-/3-course weekday lunch menus €18/19, 4-course dinner menu €44, mains €24-26; 7.30-11pm Tue, noon-2pm & 7.30-11pm Wed-Sat; Faidherbe-Chaligny), feauting modern cuisine.

Chez Paul   Bistro €€

(01 47 00 34 57; www.chezpaul.com; 13 rue de Charonne, 11e; 2-/3-course lunch menus €18/21, mains €17-27; noon-12.30am; Ledru-Rollin) This is Paris as your grandmother knew it: chequered red-and-white napkins, faded photographs on the walls, old red banquettes and traditional French dishes that could well make your hair curl: pig trotters, *andouillette* (a fiesty tripe sausage), *tête de veau et cervelle* (calf head and brains) and the like. Less offal: a steaming bowl of *pot au feu* (beef stew).

À la Biche au Bois   Traditional French €€

(01 43 43 34 38; 45 av Ledru-Rollin, 12e; 2-/3-course lunch menus €19/21.50, dinner menu €31.50; 7-10.45pm Mon, noon-2.30pm & 7-10.45pm Tue-Sat; Gare de Lyon) Game, especially *la biche,* is the specialty of convivial 'Doe in the Woods', but dishes like foie gras and coq au vin also add to the countryside ambience, as do the green awning and potted plants out front. The cheeses and wines are excellent, but game aside, top honours have to go to the sensational *frites* (fries).

Septime   Modern French €€€

(01 43 67 38 29; www.septime-charonne.fr; 80 rue de Charonne, 11e; lunch menus €28 & €55, dinner menu €58; 7.30-10pm Mon, 12.15-2pm & 7.30-10pm Tue-Fri; Charonne) The alchemists in Bertrand Grébaut's Michelin-starred kitchen produce truly beautiful creations, while blue-smocked waitstaff ensure culinary surprises are all pleasant ones: each dish on the menu is a mere listing of three ingredients, while the mystery *carte blanche* menu puts your tastebuds in the hands of the innovative chef. Snagging a table requires planning and perseverance – book three weeks in advance.

For a pre- or post-meal drink, drop by its nearby wine bar Septime La Cave (01 43 67 14 87; www.septime-charonne.fr; 3 rue Basfroi, 11e; 4-11pm Tue-Sat, 5-10pm Sun; Charonne). For stunning seafood tapas, its sister restaurant **Clamato** (www.septime-charonne.fr; 80 rue de Charonne, 11e; tapas €7-20; 7-11pm Wed-Fri, noon-11pm Sat & Sun; Charonne) is right next door.

Le Train Bleu   French €€€

(01 43 43 09 06; www.le-train-bleu.com; 26 place Louis Armand, 12e, Gare de Lyon; menus €65 & €105, mains €25-45; restaurant 11.30am-2.45pm & 7-10.45pm, bar 7.30am-10.30pm Mon-Sat, 9am-10.30pm Sun; ; Gare de Lyon) This ravishing, belle époque train-station restaurant has been an elegant port of call for hungry travellers and city workers since 1901. Cuisine is traditional French – Charolais beef tartare is prepared at your table – and even if you can't dine here, indulging in a silver pot of tea or cocktail in its comfortable lounge bar is well worth the top-end prices.

Table   Modern French €€€

(01 43 43 12 26; www.tablerestaurant.fr; 3 rue de Prague, 12e; lunch menu €29, mains €32-49; noon-3pm & 7.45-10.30pm Mon-Fri; Ledru-Rollin) Unusual and rare artisan products sourced from all over France decide the day's menu at this appealing eatery, styled very much like a *table d'hôte*, with diners sitting at the curvaceous zinc bar while talented chef Bruno Verjus performs in his

Paris on a Plate

A classic *baguette ordinaire* legally has three ingredients (flour, yeast and salt) and weighs 250g.

○ Avoid baguettes with a mesh-like patterned base or overly uniform colouring (signs they're industrially produced).

○ A baguette tradition ('une tradi') is a shorter, pointier version with a coarse, hand-crafted surface.

LUZIA ELLERT/GETTY IMAGES ©

Know Your Baguette

PHOTONONSTOP/ALAMY STOCK PHOTO ©

Daily Bread

Some 80% of Parisians eat bread with every meal, hence the near-constant aroma of freshly baking baguettes and other varieties wafting from Paris' *boulangeries* (bakeries), with around 1200 *boulangeries* city-wide, or 11.5 per sq km.

The shape of a baguette (meaning 'stick' or 'wand') evolved when Napoléon ordered army bakers to create loaves for soldiers to stuff down their trouser legs on the march.

★ Top Five Boulangeries

Besnier (Map p248; 40 rue de Bourgogne, 7e; ☉7am-8pm Mon-Fri Sep-Jul; Ⓜ Varenne) Watch baguettes being made from the viewing window.

Du Pain et des Idées (Map p250; http://du-painetdesidees.com; 34 rue Yves Toudic, 10e; pastries from €1.50; ☉6.45am-8pm Mon-Fri; Ⓜ Jacques Bonsergent) Naturally levened bread, orange-blossom brioche and decadent escargots.

Le Grenier à Pain (Map p256; 38 rue des Abbesses, 18e; sandwiches €3-4.10; ☉7.30am-8pm Thu-Mon; Ⓜ Abbesses) Past winner of Paris' 'best baguette' prize.

Poilâne (www.poilane.com; 8 rue du Cherche Midi, 6e; ☉7.15am-8.15pm Mon-Sat; Ⓜ Sèvres-Babylone) Wood-fired, sourdough loaves.

Chambelland (☎01 43 55 07 30; http://chambelland.com; 14 rue Ternaux, 11e; lunch menu €12; ☉9am-8pm Tue-Sun; Ⓜ Parmentier) 100% gluten-free bakery.

open kitchen. Delicious meats come out of his rotisserie and the chef delights in talking food with diners.

Dersou   Neobistro €€€

(📞09 81 01 12 73; www.dersouparis.com; 21 rue St-Nicolas, 12e; 5-/6-/7-course tasting menus incl drinks €95/115/135; ⏱7.30pm-midnight Tue-Fri, noon-3.30pm & 7.30pm-midnight Sat, noon-3.30pm Sun; Ⓜ Ledru-Rollin) Leave any preconceptions you might have at the door, ignore or enjoy the brutishly understated decor, and be wooed by the creative fusion cuisine of Taku Sekine. Much of the seating is at the counter, meaning first-class views of the Japanese chef at work, and options are limited to tasting menus, with each course exquisitely paired with a bespoke cocktail. Reservations essential.

✖ The Islands

Berthillon   Ice Cream €

(Map p254; www.berthillon.fr; 31 rue St-Louis en l'Île, 4e; 1/2/3 scoops take away €3/4/6.50, eat in €4.50/7.50/10.50; ⏱10am-8pm Wed-Sun, closed Aug; Ⓜ Pont Marie) Founded here in 1954, this esteemed *glacier* (ice-cream maker) is still run by the same family today. Its 70 all-natural, chemical-free flavours include fruit sorbets such as blackcurrant or pink grapefruit, and richer ice creams made from fresh milk and eggs, such as salted caramel, *marrons glacés* (candied chestnuts) and *agenaise* (Armagnac and prunes), along with seasonal flavours like gingerbread.

Café Saint Régis   Cafe €

(Map p250; www.cafesaintregisparis.com; 6 rue Jean du Bellay, 4e; breakfast & snacks €3.50-14.50, mains €18-32; ⏱8am-2am; 📶; Ⓜ Pont Marie) Waiters in long white aprons, a white ceramic-tiled interior, and retro vintage decor make hip Le Saint Régis (as regulars call it) a deliciously Parisian hang-out any time of day, from breakfast pastries to mid-morning pancakes, lunchtime salads and burgers and early-evening oyster platters. Come midnight it morphs into a late-night hotspot.

Le Caveau du Palais   Modern French €€

(Map p250; 📞01 43 26 04 28; www.caveaudupalais.fr; 19 place Dauphine, 1er; mains €21-27; ⏱noon-2.30pm & 7-10pm Mon-Sat; Ⓜ Pont Neuf) Even when the western Île de la Cité shows few other signs of life, the Caveau's half-timbered dining areas and (weather permitting) alfresco terrace are packed with diners tucking into bountiful fresh fare: steak tartare with quail's egg, artichoke and mushroom risotto with braised spinach, turbot with sweet-potato-and-sea-salt mash, and deconstructed lemon tart.

More informal dishes are served up at its adjacent wine bar, **Le Bar du Caveau** (Map p250; www.caveaudupalais.fr; 17 place Dauphine, 1er; ⏱8am-6.30pm Mon-Wed & Fri, to 10pm Thu; Ⓜ Pont Neuf).

Les Voyelles   Modern French €€

(Map p250; 📞01 46 33 69 75; www.les-voyelles.com; 74 quai des Orfèvres, 4e; 2-/3-course menus €17/22.50; ⏱noon-3pm & 7-10.30pm Tue-Sat; Ⓜ Pont Neuf) Worth the short walk from Notre Dame, the Vowels – spot the letters scattered between books and beautiful objects on the shelves lining the intimate 'library' dining room – is thoroughly contemporary, with fare ranging from finger food (including a daily burger) to full-blown *menus*, which might feature *onglet de bœuf* (hanger steak) with Béarnaise sauce. Its pavement terrace is Paris gold.

Ma Salle à Manger   Bistro €€

(Map p250; 📞01 43 29 52 34; www.masalle-amanger.fr; 26 place Dauphine, 1er; 2-/3-course lunch menus €20.50/25.50, 2-/3-course dinner menus €23.50/28.50; ⏱9am-10.30pm; Ⓜ Pont Neuf) Framed by a pretty-as-a-picture blue-and-white striped awning and pavement tables, on tucked-away Place Dauphine, convivial little bistro-wine bar 'My Dining Room' chalks its changing menu on the blackboard. Simple yet inspired dishes might include French onion soup, Camembert baked with wine, confit of duck with baked apple, filet mignon with potato *dauphinoise* (grated baked potatoes) and a feather-light crème brûlée.

Mon Vieil Ami · · · · · · French €€€

(Map p254; ☑01 40 46 01 35; www.mon-vieil-ami.
com; 69 rue St-Louis en l'Île, 4e; menu €48, mains
€14-25; ☺noon-2.30pm & 7-11pm; ☎; Ⓜ Pont
Marie) Alsatian chef Antoine Westermann is
the creative talent behind this sleek black
neobistro where guests are treated like old
friends (hence the name) and vegetables get
star billing. From Wednesday to Sunday only,
the good-value lunchtime *plat du jour* (dish
of the day), such as wintertime kale with
smoked bacon and roast chicken, is a perfect
reflection of the season.

✕ Latin Quarter

Shakespeare & Company Café · · · · · · · · · · · Cafe €

(Map p254; www.shakespeareandcompany.com;
2 rue St-Julien le Pauvre, 5e; dishes €4-9.50;
☺10am-6.30pm Mon-Fri, to 7.30pm Sat & Sun;
☎✐♿; Ⓜ St-Michel) ✐ Instant history was
made when this light-filled, literary-inspired
cafe opened in 2015 adjacent to magical
bookshop Shakespeare & Company (p157). It
was designed from long-lost sketches to fulfil
a dream of late bookshop founder George
Whitman from the 1960s. Its primarily
vegetarian menu (with vegan and gluten-free
dishes available) includes homemade bagels,
rye bread, soups, salads and pastries, plus
Parisian-roasted Café Lomi coffee.

Picnic hampers (named 'A Moveable
Feast' and including a short story) are in
the works.

Odette · · · · · · · · · · · · · · · · Patisserie €

(Map p254; www.odette-paris.com; 77 rue Galande,
5e; 1/6/12 pastry puffs €1.90/9.90/19.80;
☺10.30am-7.30pm; Ⓜ St-Michel) Odette's
ground-floor space sells *choux* pastry with
seasonal flavoured cream fillings (nine at any
one time), such as coffee, lemon, green tea,
salted caramel, pistachio and forest berries.
Upstairs, its art deco tearoom plays 1920s
music and serves *choux* along with tea,
coffee and Champagne. The black-painted
timber façade, fronted by tables, and gerani-
um-filled 1st-floor window box are charming.

Le Comptoir du Panthéon · · · · · · Cafe, Brasserie €

(Map p254; ☑01 43 54 75 36; 5 rue Soufflot, 5e;
salads €11-13, mains €12.40-15.40; ☺kitchen
7am-11pm Mon-Sat, 8am-11pm Sun; ☎; Ⓜ Cardinal
Lemoine or RER Luxembourg) Enormous,
creative meal-size salads are the reason to
choose this as a dining spot. Magnificently
placed across from the domed Panthéon on
the shady side of the street, its pavement terrace is big, busy and quintessentially Parisian
– turn your head away from Voltaire's burial
place and the Eiffel Tower pops into view. The
bar closes at 1.45am every day.

La Salle à Manger · · · · · · · · · French €

(☑01 55 43 91 99; 138 rue Mouffetard, 5e; mains
€10-15, weekend brunch €22; ☺8.30am-6.30pm;
Ⓜ Censier Daubenton) With a sunny pavement terrace beneath trees enviably placed
at the foot of foodie street rue Mouffetard,
the 'Dining Room' is prime real estate. Its
360-degree outlook – market stalls, fountain, church and garden with a playground
for tots – couldn't be prettier, and its
salads, *tartines* (open-faced sandwiches),
tarts and pastries ensure packed tables at
breakfast, lunch and weekend brunch.

Café de la Nouvelle Mairie · · · Cafe €€

(Map p254; ☑01 44 07 04 41; 19 rue des
Fossés St-Jacques, 5e; mains €12-32; ☺kitchen
8am-midnight Mon-Fri; Ⓜ Cardinal Lemoine)
Shhhh...just around the corner from the
Panthéon but hidden away on a small,
fountained square, this narrow wine bar is
a neighbourhood secret, serving black-
board-chalked natural wines by the glass
and delicious seasonal bistro fare from oysters and ribs (*à la française*) to grilled lamb
sausage over lentils. It takes reservations
for dinner but not lunch – arrive early.

Le Coupe-Chou · · · · · · · · · · French €€

(Map p254; ☑01 46 33 68 69; www.lecoupechou.
com; 9 & 11 rue de Lanneau, 5e; 2-/3-course
menus €27/33; ☺noon-2pm & 7-10.45pm Sep-
Jul, 7-10.45pm Aug; Ⓜ Maubert-Mutualité) This
maze of candlelit rooms inside a vine-clad
17th-century townhouse is overwhelmingly
romantic. Ceilings are beamed, furnishings

are antique, open fireplaces crackle and background classical music mingles with the intimate chatter of diners. As in the days when Marlene Dietrich dined here, advance reservations are essential. Timeless French dishes include Burgundy snails, steak tartare and bœuf bourguignon.

Les Papilles   Bistro €€

(Map p254; ✆01 43 25 20 79; www.lespapilles-paris.com; 30 rue Gay Lussac, 5e; 2-/3-course menus from €20/35, mains €18-35; ◷noon-2pm & 7-10.30pm Tue-Sat; Ⓜ Raspail or RER Luxembourg) This hybrid bistro, wine cellar and *épicerie* (specialist grocer) with a sunflower-yellow façade is one of those fabulous Parisian dining experiences. Meals are served at simply dressed tables wedged beneath bottle-lined walls, and fare is market driven: each weekday cooks up a different *marmite du marché* (market casserole). But what really sets it apart is its exceptional wine list.

Terroir Parisien   Bistro €€

(Map p254; ✆01 44 31 54 54; www.yannick-alleno.com; 20 rue St-Victor, 5e; 2-/3-course lunch menus €24/32, mains €16-29; ◷noon-2.30pm & 7-10.15pm; Ⓜ Maubert-Mutualité) A focus on exclusively Île-de-France-sourced ingredients and an airy, modern interior make for a winning combination. Contemporary creations span from pan-seared scallops with Jerusalem-artichoke purée, ham and chicory gratin to green cabbage stuffed with roast pigeon. A few quick bites (eg croque monsieur) are also served. Do note that portions are small.

Restaurant AT   Gastronomic €€€

(Map p254; ✆01 56 81 94 08; http://atsush-itanaka.com; 4 rue du Cardinal Lemoine, 5e; 4-/6-course lunch menus €35/55, 12-course dinner tasting menu €95; ◷12.15-2pm & 8-9.30pm Tue-Sat; Ⓜ Cardinal Lemoine) Trained by some of the biggest names in gastronomy (Pierre Gagnaire included), chef Atsushi Tanaka showcases abstract-art-like masterpieces incorporating rare ingredients (charred bamboo, kohlrabi turnip cabbage, juniper-berry powder, wild purple fennel, Nepalese

🍽 Speciality Shops

Many Parisians buy at least some of their food from a series of small neighbourhood shops, each with its own speciality. *Boulangeries* (bakeries) and *fromageries* (cheese shops) aside, look out for the following:

Patisseries (pastry shops) Similar to but generally more sophisticated than bakeries. Although they sell different varieties of pastries and cakes, each one is often known for a particular speciality: Ladurée (p121) does macarons, Gérard Mulot (p137) does cakes and tartes, and so on. A chocolatier specialises in chocolates, generally sold in 100g increments.

Boucheries The neighbourhood butcher's shop is a common fixture in Paris. They will also have a selection of charcuterie such as pâtés, terrines, *saucissons* (salami) and *rillettes* (meat spreads).

Traiteurs Similar to a deli, the *traiteur* specialises in prepared dishes – in its earliest form, this was the origin of the modern-day restaurant. You'll find a selection of charcuterie along with salads, baked goods (eg quiches) and sometimes sandwiches.

Cavistes These neighbourhood wine shops generally have passionate staff – helpful as wines are classified by region, not grape variety. To sample French wine paired with a good meal, your best bet is to visit a *bar à vins* (wine bar) or a *cave à manger* (a *caviste* that serves meals in addition to selling wine).

Macarons from Ladurée (p121)

7-10.30pm Tue-Sat Sep-Jul; MCardinal Lemoine)
The venerable Michelin-starred 'Silver
Tower' is famous for its *caneton* (duckling),
rooftop garden with glimmering Notre
Dame views and fabulous history harking
back to 1582 – from Henry III's inaugura-
tion of the first fork in France to inspiration
for the winsome animated film *Ratatouille*.
Its wine cellar is one of Paris' best; dining is
dressy and exceedingly fine.

Reserve eight to 10 days ahead for lunch,
three weeks ahead for dinner – and don't
miss its chocolate soufflé with bitter orange
ice cream for dessert.

Buy fine food and accessories in La
Tour d'Argent's **boutique** (Map p254; www.
latourdargent.com; 2 rue du Cardinal Lemoine, 5e;
⊙11.15am-7.15pm Tue-Sat; MCardinal Lemoine)
directly across the street, near its casual
bistro **La Rôtisserie** (Map p254; ⏰01 43 54
17 47; www.larotisseriedelatour.com; 19 quai de la
Tournelle, 5e; mains €22-28; ⊙noon-2.15pm &
7-10.30pm; MCardinal Lemoine).

Timut pepper) on stunning outsized plates
in a blank-canvas-style dining space. Just
off the entrance, steps lead to his cellar
wine bar, **Bar à Vins AT** (Map p254; ⏰01
56 81 94 08; http://atsushitanaka.com; 4 rue du
Cardinal Lemoine, 5e; dishes €12-16; ⊙7pm-2am
Tue-Sun; MCardinal Lemoine).

Sola — Fusion €€€

(Map p254; ⏰dinner 01 43 29 59 04, lunch 09
65 01 73 68; www.restaurant-sola.com; 12 rue de
l'Hôtel Colbert, 5e; menus lunch €48-78, dinner
€98; ⊙noon-1.30pm & 7.30-9pm Tue-Sat;
MSt-Michel) Pedigreed chef Hiroki Yoshitake
combines French technique with Japanese
sensibility, resulting in gorgeous signature
creations (such as miso-marinated foie
gras on *feuille de brick* served on sliced tree
trunk). The artful presentations and atten-
tive service make this a perfect choice for a
romantic meal – go for the full experience
and reserve a table in the Japanese dining
room downstairs.

La Tour d'Argent — Gastronomic €€€

(Map p254; ⏰01 43 54 23 31; www.latourdargent.
com; 15 quai de la Tournelle, 5e; menus lunch €85,
dinner €180-200, mains €75-100; ⊙12.30-2pm &

✖ St-Germain & Les Invalides

L'Avant Comptoir de la Mer — Seafood Tapas €

(Map p254; www.hotel-paris-relais-saint-germain.
com; 3 Carrefour de l'Odéon, 6e; tapas €4-30;
⊙noon-11pm; MOdéon) The latest in Yves
Camdeborde's stunning line-up of Carrefour de l'Odéon eateries, alongside **Le
Comptoir** (Map p254; ⏰01 44 27 07 97; www.
hotel-paris-relais-saint-germain.com; 9 Carrefour
de l'Odéon, 6e; mains €14-39, dinner menu €60;
⊙noon-6pm & 8.30-11.30pm Mon-Fri, noon-11pm
Sat & Sun; MOdéon) and **L'Avant Comptoir**
(Map p254; www.hotel-paris-relais-saint-germain.
com; 3 Carrefour de l'Odéon, 6e; tapas €5-10;
⊙noon-midnight; MOdéon), serves succulent
oysters (Bloody Mary–style or with chipolata
sausages), herring *tartine*, cauliflower and
trout roe, blood-orange razor clams, lobster
with almond-milk foam, roasted scallops and
salmon croquettes, complemented by its
bar's artisan bread, flavoured butters, sea salt
and Kalamata olives.

Au Pied de Fouet
Bistro €

(Map p250; 📞01 43 54 87 83; www.aupied-defouet.com; 3 rue St-Benoît, 6e; mains €9-12.50; 🕑noon-2.30pm & 7-11pm Mon-Sat; Ⓜ St-Germain des Prés) At this tiny, lively, cherry-red-coloured bistro, wholly classic dishes such as *entrecôte* (steak), *confit de canard* (duck cooked slowly in its own fat) with creamy potatoes and *foie de volailles sauté* (pan-fried chicken livers) are astonishingly good value. Round off your meal with a *tarte Tatin* (upside-down apple tart), wine-soaked prunes, or deliciously rich *fondant au chocolat*.

Cuisine de Bar
Sandwiches €

(www.cuisinedebar.fr; 8 rue du Cherche Midi, 6e; dishes €9.20-13.50; 🕑8.30am-7pm Mon-Sat, 9.30am-3.30pm Sun; 🛜; Ⓜ Sèvres-Babylone) As next-door neighbour to one of Paris' most famous bakers, this isn't your average sandwich bar. Instead, between shopping in designer boutiques, it's an ultrachic spot to lunch on open sandwiches cut from that celebrated Poilâne bread (p22) and fabulously topped with gourmet goodies such as foie gras, smoked duck, gooey St-Marcellin cheese and Bayonne ham.

Little Breizh
Crêperie €

(Map p250; 📞01 43 54 60 74; 11 rue Grégoire de Tours, 6e; crêpes €4.70-12; 🕑noon-2.15pm & 7-10.15pm; 📷; Ⓜ Odéon) As authentic as you'd find in Brittany, but with some innovative twists (such as Breton sardines, olive oil and sundried tomatoes; goat's cheese, stewed apple, hazelnuts, rosemary and honey; smoked salmon, dill cream, pink peppercorns and lemon), the crêpes at this sweet spot are infinitely more enticing than those sold on nearby street corners. Hours can fluctuate; book ahead.

L'Amaryllis de Gérard Mulot
Patisserie €

(Map p254; www.gerard-mulot.com; 12 rue des Quartre Vents, 6e; dishes €6.60-20, lunch menu €25; 🕑11am-6.30pm Tue-Sat; Ⓜ Odéon) Pastry maestro Gérard Mulot has three boutiques in Paris, including one on nearby **rue de**

Seine (Map p254; www.gerard-mulot.com; 76 rue de Seine, 6e; 🕑6.45am-8pm Thu-Tue; Ⓜ Mabillon), but this branch also incorporates a *salon de thé* (tearoom) where you can sit down to savour his famous fruit tarts on the spot. Other dishes include quiches, gourmet salads, omelettes, and more filling lunch meals including a meat or fish *suggestion du chef*.

Bouillon Racine
Brasserie €€

(Map p254; 📞01 73 20 21 12; www.bouillonracine.com; 3 rue Racine, 6e; weekday lunch menu €16, menus €31-42; 🕑noon-11pm; 👶; Ⓜ Cluny-La Sorbonne) Inconspicuously situated in a quiet street, this heritage-listed 1906 art nouveau 'soup kitchen', with mirrored walls, floral motifs and ceramic tiling, was built in 1906 to feed market workers. Despite the magnificent interior, the food – inspired by age-old recipes – is no afterthought but superbly executed (stuffed, spit-roasted suckling pig, pork shank in Rodenbach red beer, scallops and shrimps with lobster coulis).

Chez Dumonet
Bistro €€

(Joséphine; 📞01 45 48 52 40; 117 rue du Cherche Midi ; mains €25-42; 🕑noon-2.30pm & 7.30-9.30pm Mon-Fri; Ⓜ Duroc) Fondly known by its former name, Joséphine, this lace-curtained, mosiac-tiled place with white-clothed tables inside and out is the Parisian bistro of many people's dreams, serving timeless standards such as confit of duck, *millefeuille* of pigeon, and grilled *châteaubriand* steak with Bearnaise sauce. Be sure to order its enormous signature Grand Marnier soufflé at the start of your meal.

Huîtrerie Regis
Seafood €€

(Map p250; http://huitrerieregis.com; 3 rue de Montfaucon, 6e; dozen oysters from €16; 🕑noon-2.30pm & 6.30-10.30pm Mon-Fri, noon-10.45pm Sat, noon-10pm Sun; Ⓜ Mabillon) Hip, trendy, tiny and white, this is *the* spot for slurping oysters on crisp winter days. They come only by the dozen, along with fresh bread and butter, but wash them down with a glass of chilled Muscadet and *voilà,* one perfect lunch. A twinset of tables loiter on

🍴◯🔪 The Five Basic Cheese Types

The choices on offer at a *fromagerie* (cheese shop) can be overwhelming, but vendors are usually very generous with their guidance and pairing advice.
Fromage à pâte demi-dure 'Semi-hard cheese' means uncooked, pressed cheese. Among the finest are Tomme de Savoie, Cantal, St-Nectaire and Ossau-Iraty.
Fromage à pâte dure 'Hard cheese' is always cooked and then pressed. Popular varieties are Beaufort, Comté, Emmental and Mimolette.
Fromage à pâte molle 'Soft cheese' is moulded or rind-washed. Camembert and Brie de Meaux are both made from raw cow's milk. Munster, Chaource, Langres and Époisses de Bourgogne are rind-washed, fine-textured cheeses.
Fromage à pâte persillée 'Marbled' or 'blue cheese' is so called because the veins often resemble *persille* (parsley). Roquefort is a ewe's-milk veined cheese that is to many the king of French cheeses. Fourme d'Ambert is a mild cow's-milk cheese from Rhône-Alpes. Bleu du Haut Jura is a mild, blue-veined mountain cheese.
Fromage de chèvre 'Goat's-milk cheese' is usually creamy and both sweet and slightly salty when fresh, but hardens and gets much saltier as it matures. Among the best varieties are Ste-Maure de Touraine, Crottin de Chavignol, Cabécou de Rocamadour and soft, slightly aged Chabichou.

JEANGILL/GETTY IMAGES ©

the pavement; otherwise it's all inside. No reservations, so arrive early.

Semilla   Neobistro €€
(Map p250; 📞01 43 54 34 50; 54 rue de Seine, 6e; lunch menu €24, mains €20-50; 🕐12.30-2.30pm & 7-10.45pm; Ⓜ Mabillon) Stark concrete, exposed pipes and an open kitchen (in front of which you can book front-row 'chef seats') set the factory-style scene for edgy, modern, daily changing dishes such as pork spare ribs with sweet potato and cinnamon, mushrooms in hazelnut butter, and trout with passionfruit and ginger (all suppliers are listed). Desserts here are outstanding. Be sure to book.

If you haven't made a reservation, head to its adjoining walk-in wine bar, **Freddy's** (Map p250; 54 rue de Seine, 6e; small plates €5-15; 🕐noon-midnight; Ⓜ St-Germain des Prés), serving small tapas-style plates.

À la Petite Chaise   Traditional French €€
(Map p248; 📞01 42 22 13 35; www.alapetitechaise. fr; 36 rue de Grenelle, 6e; menus lunch/dinner €25/33, mains €21; 🕐noon-2pm & 7-11pm; Ⓜ Sèvres-Babylone) Paris' oldest restaurant hides behind an iron gate that's been here since it opened in 1680, when wine merchant Georges Rameau served food to the public to accompany his wares. Classical decor and cuisine (onion soup, foie gras, duck, lamb and unexpected delights like venison terrine with hazelnuts) make it worth a visit above and beyond its history.

Clover   Neobistro €€
(Map p248; 📞01 75 50 00 05; www.clover-paris. com; 5 rue Perronet, 7e; 2-/3-course lunch menus €28/42, 3-/5-course dinner menus €58/73; 🕐12.30-2pm & 7.30-10pm Tue-Sat; Ⓜ St-Germain des Prés) Dining at hot-shot chef Jean-François Piège's casual bistro is like attending a private party: the galley-style open kitchen adjoining the 20 seats (reserve ahead!) is part of the dining-room decor, putting customers at the front and centre of the culinary action. Light, luscious dishes span from quinoa chips with aubergine and black sesame to cabbage leaves with smoked-herring *crème* and chestnuts.

KALEIDOSCOPIK PHOTOGRAPHY/SHUTTERSTOCK ©

Brioche

Polidor   Traditional French €€
(Map p254; ☎01 43 26 95 34; www.polidor.com; 41 rue Monsieur le Prince, 6e; menus €22-35, mains €12-20; ⊙noon-2.30pm & 7pm-12.30am Mon-Sat, noon-2.30pm & 7-11pm Sun; 👬; Ⓜ Odéon) A meal at this quintessentially Parisian *crèmerie-restaurant* is like a trip to Victor Hugo's Paris: the restaurant and its decor date from 1845. *Menus* of tasty, family-style French cuisine ensure a stream of diners eager to sample *bœuf bourguignon*, *blanquette de veau à l'ancienne* (veal in white sauce) and Polidor's famous *tarte Tatin*. Expect to wait. No credit cards.

Restaurant
Guy Savoy   Gastronomic €€€
(Map p250; ☎01 43 80 40 61; www.guysavoy. com; Monnaie de Paris, 11 quai de Conti, 6e; lunch menu via online booking €110, 12-/18-course tasting menus €420/490; ⊙noon-2pm & 7-10.30pm Tue-Fri, 7-10.30pm Sat; Ⓜ Pont Neuf) If you're considering visiting a three-Michelin-star temple of gastronomy, this should certainly be on your list. The world-famous chef needs no introduction (he trained Gordon Ramsay, among others) but now his flag-

ship, entered via a red-carpeted staircase, is ensconced in the gorgeously refurbished neoclassical **Monnaie de Paris** (Map p250; ☎01 40 46 56 66; www.monnaiedeparis.fr; 11 quai de Conti, 6e; Ⓜ Pont Neuf). Monumental cuisine to match includes Savoy icons like artichoke and black-truffle soup with layered brioche.

Look out for his casual courtyard brasserie/cafe on the same site. Or try his famed brioche for a fraction of the price in his eponymous restaurant by heading around the corner to his brioche boutique, **Goût de Brioche** (Map p250; www.goutde-brioche.com; 54 rue Mazarine, 6e; brioche €4-7; ⊙8.30am-7.30pm Tue-Fri, 8am-7.30pm Sat & Sun; Ⓜ Odéon).

Les Climats   Traditional French €€€
(Map p248; ☎01 58 62 10 08; http://lesclimats. fr; 41 rue de Lille, 7e; 2-/3-course lunch menus €36/42, 5-course dinner menu €98, mains €44-58, bar snacks €7-22; ⊙restaurant noon-2.30pm & 7-10pm Tue-Sat, bar noon-2.30pm & 7-10.30pm Tue-Sat; Ⓜ Solférino) Like the neighbouring Musée d'Orsay, this is a magnificent art nouveau treasure – a 1905-built former

home for female telephone, telegram and postal workers – featuring soaring vaulted ceilings and original stained glass, along with a lunchtime summer garden and glassed-in winter garden. Exquisite Michelin-starred dishes complement its 150-page list of wines, sparkling wines and whiskies purely from the Burgundy region.

Restaurant David Toutain   Gastronomic €€€

(Map p248; ☏ 01 45 51 11 10; http://davidtoutain. com; 29 rue Surcouf, 7e; 9-/15-course tastings menu €80/110; ☉ noon-2pm & 8-10pm Mon-Fri; Ⓜ Invalides) Prepare to be wowed: David Toutain pushes the envelope at his eponymous Michelin-starred restaurant with some of the most creative high-end cooking in Paris. Mystery degustation courses include unlikely combinations such as smoked eel in green-apple-and-black-sesame mousse, cauliflower, white chocolate and coconut truffles, or candied celery and truffled rice pudding with artichoke praline (stunning wine pairings available).

Le Dôme brasserie

DENNIS K JOHNSON/GETTY IMAGES ©

✕ Montparnasse & Southern Paris

L'Atelier B   Burgers €

(www.latelierb.fr; 129 rue du Château, 14e; burgers €11-13; ☉ noon-2.30pm & 6pm-2am Tue-Sat; Ⓜ Pernety) The best thing about this brilliant spot isn't the late closing time, friendly service or even the cocktails, wine and beers but the burgers themselves. Choices include Mon Bougnat (black Angus, confit onion, ruccola and blue cheese), Mon Basse Cour (chicken, aubergine, red onion, pickles and homemade BBQ sauce) and Mon Bia (chickpea patty, coleslaw, spinach, mushrooms and brie).

Le Beurre Noisette   Neobistro €€

(☏ 01 48 56 82 49; 68 rue Vasco de Gama, 15e; 2-/3-course lunch menus €23/32, mains €18; ☉ noon-2pm & 7-10.30pm Tue-Sat; Ⓜ Lourmel) *Beurre noisette* (brown butter sauce, named for its hazelnut colour) features in dishes such as scallops with cauliflower purée, and tender *bœuf fondante* with artichokes, courgette and carrot at pedigreed chef Thierry Blanqui's neighbourhood neobistro. Other treats include homemade blood sausage with apple compote. Filled with locals, the chocolate-toned dining room is wonderfully convivial – be sure to book.

Le Casse Noix   Modern French €€

(Map p248; ☏ 01 45 66 09 01; www.le-cassenoix. fr; 56 rue de la Fédération, 15e; 2-/3-course lunch menus €21/28, 3-course dinner menu €35; ☉ noon-2.30pm & 7-10.30pm Mon-Fri; Ⓜ Bir Hakeim) Proving that a location footsteps from the Eiffel Tower doesn't mean compromising on quality, quantity or authenticity, 'The Nutcracker' is a neighbourhood gem with a cosy retro interior, affordable prices, and exceptional cuisine that changes by season and by the inspiration of owner-chef Pierre Olivier Lenormand, who has honed his skills in some of Paris' most fêted kitchens. Book ahead.

Jeu de Quilles   Bistro €€

(📞01 53 90 76 22; 45 rue Boulard, 14e; 2-/3-course lunch menus €18/21, 4-course dinner menu €35, mains €23-37; ⏱8-10pm Tue, noon-2pm & 8-10pm Wed-Fri, noon-2pm & 7.30-10pm Sat; Ⓜ Mouton-Duvernet) When your next-door neighbour is the original premises of celebrated butcher Hugo Desnoyer, you have an inside track to serve exceptional meat-based dishes, and chef Benoît Reix does at this fabulous bistro. Creations such as artichoke-paste-encrusted pork or veal carpaccio pair with an extensive selection of natural wines. Reserve ahead: there are just 18 seats and locals love it.

Le Clos Y   Modern French €€

(📞01 45 49 07 35; www.leclosy.com; 27 av du Maine, 15e; 2-/3-course lunch menus €26/31, 4-/6-course dinner menus €45/65; ⏱noon-2pm & 7.30-10pm Tue-Sat; Ⓜ Montparnasse Bienvenüe) One of Paris' rapidly rising star chefs, Yoshi-taka Ikeda creates utterly original *menus* that change daily but might start with foie gras ice cream and move on to perch sashimi with beetroot, apple and powdered olive oil; green peas in pea jelly with mascarpone; smoked salmon and egg with raspberry foam; and Madeira-marinated beef with butternut squash and carrot purée.

La Rotonde
Montparnasse   Brasserie €€

(📞01 43 26 48 26; www.rotondemontparnasse.com; 105 bd du Montparnasse, 6e; 3-course menu €42, mains €15.50-42; ⏱6am-2am, menus noon-3pm & 7-11pm; Ⓜ Vavin) Opened in 1911 and recently restored to its former glory, La Rotonde may be awash with the same Les Montparnos history as its famous brasserie neighbours like Le Select, but the real reason to come is for the superior food. Meat comes from Pa-risian butcher extraordinaire Hugo Desnoyer, salmon and chicken are organic, and brasserie classics are cooked to perfection.

Le Grand Pan   Neobistro €€

(📞01 42 50 02 50; www.legrandpan.fr; 20 rue Rosenwald, 15e; mains €16-29; ⏱noon-2pm & 7-11pm Mon-Fri; Ⓜ Porte de Vanves) Red-leather banquettes, gorgeous mosaic-tiled floors and dark-timber tables set the stage for an atmospheric Parisian dining experience. The blackboard menu changes daily but stalwarts include foie gras ravioli with truffle shavings, *côte de veau* with cream sauce, and a chocolate cylinder filled with vanilla mousse and drizzled with salted caramel sauce. Its small-plates restaurant, Le Petit Pan, is directly opposite.

La Gauloise   Traditional French €€

(📞01 47 34 11 64; 59 av de la Motte-Picquet, 15e; 2-/3-course lunch menus €26/31, mains €19-31; ⏱noon-2.30pm & 7-11pm; Ⓜ La Motte Picquet Grenelle) With a name like La Gauloise, you wouldn't expect this venerable, terrace-front-ed restaurant to serve anything other than traditional fare, which it does, very well. From onion soup to pan-sautéed calf's liver, preserved foie gras with pear and mustard marmalade, and profiteroles or *îles flottantes* for dessert, it refines but doesn't reinvent the classics that make French cuisine iconic.

Le Ciel
de Paris   Traditional French €€€

(📞01 40 64 77 64; www.cieldeparis.com; Level 56, Tour Montparnasse, 33 av du Maine, 14e; menus lunch/dinner from €30/45; ⏱7.30am-11pm; Ⓜ Montparnasse Bienvenüe) Views don't get much better than 'the Sky of Paris', the Tour Montparnasse's 56th-floor restaurant, accessed by private lift/elevator. Starters include snails and pig's trotters; seafood is a speciality. The gastronomic Grand Écran menu (€136), available at dinner daily and Sunday lunch, includes a guaranteed window table and bottle of Champagne per person. The bar stays open until 1am.

Le Dôme   Brasserie €€€

(📞01 43 35 25 81; 108 bd du Montparnasse, 14e; mains €44-66.50, seafood platters €75; ⏱noon-3pm & 7-11.30pm; Ⓜ Vavin) A 1930s art deco extravaganza of the formal white-tablecloth and bow-tied waiter variety, monumental Le Dôme is one of the swishest places around for shellfish platters piled high with fresh oysters, king prawns, crab claws and much more, followed by traditional creamy homemade *millefeuille* for dessert.

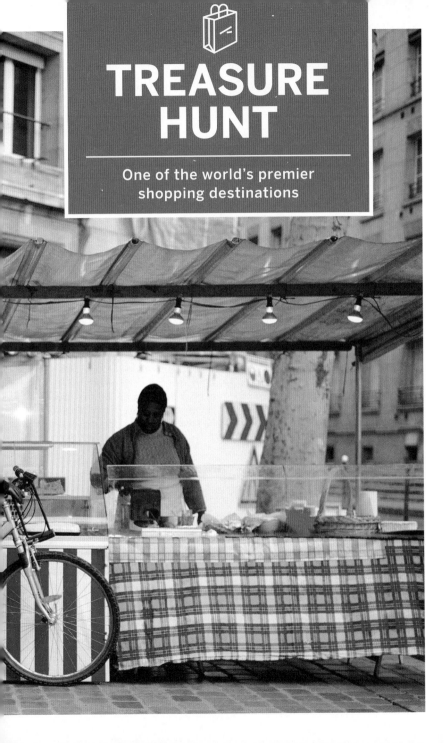

TREASURE HUNT

One of the world's premier shopping destinations

Treasure Hunt

Paris has it all: broad boulevards lined with flagship fashion houses and international labels, famous grand magasins (department stores) and fabulous markets, along with tiny speciality shops and quirky boutiques that sell everything from strawberry-scented Wellington boots to heaven-scented candles.

Fashion is Paris' forte. Browse haute couture creations, original streetwear and vintage gear, and adorable children's wear and accessories. Parisian fashion doesn't have to break the bank: there are fantastic bargains at secondhand and vintage boutiques, along with outlet shops selling previous seasons' collections, surpluses and seconds by top-line designers. But fashion is just the beginning. Paris is an exquisite treasure chest of gourmet food, wine, tea, books, stationery, art, art supplies, antiques and collectables.

In This Section

Useful Phrases

Look for signs indicating *cabines d'essayage* (fitting rooms).

Most shops offer free (and beautiful) gift wrapping – ask for *un paquet cadeau*.

A *ticket de caisse* (receipt) is essential for returning/exchanging an item (within one month of purchase).

If you're happy browsing, tell sales staff *Je regarde* (I'm just looking).

**Montmartre &
Northern Paris**
Gourmet food shops,
art, quintessential
souvenirs (p150)

**Champs-Élysées &
Grands Boulevards**
Haute couture houses,
famous department stores
(p148)

**Louvre &
Les Halles**
Cookware shops,
high-street chains,
covered arcades
(p149)

**Le Marais,
Ménilmontant &
Belleville**
Quirky homewares,
art galleries, up-and-
coming designers
(p153)

*Eiffel
Tower*

**St-Germain &
Les Invalides**
Art, antiques and
chic designer boutiques
(p159)

Seine

The Islands
Enchanting gift shops
and gourmet
boutiques (p156)

**Bastille &
Eastern Paris**
Great markets,
Viaduc des Arts
workshops (p155)

Seine

Latin Quarter
Late-opening
bookshops and
music shops (p157)

**Montparnasse
& Southern Paris**
Discount fashion
outlets, Asian
groceries (p161)

Opening Hours

Shops generally open between 10am
and 7pm Monday to Saturday. Smaller
shops often shut on Monday or may
close from around noon to 2pm for
lunch. Larger stores hold *nocturnes*
(late-night shopping), usually on Thursday, until around 10pm. Sunday shopping is limited; the Champs-Élysées,
Montmartre and Le Marais are liveliest.

Sales

Paris' twice-yearly *soldes* (sales) generally last five to six weeks. Winter sales
start around mid-January and summer
sales start around mid-June.

The Best...

Experience Paris' best shopping

Fashion Boutiques

Maison Kitsuné (p150) The secret to looking effortlessly French.

Andrea Crews (p153) Bold art and fashion collective.

La Boutique Extraordinaire (p154) Exquisite hand-knitted garments.

Antoine et Lili (pictured below; p151) All the colours of the rainbow in this iconic boutique.

Pigalle (p150) Leading Parisian menswear brand.

Gourmet Shops

Place de la Madeleine (p155) Single-item specialist shops and famous emporiums.

La Manufacture de Chocolat (p155) Alain Ducasse's bean-to-bar chocolate factory.

Fromagerie Goncourt (p154) Contemporary *fromagerie* (cheese shop) unusually styled like a boutique.

L'Éclair de Génie (p154) Sweet éclairs displayed like art.

For Kids

Chez Hélène (p154) Old-fashioned *bonbon* shop.

Smallable Concept Store (p161) One-stop shop for babies, children and teens.

Boîtes à Musique Anna Joliet (p149) Swiss music boxes to enchant in the Palais Royale.

Album (p159) Superb collection of *bandes desinées* (graphic novels) and related collectibles.

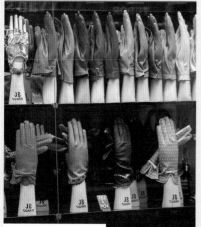

Accessories

JB Guanti (p160) Gorgeous gloves.
Marie Mercié (p161) Handmade hats.
Alexandra Sojfer (p160) Handcrafted umbrellas.

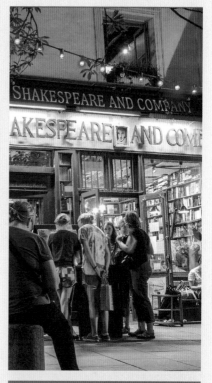

Concept Stores

Gab & Jo (p159) The country's first concept store stocking only French-made items.
Merci (pictured above; p153) Fabulously fashionable and unique: all profits go to a children's charity in Madagascar.
Colette (p150) Uberhip designer fashion and basement 'water bar'.
Hermès (p160) Housed in an art deco swimming pool.

★ Lonely Planet's Top Choices

Le Bonbon au Palais (p158) Artisan sweets from regions throughout France in a geography-classroom-themed boutique.
Didier Ludot (p149) Couture creations of yesteryear.
E Dehillerin (p149) Paris' professional chefs stock up at this opened-in-1820 cookware shop.
La Grande Épicerie de Paris (p160) Glorious food emporium.
Magasin Sennelier (p159) Historic art-supply shop with paints, canvases and paraphernalia galore.
Shakespeare & Company (p157) A 'wonderland of books', as Henry Miller described it.

🔒 Eiffel Tower & Western Paris

Patrick Roger Chocolate
(Map p248; 📞01 45 01 66 71; www.patrickroger.com; 45 av Victor Hugo, 16e; 🕙10.30am-7.30pm Mon-Sat; Ⓜ Victor Hugo) The creations of chocolate artist and sculptor Patrick Roger are extraordinary (and often very large – 80kg or so), rendering a visit to his swish boutiques an eye-opening experience. More modest, take-home boxes of one-bite chocolates, truffles, fruit jellies or coated almonds are as beautiful.

🔒 Champs-Élysées & Grands Boulevards

Galeries Lafayette Department Store
(http://haussmann.galerieslafayette.com; 40 bd Haussmann, 9e; 🕙9.30am-8pm Mon-Wed, Fri & Sat, to 9pm Thu; 📶; Ⓜ Chaussée d'Antin or RER Auber) Grande dame department store Galeries Lafayette is spread across the main store (its magnificent stained-glass dome is over a century old), **men's store**
(bd Haussmann, 9e; 🕙9.30am-8pm Mon-Wed, Fri & Sat, to 9pm Thu; 📶; Ⓜ Chaussée d'Antin or RER Auber) and **homewares** (bd Haussmann, 9e; 🕙9.30am-8pm Mon-Wed, Fri & Sat, to 9pm Thu; 📶; Ⓜ Havre Caumartin or RER Auber) store, and includes a gourmet emporium (bd Haussmann, 9e; 🕙9.30am-8pm Mon-Sat, to 9pm Thu; Ⓜ Havre Caumartin or RER Auber).

Catch modern art in the **gallery** (www.galeriedesgaleries.com; 1st fl, Galeries Lafayette; 🕙11am-7pm Tue-Sat; Ⓜ Chaussée d'Antin or RER Auber) FREE, take in a **fashion show** (📞bookings 01 42 82 30 25; 🕙3pm Fri Mar-Jun & Sep-Dec by reservation), ascend to a free, windswept rooftop panorama, or take a break at one of its 24 restaurants and cafes.

Guerlain Perfume
(Map p248; 📞spa 01 45 62 11 21; www.guerlain.com; 68 av des Champs-Élysées, 8e; 🕙10.30am-8pm Mon-Sat, noon-7pm Sun; Ⓜ Franklin D Roosevelt) Guerlain is Paris' most famous parfumerie, and its shop (dating from 1912) is one of the most beautiful in the city. With its shimmering mirror and marble art deco interior, it's a reminder of the former glory of the Champs-Élysées. For total

Galeries Lafayette

indulgence, make an appointment at its decadent spa.

Marché aux Fleurs Madeleine   Market
(Map p248; place de la Madeleine, 8e; ☺8am-7.30pm Mon-Sat; Ⓜ Madeleine) This colourful flower market has been trading since 1832.

Publicis Drugstore   Concept Store
(www.publicisdrugstore.com; 133 av des Champs-Élysées, 8e; ☺8am-2am; Ⓜ Charles de Gaulle-Étoile) An institution since 1958, Publicis incorporates cinemas and late-opening shops, including an *épicerie* (specialist grocer), pharmacy, beauty counter, international newsagent, a wine *cave* (cellar) and cigar bar. At street level there's a glassed-in brasserie and steakhouse; downstairs is the overrated black-and-red Étoile branch of L'Atelier de Joël Robuchon.

À la Mère de Famille   Confectionery
(www.lameredefamille.com; 35 rue du Faubourg Montmartre, 9e; ☺9.30am-8pm Mon-Sat, 10am-1pm Sun; Ⓜ Le Peletier) Founded in 1761, this is the original location of Paris' oldest chocolatier. Its beautiful belle époque façade is as enchanting as the rainbow of sweets, caramels and chocolates inside.

🛍 Louvre & Les Halles

Didier Ludot   Fashion
(Map p250; ☎01 42 96 06 56; www.didierludot.fr; 19-20 & 23-24 Galerie de Montpensier, 1er; ☺10.30am-7pm Mon-Sat; Ⓜ Palais Royal–Musée du Louvre) In the rag trade since 1975, collector Didier Ludot sells the city's finest couture creations of yesteryear in his exclusive twinset of boutiques, hosts exhibitions and has published a book portraying the evolution of the little black dress.

E Dehillerin   Homewares
(Map p250; www.e-dehillerin.fr; 18-20 rue Coquillière, 1er; ☺9am-12.30pm & 2-6pm Mon, 9am-6pm Tue-Sat; Ⓜ Les Halles) Founded in 1820, this extraordinary two-level store – think old-fashioned warehouse rather than shiny, chic boutique – carries an incredible selection of professional-quality *matériel*

Bouquinistes along the Seine

With some 3km of forest-green boxes lining the Seine, containing over 300,000 secondhand, often out-of-print, books, rare magazines, postcards and old advertising posters, Paris' **bouquinistes** (quai Voltaire, 7e to quai de la Tournelle, 5e & Pont Marie, 4e to quai du Louvre, 1er; ☺11.30am-dusk), or used-book sellers, are as integral to the cityscape as Notre Dame. Many open only from spring to autumn (and many shut in August), but year-round you'll still find some to browse.

The *bouquinistes* have been in business since the 16th century, when they were itinerant peddlers selling their wares on Parisian bridges – back then their sometimes-subversive (eg Protestant) materials would get them in trouble with the authorities. By 1859 the city had finally wised up: official licenses were issued, space was rented (10m of railing) and eventually the permanent green boxes were installed.

Today, *bouquinistes* (the official count ranges from 200 to 240) are allowed to have four boxes, only one of which can be used to sell souvenirs. Look hard enough and you just might find some real treasures: old comic books, forgotten 1st editions, maps, stamps, erotica and prewar newspapers – as in centuries past, it's all there, waiting to be rediscovered.

de cuisine (kitchenware). Poultry scissors, turbot poacher, professional copper cookware or Eiffel Tower–shaped cake tin – it's all here.

Boîtes à Musique Anna Joliet   Gifts, Souvenirs
(Map p250; Passage du Perron, 1er; ☺noon-7pm Tue-Sat; Ⓜ Pyramides) This wonderful shop at the northern end of the Jardin du Palais

Historic Haute Couture

A stroll around the legendary Triangle d'Or (Golden Triangle; bordered by avs George V, Champs-Élysées and Montaigne, 8e) or on rue du Faubourg St-Honoré constitutes the walk of fame of top French fashion. Rubbing shoulders with the world's top international designers are Paris' most influential French fashion houses: Chanel, Chloé, Dior, Givenchy, Hermès, Lanvin, Louis Vuitton and Yves Saint Laurent.

Royal specialises in music boxes, new and old, from Switzerland.

Colette Concept Store
(Map p248; www.colette.fr; 213 rue St-Honoré, 1er; ⊙11am-7pm Mon-Sat; MTuileries) Uberhip is an understatement. Ogle designer fashion on the 1st floor, and streetwear, limited-edition sneakers, art books, music, gadgets and other high-tech, inventive and/ or plain unusual items on the ground floor. End with a drink in the basement 'water bar' and pick up free design magazines and flyers for some of the city's hippest happenings by the door upon leaving.

Kiliwatch Fashion
(Map p250; ☑01 42 21 17 37; http://espacekili-watch.fr; 64 rue Tiquetonne, 2e; ⊙10.30am-7pm Mon, to 7.30pm Tue-Sat; MÉtienne Marcel) A Parisian institution, Kiliwatch gets jam-packed with hip guys and gals rummaging through racks of new and used streetwear. Startling vintage range of hats and boots plus art/ photography books, eyewear and the latest sneakers.

Legrand Filles & Fils Food & Wine
(Map p250; www.caves-legrand.com; 1 rue de la Banque, 2e; ⊙10am-7.30pm Tue-Sat, 11am-7pm Sun; MPyramides) Tucked inside Galerie Vivienne since 1880, Legrand sells fine wine and all the accoutrements: corkscrews, tasting glasses, decanters etc. It also has a fancy wine bar, école du vin (wine school)

and éspace dégustation (tasting room) with several tastings a month; check its website for details.

Antoine Fashion
(Map p250; 10 av de l'Opéra, 1er; ⊙10.30am-1pm & 2-6.30pm Mon-Sat; MPyramides, Palais Royal-Musée du Louvre) Antoine has been the Parisian master of bespoke canes, umbrellas, fans and gloves since 1745.

MORA Homewares
(Map p250; 13 Rue Montmartre, 1er; ⊙9am-6.15pm Mon-Fri, 10am-1pm & 1.45-6.30pm Sat; MLes Halles) Both amateur and professional pastry chefs will want to stop by MORA to pick up all manner of specialist culinary items, from unique cake and pastry moulds to macaron mats, pasta makers, piping bags and cream chargers (in case you're considering some fresh-baked éclairs back home).

Nose Perfume
(Map p250; ☑01 40 26 46 03; http://nose.fr; 20 rue Bachaumont, 2e; ⊙10.30am-7.30pm Mon-Sat; MSentier) Come to this concept shop for a personal perfume diagnosis, after which the knowledgable staff (English spoken) will be able to narrow down a selection of fragrances that suit you best. You could easily spend over an hour here, so come with time to spare. Perfumes and cosmetics available for both men and women.

🏠 Montmartre & Northern Paris

Maison Kitsuné Fashion
(Map p256; https://shop.kitsune.fr; 68 rue Condorcet, 9e; ⊙1.30-7pm Mon-Sat, noon-6.30pm Sun; MPigalle) Paris fashion label Kitsuné is the secret to looking effortlessly French. Shop here for ready-to-wear fashion, accessories and must-have everyday items for men and women.

Pigalle Fashion
(Map p256; www.pigalle-paris.com; 7 rue Henry Monnier, 9e; ⊙noon-8pm Mon-Sat, 2-8pm Sun; MPigalle) Blend in with local hipsters with a hoodie emblazoned with the B&W Pigalle logo from this leading Parisian menswear

brand, created by wild-child designer and amateur basketball player Stéphane Ashpool, who grew up in the 'hood.

Antoine et Lili   Fashion, Homewares
(www.antoineetlili.com; 95 quai de Valmy, 10e; ⊙11am-8pm Tue-Fri, to 7pm Sun & Mon; MJacques Bonsergent, Gare de l'Est) All the colours of the rainbow and all the patterns in the world congregate in this wonderful Parisian institution with designer clothing for women (pink store) and children (green store), and hip home decorations (yellow store).

Belle du Jour   Accessories
(Map p256; www.belle-de-jour.fr; 7 rue Tardieu, 18e; ⊙10.30am-1pm & 2-7pm Tue-Fri, 10.30am-1pm & 2-6pm Sat; MAnvers) Be whisked back in time to the elegance of belle époque Paris with this sweet-smelling Montmartre shop specialising in perfume bottles. Gorgeous 19th-century atomisers, smelling salts and powder boxes in engraved or enamelled Bohemian, Baccarat and St-Louis crystal jostle for the limelight with more contemporary designs. Art deco or art nouveau, pink-frosted or painted glass, it's here.

Fromagerie Alléosse   Cheese
(www.alleosse.com; 13 rue Poncelet, 17e; ⊙9am-1.15pm & 3-7.15pm Tue-Fri, 9am-7pm Sat, 9am-1pm Sun; MTernes) Although there are cheese shops throughout the city, this one is actually worth a trip across town. Cheeses are sold as they should be, grouped into five main categories: *fromage de chèvre* (goat's-milk cheese), *fromage à pâte persillée* (veined or blue cheese), *fromage à pâte molle* (soft cheese), *fromage à pâte demi-dure* (semihard cheese) and *fromage à pâte dure* (hard cheese).

Jeremie Barthod   Jewellery
(Map p256; www.jeremiebarthod.com; 7 rue des Trois Frères, 18e; ⊙11.15am-7.15pm; MAbbesses) Fantasy necklaces, bracelets and other jewellery pieces are crafted from metal springs dipped in antique silver, bronze or copper at this hybrid boutique-atelier in Montmartre.

Kann Design   Homewares, Fashion
(☎09 53 40 86 98; www.kanndesign.com; 28 rue des Vinaigriers, 10e; ⊙10.30am-1pm & 2-7pm Tue-Fri, 1-7pm Sat; MJacques Bonsergent) This stylish concept store near Canal St-Martin is a wonderful one-stop shop for hipster-cool T-shirts, sneakers, stationery, games and candles as well as cushions, lamps, furniture and other beautiful objects for your pad back home.

Marché aux Puces de St-Ouen   Market
(www.marcheauxpuces-saintouen.com; rue des Rosiers; ⊙varies; MPorte de Clignancourt) This vast flea market, founded in the late 19th century and said to be Europe's largest, has more than 2500 stalls grouped into 15 *marchés* (markets), each with its own speciality (eg Marché Paul Bert Serpette for 17th-century furniture, Marché Malik for casual clothing, Marché Biron for Asian art). Each market has different opening hours – check its website for details.

Hotel Plaza Athénée on fashionable Avenue Montaigne

5 Must-Buy Mementos

1 Artistic Masterpieces

At major museums, the Boutiques de Musées (www.boutiquesdemusees.fr) have digital painting-and-frame services so you can get replicas mailed to your home.

2 Perfume

Browse for perfume at new innovators or department stores, or buy a bottle of Champs-Élysées from Guerlain's century-old premises (p148) on its namesake street.

3 Macarons

Pick up a box of ganache-filled, ground-almond meringue *macarons* in a kaleidoscope of colour and flavour combinations from *pâtissier* Pierre Hermé (p160).

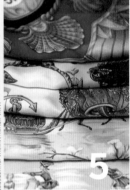

5 Scarves

The secret to French fashion is accessorising, and the ultimate Parisian accessory is a scarf. Timeless silk designs are produced by Hermès (p160).

4 Candles

Candle-makers in the City of Light span from the world's oldest, Cire Trudon (p160), to La Note Parisienne's contemporary designs found at Gab & Jo (p159).

Spree
Fashion

(Map p256; ☎01 42 23 41 40; http://spree.fr; 16 rue de la Vieuville, 18e; ⊙11am-7.30pm Tue-Sat, 3-7pm Mon & Sun; MAbbesses) Sift through Montmartre's tourist shops to find its super stylish boutique-gallery, with a carefully curated collection of vintage fashion (1950s to 1980s) put together by Paris stylist Roberta Oprandi. What makes shopping here fun is that all the furniture – several lovely 1950s and 1960s pieces by Eames et al – is also for sale, as is the contemporary artwork on the walls. Allow plenty of time to mooch.

🛍 Le Marais, Ménilmontant & Belleville

Merci
Concept Store

(Map p250; ☎01 42 77 00 33; www.merci-merci. com; 111 bd Beaumarchais, 3e; ⊙10am-7pm Mon-Sat; MSt-Sébastien-Froissart) A Fiat Cinquecento marks the entrance to this unique concept store, which donates all its profits to a children's charity in Madagascar. Shop for fashion, accessories, linens, lamps and nifty designs for the home; and complete the experience with a coffee in its hybrid used-bookshop-cafe or lunch in its stylish basement **La Cantine de Mercia** (Map p250; ☎01 42 77 79 28; www.merci-merci. com; 111 bd Beaumarchais, 3e; soups €8-10, salads & tarts €10-17; ⊙noon-6pm Mon-Sat; MSt-Sébastien-Froissart).

Andrea Crews
Fashion

(Map p250; www.andreacrews.com; 83 rue de Turenne, 3e; ⊙11am-7pm Mon-Fri, 12.30-7.30pm Sat; MSt-Sébastien-Froissart) Using everything from discarded clothing to electrical fittings and household bric-a-brac, this bold art and fashion collective sews, recycles and reinvents to create the most extraordinary pieces. Watch out for 'happenings' in this Marais boutique.

Belleville Brûlerie
Coffee

(☎09 83 75 60 80; http://cafesbelleville.com; 10 rue Pradier, 19e; ⊙11.30am-5.30pm Sat; MBelleville) With its understated steel-grey

🛍 Secret Shopping

Some of the Marais' sweetest boutique shopping is secreted down peaceful alleyways and courtyards, free of cars, as they were centuries ago. Take **Rue du Trésor** (a pedestrian dead-end passage off rue du Vieille du Temple), encrusted with an exclusive handful of hip boutiques, such as **Trésor** (Map p250; 5 rue du Trésor, 4e; ⊙11am-7.30pm Tue-Sat; MHôtel de Ville, St-Paul) by Brigitte Masson, a bohemian boutique with a catchy salmon-orange façade strung with old-fashioned fairy lights and fresh, individual women's fashion inside. End with a drink or lunch on the buzzing pavement terrace of **La Chaise au Plafond** (Map p250; 10 rue du Trésor, 4e; ⊙9am-2am; MHôtel de Ville, St-Paul) or neighbouring **Les Philosophes** (Map p250; www.cafeine. com/philosophes; 28 rue Vieille du Temple, 4e; ⊙9am-2am, kitchen noon-1.15am; ☎; MHôtel de Ville).

From Monday to Friday the area's cobbled alleys are mostly mouse quiet, but come the weekend savvy trendsetters mingle at **Village St-Paul** (Map p250; rue St-Paul, des rue Jardins St-Paul & rue Charlemagne, 4e; MSt-Paul), a designer set of five vintage courtyards, refashioned in the 1970s from the 14th-century walled gardens of King Charles V. Meander away Saturday afternoon with a courtyard-to-courtyard stroll, with old stone paving, ancient fountains and tiny artisan boutiques, galleries and antique shops.

façade, this ground-breaking roastery in Belleville is easy to miss. Don't! These are the guys who brought good coffee to Paris and its beans go into some of the best espressos and cappucinos in town. Taste the week's selection, compare tasting notes and buy a bag to take home. Online shop too.

Fromagerie Beaufils   Cheese

(www.fromagerie-beaufils.com; 118 rue de Belle-ville, 20e; ⊙8am-1pm & 3.30-7.45pm Tue-Sat, 8.30am-1pm Sun; MJourdain) The queue outside the door, especially at weekends, says it all. This family-run *fromagerie* (cheese shop) and *affineur* (ripener) in Belleville is among the best in Paris, with dozens of French cheeses you're unlikely to see – and, more importantly, taste – elsewhere.

Chez Hélène   Confectionery

(Map p250; www.chezhelene-paris.com; 28 rue Saint-Gilles, 3e; ⊙11am-2pm & 3-7.30pm Mon-Sat; MChemin Vert) Pure indulgence is what this irresistible bonbon boutique – a child's dream come true – is about. Old-fashioned toffees and caramels, fudge, liquorice, Eiffel Tower sugar cubes, designer lollipops, artisanal marshmallows, Provençal *calissons* (diamond-shaped icing-sugar-topped ground fruit and almonds)...the choice of quality, well-made bonbons and *gourmandises* (sweet treats) is outstanding.

L'Éclair de Génie   Food

(Map p250; http://leclairdegenie.com; 14 rue Pavée, 4e; ⊙11am-7pm Mon-Fri, 10am-7.30pm Sat & Sun; MSt-Paul) You will never look at a simple éclair again after visiting the swish boutique of highly creative pastry chef Christophe Adam. Exquisitely filled and decorated éclairs are displayed with military precision in rows beneath glass. Like fashion, flavours change with the seasons. Count on between €5 and €7 a shot.

Fromagerie Goncourt   Cheese

(☑01 43 57 91 28; 1 rue Abel Rabaud, 11e; ⊙9am-1pm & 4-8.30pm Tue-Fri, 9am-8pm Sat; MGoncourt) Styled like a boutique, this contemporary *fromagerie* (cheese shop) is a must-discover. Clément Brossault ditched a career in banking to become a *fromager* and his cheese selection – 70-odd types – is superb. Cheeses flagged with a bicycle symbol are varieties he discovered in situ during a two-month French cheese tour he embarked on as part of his training.

Le Creuset   Homewares

(Map p250; www.lecreuset.fr; 26 rue des Rosiers, 4e; ⊙10.30am-7.30pm; MHôtel de Ville) French cooks have been using Le Creuset's colourful cast-iron and stainless pots and pans since 1925. Now you can do the same thanks to this gorgeous Marais boutique. Pepper mills, spatulas, eggs cups, crêpe turners and far, far more than just very heavy saucepans.

Les Exprimeurs   Souvenirs

(Map p250; www.lesexprimeurs.fr; 4 rue du Pont Louis-Philippe, 4e; ⊙9am-1pm & 2-6pm Tue, Thu & Fri, 9am-noon Wed, 11am-1pm & 2-7pm Sat; MHôtel de Ville) For an exquisite paper cut-out of the Eiffel Tower, a bookmark shaped like the Panthéon rooftop or a quality sketchbook or ink pen, look no further than this wonderful stationery shop. It sells both fabulously classy souvenirs as well as daily essentials.

La Boutique Extraordinaire   Fashion

(Map p250; www.laboutiqueextraordinaire.com; 67 rue Charlot, 3e; ⊙11am-8pm Tue-Sat, 1-7pm Sun; MFilles du Calvaire) Mohair, silk and other natural, organic and ethical materials are hand-knitted into exquisite garments, almost too precious to wear, at this unusual and captivating Haut Marais boutique.

Made by Moi   Fashion, Homewares

(☑01 58 30 95 78; www.madebymoi.fr; 86 rue Oberkampf, 11e; ⊙2.30-8pm Mon, 10am-8pm Tue-Sat; MParmentier) 'Made by Me', ie handmade, is the driver of this appealing boutique on trendy rue Oberkampf – a perfect address to buy unusual gifts. Mooch here for women's fashion, homewares and other beautiful objects like coloured glass carafes, feathered headdresses, funky contact-lens boxes and retro dial telephones. The ultimate Paris souvenir: 'Bobo brunch' scented candles by Bougies La Française.

Mariage Frères   Drink

(Map p250; www.mariagefreres.com; 30, 32 & 35 rue du Bourg Tibourg, 4e; ⊙10am-7.30pm; MHôtel de Ville) Founded in 1854, this is Paris' first and arguably finest teashop. Choose from more than 500 varieties of tea sourced from some 35 countries. Mariage Frères has four other outlets, including branches in the 6e and 8e.

Paris Rendez-Vous   Concept Store

(Map p250; http://rendezvous.paris.fr; 29 rue de Rivoli, 4e; ⊙10am-7pm Mon-Sat; MHôtel de Ville) Only the city of Paris could be so chic as to have its own designer line of souvenirs, sold in its own ubercool concept store inside Hôtel de Ville (City Hall). Shop here for everything from clothing and homewares to Paris-themed books, toy sailing boats and signature Jardin du Luxembourg's Fermob chairs. *Quel style!*

Vert d'Absinthe   Drink

(Map p250; www.vertdabsinthe.com; 11 rue d'Ormesson, 4e; ⊙noon-7pm Tue-Sat; MSt-Paul) Fans of the *fée verte* (green fairy), as absinthe was known during the belle époque, will think they've died and gone to heaven. Here, you can buy not only bottles of the best-quality hooch but all the paraphernalia as well: glasses, water jugs and tiny slotted spoons for the all-important sugar cube.

🏛 Bastille & Eastern Paris

La Manufacture
de Chocolat   Chocolate

(www.lechocolat-alainducasse.com; 40 rue de la Roquette, 11e; ⊙10.30am-7pm Tue-Sat; MBastille) If you dine at superstar chef Alain Ducasse's restaurants, the chocolate will have been made here at Ducasse's own chocolate factory (the first in Paris to produce 'bean-to-bar' chocolate), which he set up with his former executive pastry chef Nicolas Berger. Deliberate over ganaches, pralines and truffles and no fewer than 44 flavours of chocolate bar.

You can also buy Ducasse's chocolates at his Left Bank boutique, **Le Chocolat Alain Ducasse** (Map p250; www.lechocolat-alainducasse.com; 26 rue St-Benoît, 6e; ⊙1.30-7.30pm Mon, 10.30am-7.30pm Tue-Sat; MSt Germain des Prés).

🛍 Place de la Madeleine

Ultragourmet food shops garland **place de la Madeleine** (Map p248; place de la Madeleine, 8e; MMadeleine); many have in-house dining options, too. Notable names include truffle dealers **La Maison de la Truffe** (Map p248; 📞01 42 65 53 22; www.maison-de-la-truffe.com; 19 place de la Madeleine, 8e; ⊙10am-10pm Mon-Sat; MMadeleine); luxury food shop **Hédiard** (Map p248; www.hediard.fr; 21 place de la Madeleine, 8e; ⊙9am-8pm Mon-Sat; MMadeleine); mustard specialist **Boutique Maille** (Map p248; 📞01 40 15 06 00; www.maille.com; 6 place de la Madeleine, 8e; ⊙10am-7pm Mon-Sat; MMadeleine); and Paris' most famous caterer, **Fauchon** (Map p248; 📞01 70 39 38 00; www.fauchon.fr; 26 & 30 place de la Madeleine, 8e; ⊙10am-8.30pm Mon-Sat; MMadeleine), selling incredibly mouth-watering delicacies, from truffles to jams, chocolates and pastries. Check out the extravagant chocolate sculptures at **Patrick Roger** (Map p248; www.patrickroger.com; 3 place de la Madeleine; ⊙10.30am-7.30pm; MMadeleine).

La Cocotte   Homewares

(www.lacocotte.net; 5 rue Paul Bert, 11e; ⊙noon-7pm Tue-Sat; MFaidherbe-Chaligny) If the slew of gourmet restaurants along rue Paul Bert has inspired you to get into the kitchen, stop by this cute boutique for stylish, often Paris- and/or French-themed accoutrements such as tea towels, oven mitts, aprons, cookware, mugs, shopping bags and more.

Viaduc des Arts
Arts & Crafts

(www.leviaducdesarts.com; 1-129 av Daumesnil, 12e; ⊙variable; Ⓜ Bastille, Gare de Lyon) Located beneath the red-brick arches of Promenade Plantée (p200) is the Viaduc des Arts, a line-up of craft shops where traditional artisans and contemporary designers carry out antique renovations and create new items using traditional methods. Artisans include furniture and tapestry restorers, interior designers, cabinet-makers, violin- and flute-makers, embroiderers and jewellers.

Marché aux Puces d'Aligre
Market

(Place d'Aligre, 12e; ⊙8am-1pm Tue-Sun; Ⓜ Ledru-Rollin) Smaller but more central than Paris' other flea markets, here you can rummage through boxes of clothes and accessories worn decades ago, as well as assorted bric-a-brac.

> *Traditional and contemporary design intersect at Viaduc des Arts*

Printmaker at an atelier in Viaduc des Arts

🔒 The Islands

Marché aux Fleurs Reine Elizabeth II
Market

(Map p250; place Louis Lépin, 4e; ⊙8am-7.30pm Mon-Sat; Ⓜ Cité) Blooms have been sold at this flower market since 1808, making it the oldest market of any kind in Paris. On Sunday, between 8am and 7pm, it transforms into a cacophonous bird market, the Marché aux Oiseaux (Map p250; place Louis Lépin, 4e; ⊙8am-7pm Sun; Ⓜ Cité).

38 Saint Louis
Food & Wine

(Map p254; 38 rue St-Louis en l'Île, 4e; ⊙8.30am-10pm Tue-Sat, 9.30am-4pm Sun; Ⓜ Pont Marie) Not only does this contemporary, creamy white-fronted *fromagerie* run by a young, dynamic, food-driven duo have an absolutely superb selection of first-class French *fromage* (cheese), it also offers Saturday wine tastings, artisan fruit juices, prepared dishes to go, such as sheep's-cheese salad with truffle oil, and wooden boxes filled with vacuum-packed cheese to take home.

MATT MUNRO/GETTY IMAGES ©

L'Îles aux Images Arts & Crafts

(Map p254; ☎01 56 24 15 22; www.lileauximages.com; 51 rue Saint-Louis en l'Île, 4e; ⊙2-7pm Mon-Sat & by appointment; ⓂPont Marie) Original and rare vintage posters, photographs and lithographs dating from 1850 onwards from artists including Man Ray, Salvador Dalí, Paul Gauguin and Picasso are stocked at this gallery-boutique. Many depict Parisian scenes and make evocative home decorations. Framing can be arranged.

Clair de Rêve Toys

(Map p254; www.clairdereve.com; 35 rue St-Louis en l'Île, 4e; ⊙11am-1pm & 1.30-7.15pm Mon-Sat; ⓂPont Marie) Stringed marionettes made of papier mâché, leather and porcelain bob from the ceiling of this endearing little shop. It also sells wind-up toys and music boxes.

🏛 Latin Quarter

Shakespeare & Company Books

(Map p254; ☎01 43 25 40 93; www.shakespeareandcompany.com; 37 rue de la Bûcherie, 5e; ⊙10am-11pm; ⓂSt-Michel) Shakespeare's enchanting nooks and crannies overflow with new and secondhand English-language books. The original shop (12 rue l'Odéon, 6e; closed by the Nazis in 1941) was run by Sylvia Beach and became the meeting point for Hemingway's 'Lost Generation'. Readings by emerging and illustrious authors take place at 7pm most Mondays. There's a wonderful **cafe** (p134) and various workshops and festivals.

It's fabled for nurturing writers, and at night its couches turn into beds where writers stay in exchange for stacking shelves.

American-born George Whitman opened the present incarnation in 1951, attracting a beat-poet clientele, and scores of authors have since passed through its doors. In 2006 Whitman was awarded the Officier des Arts et Lettres by the French Minister of Culture, recognising 'significant contribution to the enrichment of the French cultural inheritance'. Whitman died in 2011, aged 98; he is buried in division 73 of Cimetière du Père

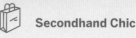

Secondhand Chic

When St-Germain's well-heeled residents spring-clean their wardrobes, they take their designer and vintage cast-offs to *dépôt-vente* (secondhand) boutiques, where savvy locals snap up serious bargains. Try your luck at the following addresses:

Catherine B (Map p254; http://les-3marchesdecatherineb.com; 1-3 rue Guisarde, 6e; ⊙11am-7pm Mon-Sat; ⓂMabillon) Serious fans of Chanel and Hermès should call into this exceptionally curated boutique, which specialises exclusively in items from these two iconic French fashion houses.

Chercheminippes (www.chercheminippes.com; 102, 106, 109-111, 114 & 124 rue du Cherche Midi, 6e; ⊙11am-7pm Mon-Sat; ⓂVaneau) Seven beautifully presented boutiques on one street selling secondhand pieces by current designers. Each specialises in a different genre (*haute couture*, kids, menswear etc), perfectly ordered by size and designer. There are even changing rooms.

Les Dépôts Chics (Map p248; 173 rue de Grenelle, 7e; ⊙10.45am-7pm Mon-Sat; ⓂÈcole Militaire) Ultra-luxe labels (Dior et al) are stocked at this elegant boutique.

Lachaise. Today his daughter, Sylvia Beach Whitman, maintains Shakespeare & Company's serendipitous magic.

The Art of Flânerie

Parisian writer Charles Baudelaire (1821–67) came up with the whimsical term *flâneur* to describe a 'gentleman stroller of city streets' or a 'detached pedestrian observer of a metropolis'.

Paris' ornate arcades were closely tied to the concept of *flânerie* in philosopher Walter Benjamin's *Arcades Project* (written between 1927 and 1940, and published posthumously). Known as *passages couverts* (covered passages), these marble-floored, iron-and-glass-roofed shopping arcades, streaming with natural light, were the elegant forerunners to department stores and malls.

The term *flânerie* is now widely used, especially in the context of architecture and town planning. But Paris – with its village-like backstreets, its riverbank paths, parks and gardens and its passages – remains the ultimate place for a *flâneur* to meander without any particular destination in mind.

The finest remaining *passages couverts* include **Galerie Véro Dodat** (Map p250; btwn rue Jean-Jacques-Rousseau & 2 rue du Bouloi; ⊙hours vary; ⓂLouvre Rivoli) and **Passage des Panoramas** (Map p250; 10 rue St-Marc, 2e; ⊙6am–midnight; ⓂBourse).

Galerie Véro Dodat
TUPUNGATO/GETTY IMAGES ©

Le Bonbon au Palais   Sweets

(Map p254; http://bonbonsaupalais.fr; 19 rue Monge, 5e; ⊙10.30am-7.30pm Tue-Sat; ⓂCardinal Lemoine) Kids and kids-at-heart will adore this sugar-fuelled *tour de France*. The school-geography-themed boutique stocks rainbows of artisan sweets from around the country. Old-fashioned glass jars brim with treats like *calissons* (diamond-shaped, icing-sugar-topped ground fruit and almonds from Aix-en-Provence), *rigolettes* (fruit-filled pillows from Nantes), *berlingots* (striped, triangular boiled sweets from Carpentras and elsewhere) and *papalines* (herbal-liqueur-filled pink-chocolate balls from Avignon).

Androuet   Cheese

(http://androuet.com; 134 rue Mouffetard, 5e; ⊙9.30am-1pm & 4-7.30pm Tue-Fri, 9.30am-7.30pm Sat, to 1.30pm Sun; ⓂCensier Daubenton) All of the cheeses at this great *fromagerie* can be vacuum-packed for free to take home. Be sure to look up to see the beautiful murals on the building's façade.

Abbey Bookshop   Books

(Map p254; ☎01 46 33 16 24; 29 rue de la Parcheminerie, 5e; ⊙10am-7pm Mon-Sat, 2-7pm Sun; ⓂCluny–La Sorbonne) In a heritage-listed townhouse, this welcoming Canadian-run bookshop serves free coffee (sweetened with maple syrup) to sip while you browse tens of thousands of new and used books, and organises literary events and countryside hikes.

Crocodisc   Music

(Map p254; www.crocodisc.com; 40 & 42 rue des Écoles, 5e; ⊙11am-7pm Tue-Sat mid-Aug–late Jul; ⓂMaubert-Mutualité) Music might be more accessible than ever before in the digital age, but for many it will never replace rummaging through racks for treasures. New and secondhand CDs and vinyl discs at 40 rue des Écoles span world music, rap, reggae, salsa, soul and disco, while No 42 has pop, rock, punk, new wave, electro and soundtracks.

Its nearby sister shop **Crocojazz** (Map p254; www.crocojazz.com; 64 rue de la Montagne Ste-Geneviève, 5e; ⊙11am-1pm & 2-7pm Tue-Sat mid-Aug–late Jul; ⓂMaubert-Mutualité) specialises in jazz, blues, gospel and timeless crooners, with books and DVDs as well as recordings.

Le Bon Marché

Album   Comics

(Map p254; http://album.fr; 67 bd St-Germain, 5e; ⏱10am-8pm Mon-Sat, noon-7pm Sun; Ⓜ Cluny-La Sorbonne) Album specialises in *bandes dessinées* (comics and graphic novels), which have an enormous following in France, with everything from Tintin and Babar to erotic comics and the latest Japanese manga. Serious comic collectors – and anyone excited by Harry Potter wands, Star Wars, Superman and other superhero figurines and T-shirts (you know who you are!) – shouldn't miss it.

🛍 St-Germain & Les Invalides

Magasin Sennelier   Arts & Crafts

(Map p250; www.magasinsennelier.com; 3 quai Voltaire, 7e; ⏱2-6.30pm Mon, 10am-12.45pm & 2-6.30pm Sat; Ⓜ St-Germain des Prés) Cézanne and Picasso were among the artists who helped develop products for this venerable 1887-founded art supplier on the banks of the Seine, and it remains an exceptional place to pick up canvases, brushes, watercolours, oils, pastels, charcoals and more. The shop's for-

est-green façade with gold lettering, exquisite original timber cabinetry and glass display cases also fuel artistic inspiration.

Gab & Jo   Concept Store

(Map p250; www.gabjo.fr; 28 rue Jacob, 6e; ⏱11am-7pm Mon-Sat; Ⓜ St-Germain des Prés) 📋 Forget mass-produced, imported souvenirs: for quality local gifts, browse the shelves of the country's first-ever concept store stocking only made-in-France items. Designers include La Note Parisienne (scented candles for each Parisian *arrondissement*, such as the 6e, with notes of lipstick, cognac, orange blossom, tuberose, jasmine, rose and fig), Marius Fabre (Marseille soaps), Germaine-des-Prés (lingerie), MILF (sunglasses) and Monsieur Marcel (T-shirts).

Le Bon Marché   Department Store

(www.bonmarche.com; 24 rue de Sèvres, 7e; ⏱10am-8pm Mon-Wed & Sat, to 9pm Thu & Fri; Ⓜ Sèvres-Babylone) Built by Gustave Eiffel as Paris' first department store in 1852, Le Bon Marché is the epitome of style, with a superb concentration of men's and women's fashions, beautiful homewares, stationery, books and toys as well as chic dining options.

Marché aux Puces de la Porte de Vanves

The icing on the cake is its glorious food hall, La Grande Épicerie de Paris (www.lagrandeepicerie.com; 36 rue de Sèvres, 7e; ☺8.30am-9pm Mon-Sat; Ⓜ Sèvres-Babylone).

Cire Trudon   Candles

(Map p254; https://trudon.com; 78 rue de Seine, 6e; ☺10am-7pm Mon-Sat; Ⓜ Odéon) Claude Trudon began selling candles here in 1643, and the company – which officially supplied Versailles and Napoléon with light – is now the world's oldest candle-maker (look for the plaque to the left of the shop's awning). A rainbow of candles and candlesticks fill the shelves inside.

Pierre Hermé   Food

(Map p254; www.pierreherme.com; 72 rue Bonaparte, 6e; ☺10am-8pm; Ⓜ Odéon) It's the size of a chocolate box, but once you're in Pierre Hermé your taste buds will go wild. This boutique, one of Paris' top chocolatiers, is a veritable feast of perfectly presented petits fours, cakes, chocolates, nougats, macarons and jams. There are several other branches around Paris.

Au Plat d'Étain   Games

(Map p254; www.auplatdetain.sitew.com; 16 rue Guisarde, 6e; ☺10.30am-6.30pm Tue-Sat; Ⓜ Mabillon) Tiny tin (*étain*) and lead soldiers,

snipers, cavaliers, military drummers and musicians (great for chessboard pieces) cram this fascinating boutique. In business since 1775, the shop itself is practically a collectable.

Alexandra Sojfer   Accessories

(Map p248; www.alexandrasojfer.com; 218 bd St-Germain, 7e; ☺10am-7pm Mon-Sat; Ⓜ Rue du Bac) Become Parisian chic with a frivolous, frilly, fantastical or frightfully fashionable *parapluie* (umbrella), parasol or walking cane handcrafted by Alexandra Sojfer from this St-Germain boutique, in the trade since 1834.

Fermob   Homewares

(Map p248; www.paris.fermob.com; 17 bd Raspail, 7e; ☺10am-7pm Mon-Sat Apr-Oct, 10am-1pm & 2-7pm Tue-Sat Nov-Mar; Ⓜ Rue du Bac) Famed for manufacturing iconic French garden furniture, including the Jardin du Luxembourg's signature chairs, Fermob has now opened this large, white 120-sq-metre Left Bank boutique in addition to its **Bastille premises** (www.paris.fermob.com; 81-83 av Ledru-Rollin, 12e; ☺10am-7pm Mon-Sat; Ⓜ Ledru-Rollin). Choose from a spectacular array of colours (23 at last count) for your own garden or terrace. Seasonal opening hours can vary.

JB Guanti   Accessories

(http://jbguanti.com; 59 rue de Rennes, 6e; ☺10am-7pm Mon-Sat; Ⓜ St-Sulpice) For the ultimate finishing touch, the men's and women's gloves at this boutique, which specialises solely in gloves, are the epitome of both style and comfort, whether unlined, silk lined, cashmere lined, lambskin lined or trimmed with rabbit fur.

Buying for someone else? To get their glove size, measure the length in centimetres of their middle finger from the top to where it joins their palm – the number of centimetres equals the size (eg 5cm is a size 5).

Hermès   Concept Store

(www.hermes.com; 17 rue de Sèvres, 6e; ☺10.30am-7pm Mon-Sat; Ⓜ Sèvres-Babylone) A stunning art deco swimming pool now houses luxury label Hermès' inaugural concept store. Retaining its original mosaic tiles and iron balustrades and adding enormous timber pod-like 'huts', the vast, tiered space showcases new directions in home furnishings, including fabrics and wallpaper, along with classic lines such as its signature scarves. There's also an appropriately chic cafe, Le Plongeoir (the Diving Board).

Marie Mercié   Fashion

(Map p254; www.mariemercie.com; 23 rue St-Sulpice; ☺11am-7pm Mon-Sat; ⓂMabillon) Stand out in the crowd in a unique hat handcrafted by Fontainebleau-born milliner Marie Mercié, who has collaborated with designers including Hermès, Kenzo, John Galliano and Agnès B and combines traditional methods with modern materials and humorous twists. She's also authored two books on her work and the history of millinery.

Quatrehomme   Cheese

(www.quatrehomme.fr; 62 rue de Sèvres, 7e; ☺9am-7.45pm Tue-Sat; ⓂVaneau) Buy the best of French cheeses, many with an original take (eg Epoisses boxed in chestnut leaves, Mont d'Or flavoured with black truffles, spiced honey and Roquefort bread), at this king of *fromageries*. The smell alone as you enter is heavenly.

There's a local branch near **Butte aux Cailles** (wwwquatrehomme.fr; 32 rue de l'Espérance, 13e; ☺9am-1pm & 4-7.45pm Tue-Fri, to 7.45pm Sat, to 1pm Sun; ⓂCorvisart).

Sabbia Rosa   Accessories

(Map p248; ☎01 45 48 88 37; 73 rue des Sts-Pères, 6e; ☺10am-7pm Mon-Sat; ⓂSt-Germain des Prés) Only French-sourced fabrics (silk from Lyon, lace from Calais) are used by lingerie designer Sabbia Rosa for her ultra-luxe range. Every piece is unique; measurements can be taken and gorgeous items custom-made in just 48 hours. The list of celebrity clients reads like a who's who: Madonna, Naomi Campbell, Claudia Schiffer and George Clooney have all shopped here.

Smallable Concept Store   Children

(www.smallable.com; 81 rue du Cherche Midi, 6e; ☺2-7.30pm Mon, 10.30am-7.30pm Tue-Sat; ⓂVaneau) Set back behind a covered polished-concrete courtyard, this deceptively large Parisian-chic space is a one-stop-shop for babies, children and teens, with over 20,000 items (strollers, shoes, furniture, clothes and toys) from 450 premium brands (Little Eleven, Chloé Kids, Petit Bateau, Pom d'Api, Zadig and many more).

La Dernière Goutte   Wine

(Map p250; ☎01 43 29 11 62; www.laderniere-goutte.net; 6 rue du Bourbon le Château, 6e; ☺3-8pm Mon, 10.30am-1.30pm & 3-8pm Tue-Fri, 11am-7pm Sat; ⓂMabillon) 'The Last Drop' is the brainchild of Cuban-American sommelier Juan Sánchez, whose tiny wine shop is packed with exciting, mostly organic French *vins de propriétaires* (estate-bottled wines) made by small independent producers. Wine classes lasting two hours (seven tastings) take place in English from Wednesday to Saturday (per person €55); check the website for the program.

🔒 Montparnasse & Southern Paris

Adam Montparnasse   Art & Crafts

(www.adamparis.com; 11 bd Edgar Quinet, 14e; ☺9.30am-7pm Mon-Sat; ⓂEdgar Quinet) If Paris' art galleries have inspired you, pick up paint brushes, charcoals, pastels, sketchpads, watercolours, oils, acrylics, canvases and more at this historic shop. Picasso, Brancusi and Giacometti were among Édouard Adam's clients. Another seminal client was Yves Klein, with whom Adam developed the ultramarine 'Klein blue' – the VLB25 'Klein Blue' varnish is sold exclusively here.

Marché aux Puces de la Porte de Vanves   Market

(www.pucesdevanves.fr; av Georges Lafenestre & av Marc Sangnier, 14e; ☺7am-2pm Sat & Sun; ⓂPorte de Vanves) The Porte de Vanves flea market is the smallest and one of the friendliest of the lot. Av Georges Lafenestre has lots of 'curios' that don't quite qualify as antiques. Av Marc Sangnier is lined with stalls of new clothes, shoes, handbags and household items for sale.

BAR OPEN

Coffee roasteries, cocktails, classic cafes, and cutting-edge wine bars

Bar Open

For the French, drinking and eating go together like wine and cheese, and the line between a cafe, salon de thé *(tearoom), bistro, brasserie, bar, and even* bar à vins *(wine bar) is blurred. The line between drinking and clubbing is often non-existent – a cafe that's quiet midafternoon might have DJ sets in the evening and dancing later on.*

Many Parisians live in tiny apartments, and cafes and bars have tradition-ally served as the salon they don't have – a place to meet with friends over un verre *(glass of wine), read for hours over* un café *(coffee), debate politics while downing an espresso at a zinc counter, swill cocktails during* apéro *(aperitif; predinner drink) or get the party started aboard a floating club on the Seine.*

In This Section

Opening Hours

Many cafes and bars open first thing in the morning, around 7am. Closing time for cafes and bars tends to be 2am, though some have licences until dawn. Club hours vary depending on the venue, day and event.

Montmartre & Northern Paris
Local gems include canal-side cafes (p172)

Champs-Élysées & Grands Boulevards
Swanky hotel bars, glam nightclubs (p168)

Louvre & Les Halles
Eclectic mix of bars and clubs (p170)

Le Marais Ménilmontant & Belleville
Hip, edgy bars and nightlife venues (p174)

Eiffel Tower & Western Paris
Classy bars and sunny cafes (p168)

St-Germain & Les Invalides
Historic literary cafes, stylish bars (p180)

The Islands
Quaint tearooms and wine bars (p179)

Bastille & Eastern Paris
Lively clubs and bars galore (p177)

Latin Quarter
Spirited student pubs and bars (p179)

Montparnasse & Southern Paris
Boulevard-facing brasseries and backstreet cafes (p181)

Costs

A coffee starts at around €2.50, a glass of wine from €4, a cocktail €8 to €15 and a *demi* (half-pint) of beer €3.50 to €7. In clubs and chic bars, prices can be double this. Admission to clubs is free to around €20 and is often cheaper before 1am.

Tipping

Tipping is not necessary at the bar. If drinks are brought to your table, tip as you would in a restaurant.

Useful Phrases

Un café Single shot of espresso.

Un café allongé Espresso lengthened with hot water (sometimes served separately).

Un café au lait Coffee with milk.

Un café crème Shot of espresso lengthened with steamed milk.

Un double Double shot of espresso.

Une noisette Shot of espresso with a spot of milk.

The Best

Experience Paris' finest drinking establishments

Wine Bars

Le Garde Robe (p170) Affordable natural wines and unpretentious vibe.

La Quincave (p181) Bar stools fashioned from wine barrels and over 200 natural wines.

Au Sauvignon (p180) Original zinc bar and hand-painted ceiling.

Coffee

Boot Café (p175) A fashionable must, if only to snap the enchanting façade.

Caffé Juno (p179) Aromatic little Latin Quarter roaster.

Café Lomi (p173) Coffee roastery and cafe in the multi-ethnic La Goutte d'Or neighbourhood.

Coutume (p181) Artisan roastery leading the way in Paris' coffee revolution.

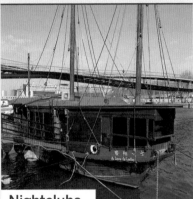

Nightclubs

Le Rex Club (p171) Mythical house and techno club with a phenomenal sound system.

Concrete (p177) Top spot for electro dance music all hours, on a barge by Gare de Lyon.

Social Club (p172) Subterranean fave and a good spot to kick off the night.

Zig Zag Club (p169) Best of the Champs-Élysées venues.

La Dame de Canton (pictured above; p181) Aboard a three-masted Chinese junk.

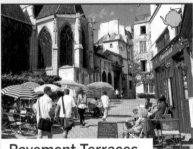

Pavement Terraces

Chez Prune (p172) The boho cafe that put Canal St-Martin on the map.

Café des Anges (p177) Wrap up in a ginger blanket and live the Paris dream.

L'Ebouillanté (p174) On sunny days there is no prettier cafe terrace.

Les Jardins du Pont-Neuf (p179) Glam floating bar with Seine-side terrace seating.

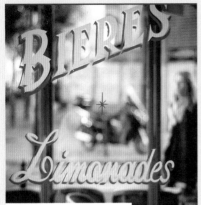

Neighbourhood Cafes

Le Petit Fer à Cheval (p176) Pocket-size cafe-bar with 1903 zinc bar and fervent crowd of regulars.

Le Progrès (p173) Old-school Montmartre cafe loaded with ambience.

Le Petit Gorille (p181) Fab neo-retro bar in the 15e.

Le Verre à Pied (p179) Old Paris charm in the Latin Quarter.

Cocktails

Experimental Cocktail Club (p170) Superb cocktails in a setting that exudes spirit and soul.

Tiger Bar (p180) Chic St-German spot with innovative mixed drinks and 45 different gins.

Baranaan (p173) New-wave cocktail bar serving Indian cocktails and veggie cuisine in the upcoming 10e.

Lulu White (p173) Absinthe-based drinks in Prohibition-era New Orleans surrounds.

Little Bastards (p179) Phenomenal house creations in a Latin Quarter backstreet.

★ Lonely Planet's Top Choices

Le Mary Céleste (p175) There are few hipper places to drink than this fashionable Marais cocktail bar.

Le Baron Rouge (pictured left; p177) Wonderfully convivial barrel-filled wine bar.

Lockwood (p171) Irrepressibly good all day long, from coffee to cocktails.

Le Batofar (p181) Red-metal tugboat with a rooftop bar and portholed club beneath.

🍷 Eiffel Tower & Western Paris

St James Paris — Bar

(📞01 44 05 81 81; www.saint-james-paris.com; 43 av Bugeaud, 16e; drinks €15-25; ⏰7pm-1am Mon-Sat; 📶; Ⓜ Porte Dauphine) It might be a hotel bar, but a drink at St James may well be one of your most memorable in Paris. Tucked behind a stone wall, this historic mansion opens its bar each evening to nonguests – and the setting redefines extraordinary.

Upper Crèmerie — Bar

(Map p248; 📞01 40 70 93 23; 71 av Marceau, 16e; ⏰9am-1am Mon-Fri; Ⓜ Kléber, George V) The sun-flooded tables at this hybrid cafe-cocktail bar in a quintessential Parisian pavement terrace heave at lunchtime and after work. The place is hip and the cocktails (and food) hit the spot. Inside, blue sofas and neon lighting reassure trendsetters that the place is anything but 'Paris-traditional'.

Café Branly — Cafe

(Map p248; 27 quai Branly, 7e; ⏰10am-7pm Tue, Wed & Sun, to 8pm Thu-Sat; Ⓜ Pont de l'Alma, Iéna) This casual spot at the Musée du Quai Branly has ringside views of the Eiffel Tower and cafe fare (foie gras salad, XL *croque monsieur*) to tuck into over a drink or three. The setting, within the museum's modernist garden, is peaceful and fantastic.

Frog XVI — Pub

(Map p248; 📞01 47 27 88 88; www.frogpubs.com; 110 av Kléber, 16e; ⏰noon-2am; Ⓜ Trocadéro) This popular Parisian pub and brewery has seven locations, but for beer drinkers this one is the saving grace, as there simply isn't much else in the way of craft brews in the posh 16e. IPA on tap, a family-friendly menu and live sports on the big screen. Pints are €5 during happy hour (5pm to 8pm).

🍷 Champs-Élysées & Grands Boulevards

PanPan — Bar

(📞01 42 46 36 06; 32 rue Drouot, 9e; ⏰11am-2am Mon-Fri, 6pm-2am Sat; Ⓜ Le Peletier) This unassuming locals' hang-out doesn't even bother with a sign, but it keeps things interesting with

Café Branly

a variety of activities throughout the week. Favourites include the cocktail workshop on Mondays (where you learn to mix your own, in French, *bien sûr*) and the Thursday-night *aperitivo* (from 7pm), where you can nibble on quiche, charcuterie and the like for €1.

Zig Zag Club   Club

(Map p248; http://zigzagclub.fr; 32 rue Marbeuf, 8e; ☺11.30pm-7am Fri & Sat; Ⓜ Franklin D Roosevelt) Some of the hippest electro beats in western Paris, with star DJs, a great sound and light system, and a spacious dance floor. It can be pricey, but it still fills up quickly, so don't start the party too late.

Wine by One   Wine Bar

(Map p248; ☎01 45 63 18 98; www.winebyone. com; 27 rue de Marignan, 8e; ☺noon-11pm Mon-Sat; Ⓜ Franklin D Roosevelt) Serve-your-self-wine off the Champs-Élysées? While it may not be quite the experience you had in mind when planning your tour of French vineyards, there's no doubt this is a fun, casual way to sample a variety of vintages without spending too much or feeling overly intimidated. Substantial cheese-and-charcuterie plates could easily turn a visit into a full meal.

ShowCase   Club

(Map p248; www.showcase.fr; Port des Champs-Élysées, 8e; ☺11.30pm-6am Thu-Sat; Ⓜ Invalides, Champs-Élysées-Clemenceau) This gigantic electro club has solved the neigh-bour-versus-noise problem that haunts so many Parisian nightlife spots: it's secreted beneath the Pont Alexandre III bridge alongside the Seine. Unlike other exclusive Champs backstreet clubs, the Showcase can pack 'em in (up to 1500 clubbers) and is less stringent about its door policy, though you'll still want to look like a star.

Blaine   Cocktail Bar

(Map p248; 65 rue Pierre Charron, 8e; ☺8pm-5am Tue-Sat; Ⓜ Franklin D Roosevelt) Hidden in plain sight is this underground speakeasy: enter through an unmarked black door, relay the password (hint: research on social media) and enter into a recreated Prohibi-tion-era bar. Good cocktails (from €13) and occasional live jazz and DJ sets.

 Wine

Wine is easily the most popular bever-age in Paris and house wine can cost less than bottled water. Of France's dozens of wine-producing regions, the principal ones are Burgundy, Bor-deaux, the Rhône and Loire Valleys, Champagne, Languedoc, Provence and Alsace. Wines are generally named after the location of the vineyard rather than the grape varietal. The best wines are Appellation d'Origine Contrôlée (AOC; soon to be relabelled Appellation d'Orig-ine Protégée, AOP), meaning they meet stringent regulations governing where, how and under what conditions they're grown, fermented and bottled.

Natural Wine

The latest trend in wine, *les vins naturels* (natural wines) have a fuzzy definition – no one really agrees on the details, but the general idea is that they are produced us-ing little or no pesticides or additives. This means natural wines do not contain sul-phites, which are added as a preservative in most wines. The good news is that this gives natural wines a much more distinct personality (or *terroir*, as the French say), the bad news is that these wines can also be more unpredictable .

Queen   Club

(Map p248; ☎01 53 89 08 90; www.queen.fr; 79 av des Champs-Élysées, 8e; ☺11.30pm-6.30am; Ⓜ George V) These days this doyen of a club is as popular with a straight crowd as it is with its namesake clientele, but Monday's

Le Garde Robe

disco nights are still prime dancing queen territory. While right on the Champs-Élysées, it's not quite as inaccessible as the other nearby clubs.

🍷 Louvre & Les Halles

Le Garde Robe   Wine Bar
(Map p250; 📞01 49 26 90 60; 41 rue de l'Arbre Sec, 1er; ⏱12.30-2.30pm Mon-Fri, 6.30-midnight Mon-Sat; Ⓜ Louvre Rivoli) The Garde Robe is possibly the only bar in the world to serve alcohol alongside a detox menu. While you probably shouldn't come here for the full-on cleansing experience, you can definitely expect excellent, affordable natural wines, a casual atmosphere and a good selection of eats, ranging from the standard cheese and charcuterie plates to more adventurous veg-friendly options.

**Experimental
Cocktail Club**   Cocktail Bar
(Map p250; 37 rue St-Saveur, 2e; ⏱7pm-2am; Ⓜ Réaumur-Sébastopol) Called ECC by tren-

dies, this fabulous speakeasy with a black curtain for a façade and old-beamed ceiling is effortlessly hip. Oozing spirit and soul, the cocktail bar – with retro-chic decor by American interior designer Cuoco Black and sister bars in London and New York – is a sophisticated flashback to those *années folles* (crazy years) of Prohibition New York.

Cocktails (€13 to €15) are individual and fabulous, and DJs set the space partying until dawn at weekends. It's not a large space, however, and fills to capacity quickly.

Angelina   Tearoom
(Map p248; 226 rue de Rivoli, 1er; ⏱8am-7pm Mon-Fri, 9am-7pm Sat & Sun; Ⓜ Tuileries) Clink china with lunching ladies, their posturing poodles and half the students from Tokyo University at Angelina, a grand dame of a tearoom dating to 1903. Decadent pastries are served here, but it's the super-thick, decadently sickening 'African' hot chocolate (€8.20), which comes with a pot of whipped cream and a carafe of water, that prompts the constant queue for a table.

Café La Fusée   Bar

(Map p250; ☎01 42 76 93 99; 168 rue St-Martin, 3e; ⏰8am-2am; Ⓜ Rambuteau, Étienne Marcel) A short walk from the Pompidou, the Rocket is a lively, laid-back indie hang-out with a red-and-white striped awning strung with fairy lights outside, and paint-peeling, tobacco-coloured walls indoors. You can grab simple meals here (€8 to €13), and it's got a decent wine selection by the glass.

Le Tambour   Bar

(Map p250; ☎01 42 33 06 90; 41 rue Montmartre, 2e; ⏰8.30am-6am; Ⓜ Étienne Marcel, Sentier) Some people will say that the 'Drummer', a Paris mecca for night owls, with generously long hours and friendly service, is a restaurant. And it does serve straightforward dishes till as late as 3.30am or 4am. But we enjoy it as a late-night drinking venue and its mixed, somewhat boisterous crowd.

Harry's New York Bar   Cocktail Bar

(Map p248; ☎01 42 61 71 14; 5 rue Daunou, 2e; ⏰noon-2am; Ⓜ Opéra) One of the most popular American-style bars in the prewar years, Harry's once welcomed writers like F Scott Fitzgerald and Ernest Hemingway, who no doubt sampled the bar's unique cocktail and creation: the Bloody Mary. The Cuban mahogany interior dates from the mid-19th century and was brought over from a Manhattan bar in 1911.

There's a basement piano bar called Ivories where Gershwin supposedly composed *An American in Paris* and, for the peckish, old-school hot dogs and generous club sandwiches to snack on. The occasional advertisement for Harry's that appears in print still reads 'Tell the Taxi Driver Sank Roo Doe Noo'.

Lockwood   Cafe

(Map p250; ☎01 77 32 97 21; 73 rue d'Aboukir, 2e; ⏰8am-2am Mon-Sat, 10am-4pm Sun; Ⓜ Sentier) A happening address for hip coffee lovers. Savour beans from the Belleville Brûlerie during the day, brunch on weekends and well-mixed cocktails in the subterranean candlelit *cave* (wine celler) at night.

🎧 Nightlife

Paris' residential make-up means nightclubs aren't ubiquitous. Lacking a mainstream scene, clubbing here tends to be underground and extremely mobile. The best DJs and their followings have short stints in a certain venue before moving on, and the scene's hippest *soirées clubbing* (clubbing events) float between venues – including the many dance-driven bars. Dedicated clubbers may also want to check out the growing suburban scene, much more alternative and spontaneous in nature, but also harder to reach.

Wherever you wind up, the beat is strong. Electronic music is of particularly high quality in Paris' clubs, with some excellent local house and techno. Funk and groove have given the predominance of dark minimal sounds a good pounding, and the Latin scene is huge; salsa dancing and Latino music nights pack out plenty of clubs. World music also has a following in Paris, where everything – from Algerian raï to Senegalese mbalax and West Indian zouk – goes at clubs. R&B and hip-hop pickings are decent, if less represented than elsewhere.

Track tomorrow's hot 'n' happening *soirée* with these finger-on-the-pulse Parisian nightlife links:

Paris DJs (www.parisdjs.com) Free downloads to get you in the groove.

Paris Bouge (www.parisbouge.com) Comprehensive listings site.

Parissi (www.parissi.com) Search by date, then *la before, la soirée* and *l'after*.

Tribu de Nuit (www.tribudenuit.com) Parties, club events and concerts galore.

Le Rex Club   Club

(Map p250; www.rexclub.com; 5 bd Poissonnière, 2e; ⏰midnight-7am Thu-Sat; Ⓜ Bonne Nouvelle) Attached to the art deco Grand Rex cinema, this is Paris' premier house and techno venue – some of the world's hottest DJs strut their stuff on a 70-speaker, multidiffusion sound system.

Social Club   Club

(Map p250; www.parissocialclub.com; 142 rue Montmartre, 2e; ⊙11pm-6am Thu-Sat; Ⓜ Bourse) These subterranean cube-themed rooms showcasing electro, hip hop, funk and live acts are a magnet for young clubbers who take their music seriously. Thursdays showcase local DJs; Fridays are gay nights.

♟ Montmartre & Northern Paris

Le Coq   Cocktail Bar

(Map p250; 12 rue du Château d'Eau, 10e; ⊙6pm-2am Tue-Sat; Ⓜ République, Jacques Bonsergent) ✐ Pop art and concrete walls set the stage for the 10e's trendy cocktail bar with austere black façade. Signature tipples incorporate French spirits – consider a Les Fleurs du Mal (absinthe and rose-infused vodka) or Initials BB (Bénédictine and bourbon). Aspiring mixologists can learn how to shake their own during Saturday-afternoon cocktail workshops; reserve in advance.

CopperBay   Cocktail Bar

(Map p250; www.copperbay.fr; 5 rue Bouchardon, 10e; ⊙6pm-2am Tue-Sat; Ⓜ Strasbourg-St-Denis, République) This sleek, faintly playful cocktail bar's floor-to-ceiling windows, polished pale-wood decor and glistening copper fixtures and fittings inject a generous dose of design flair into proceedings. The cocktail menu mixes classics with house specials like the fig-and-blackberry Black Julep.

Chez Prune   Bar

(Map p250; 71 quai de Valmy, 10e; ⊙8am-2am Mon-Sat, 10am-2am Sun; Ⓜ République) This Soho-*boho* cafe put Canal St-Martin on the map over a decade ago and its good vibes and rough-around-the-edges look show no sign of disappearing in the near future. Chez Prune remains one of those timeless classic Paris addresses, fabulous for hanging out and people-watching any time of day. Weekend brunch buzzes.

Chez Prune

Lulu White
Cocktail Bar

(Map p256; http://luluwhite.bar; 12 rue Frochot, 9e; ⊙7pm-3am Mon-Sat; Ⓜ️Pigalle) Sip absinthe-based cocktails in Prohibition-era New Orleans surrounds at this elegant, serious and supremely busy cocktail bar on rue Frochot; several more line the same street, making for a fabulous evening out. Should you be wondering, Lulu White was an infamous African American brothel owner in early 20th-century New Orleans.

Baranaan
Cafe, Cocktail Bar

(Map p250; ☑️01 40 38 97 57; www.elaichicafe.com; 7 rue du Faubourg St-Martin, 10e; ⊙cafe 3pm-12.30am Tue-Thu & Sun, 3pm-1.30am Fri & Sat, bar 6.30pm-2am Mon-Sat; 🛜; Ⓜ️Strasbourg-St-Denis, Jacques Bonsergent) One address, two ubercool identities: by day Baranaan is the hip Elaichi Café, serving tasty vegetarian food and lassi, chai and fresh juices in a smart, contemporary setting. Come dusk, the space morphs into one of Paris' most exciting new-wave cocktail bars, serving Indian cocktails and well-filled naan breads to a keen hipster crowd. Check Baranaan's Facebook page for events and happenings.

Café Lomi
Coffee

(☑️09 80 39 56 24; www.cafelomi.com; 3ter rue Marcadet, 18e; ⊙10am-7pm; Ⓜ️Marcadet Poissonniers) Curious coffee aficionados in Paris have to visit Café Lomi at least once. The coffee roastery and adjoining industrial-styled cafe is far away from the madding crowd, in the multi-ethnic La Goutte d'Or neighbourhood, but its coffee beans are personally sourced halfway around the world and roasted back home in Paris.

Alongside the regular espresso, noisette (shot of coffee with a spot of milk), latte and so forth, it serves filter coffee (mug, Aeropress or Chemex) and a whole host of wacky coffee creations like Bleu d'Auvergne cheese dipped in espresso or espresso tonic (tonic water with espresso). Breakfast, lunch and weekend brunch too.

🍾🍷 Craft Breweries

Bière artisanale (craft beer) is exploding in Paris and there are some fabulous, flavour-packed beers being brewed right in the city centre.

Behind-the-scenes tours and tastings are available at creative new breweries, including Brasserie BapBap (☑️01 77 17 52 97; www.bapbap.paris; 79 rue St-Maur, 11e; guided tour €10; ⊙5-7pm Mon-Fri, 2-7pm Sat; Ⓜ️St-Maur), Brasserie de la Goutte d'Or (Map p256; ☑️09 80 64 23 51; www.brasserielagouttedor.com; 28 rue la Goutte d'Or, 18e; ⊙5-7pm Thu & Fri, 2-7pm Sat; Ⓜ️Château Rouge) **FREE** and Brasserie La Parisienne (☑️09 52 34 94 69; http://brasserielaparisienne.com; 10 rue Wurtz, 13e; tours €15; ⊙tours by reservation; Ⓜ️Glacière).

Dedicated craft-beer shops such as Biérocratie (www.bierocratie.com; 32 rue de l'Espérance, 13e; ⊙11am-8pm Tue & Thu-Sat, 4-8pm Wed; Ⓜ️Corvisart), Hop Malt Market (☑️01 55 28 77 24; www.facebook.com/hmmarket75; 79 rue Saint-Maur, 11e; ⊙9.30am-2pm & 3.30pm-1.30am; Ⓜ️St-Maur), Bieregrad (www.bieregrad.com; 18-20 rue de la Butte aux Cailles, 13e; ⊙1-9pm Tue, 11am-2pm & 3-10pm Wed-Sat; Ⓜ️Corvisart) and Bières Cultes (Map p254; http://bierescultes.fr; 44 rue des Boulangers, 5e; ⊙3-8pm Mon, 11am-2pm & 3-9pm Tue-Thu, 11am-9pm Fri & Sat; Ⓜ️Cardinal Lemoine) also often host events.

Craft beer devotees will want to time their trip to coincide with May's Paris Beer Week.

TFOXFOTO/GETTY IMAGES ©

Le Progrès   Bar

(Map p256; 7 rue des Trois Frères, 18e; ⊘9am-2am; Ⓜ Abbesses) A real live *café du quartier* (neighbourhood cafe) perched in the heart of Abbesses, the 'Progress' occupies a corner site with huge windows and simple seating and attracts a relaxed mix of local artists, shop staff, writers and hangers-on. It's great for convivial evenings, but it's also a good place to come for meals (mains €17.90 to €20.50), coffee and well-priced cocktails (€9).

La Fourmi   Bar

(Map p256; 74 rue des Martyrs, 18e; ⊘8am-1am Mon-Thu, to 3am Fri & Sat, 10am-1am Sun; Ⓜ Pigalle) A Pigalle institution, La Fourmi hits the mark with its high ceilings, long zinc bar and unpretentious vibe. Get up to speed on live music and club nights or sit down for a reasonably priced meal and drinks.

L'Entrée des Artistes   Bar

(Map p256; ☎01 45 23 11 93; www.lentreedesartistespigalle.com; 30-32 rue Victor Massé, 9e; ⊘7pm-2am Tue-Thu, to 4am Fri & Sat; Ⓜ Pigalle) Sophisticated cocktails and gourmet nibbles grand enough to comprise an entire evening meal lure a hip set to this buzzing speakeasy, at home in a twinset of hostess bars in nightlife-busy Pigalle. Lovers of vintage will adore this address: from the salvaged 1920s bistro chairs to the candlelit tables and fabulous vinyl collection, everything at the Artists' Entrance is old and achingly cool.

Blackburn Coffee   Coffee

(Map p250; ☎01 42 41 73 31; www.blackburn-paris.com; 52 rue du Faubourg St-Martin, 10e; ⊘9am-6pm Mon-Fri, 10am-7pm Sat & Sun; 🛜; Ⓜ Strasbourg-St-Denis) Be it an Aeropress, Dirty Chai or macchiato you're craving, this specialist coffee shop in the increasingly foodie 10e doesn't disappoint. Its stylish interior is a mellow space to hang out in over detox juices, gourmet *tartines* (open sandwiches) and healthy meal-sized salads. Weekend brunch (€24) – an egg, taco, veggie side and savoury tart affair – is a big draw for the local hipster crowd.

Gravity Bar   Cocktail Bar

(44 rue des Vinaigriers, 10e; ⊘7pm-2am Tue-Sat; Ⓜ Jacques Bonsergent, Gare de l'Est) Catching the wave is the theme behind this trendsetting, surfing- and water-sports-themed bar near Canal St-Martin. Indeed, the stunning wave-like interior crafted from soft wood threatens to distract from the business at hand – serious cocktails, best partaken in the company of some excellent tapas-style small plates (€5 to €12).

Le Très Particulier   Cocktail Bar

(Map p256; ☎01 53 41 81 40; http://hotel-particulier-montmartre.com; 23 av Junot, 18e, Pavillon D; ⊘6pm-2am Tue-Sun; Ⓜ Lamarck-Caulaincourt) There is possibly no more enchanting spot for a summertime alfresco cocktail than Le Très Particulier, the utterly unique and clandestine cocktail bar of Hôtel Particulier Montmartre. Ring the buzzer at the unmarked black gated entrance to get in and make a beeline for the 1871 mansion's flowery walled garden bar with conservatory-style interior. DJs spin tunes from 10pm every Friday and Saturday.

🍸 Le Marais, Ménilmontant & Belleville

L'Ebouillanté   Cafe

(Map p250; http://ebouillante.pagespersoorange.fr; 6 rue des Barres, 4e; ⊘noon-10pm summer, to 7pm winter; Ⓜ Hôtel de Ville) On sunny days there is no prettier cafe terrace. Enjoying a privileged position on a pedestrian, stone-flagged street just footsteps from the Seine, L'Ebouillanté buzzes with savvy Parisians sipping refreshing glasses of homemade *citronnade* (ginger lemonade), hibiscus-flower cordial and herbal teas. Delicious cakes, jumbo salads, savoury crêpes and Sunday brunch (€21) complement the long drinks menu.

PasDeLoup   Cocktail Bar

(Map p250; ☎09 54 74 16 36; www.facebook.com/pasdelouparis; 108 rue Amelot, 11e; ⊘6pm-2am Tue-Sun; Ⓜ Filles du Calvaire) This trendy cocktail

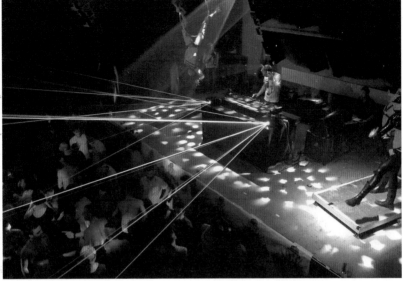

La Machine du Moulin Rouge

bar next to the Cirque d'Hiver in Le Marais is a small place with a simple wood bar and copper-tube shelving evoking Scandinavia in its design. But what makes it stand out for the city's increasingly discerning cocktail crowd is its interesting and superbly gourmet food pairings (from €10).

Boot Café   Coffee
(Map p250; 19 rue du Pont aux Choux, 3e; ☺10am-6pm; Ⓜ St-Sébastien-Froissart) The charm of this three-table ode to good coffee is its façade, which must win a prize for 'most photographed'. An old cobbler's shop, with the original washed-blue exterior, 'Cordonnerie' lettering and fantastic red boot sign above beautifully preserved. Excellent coffee, roasted in Paris, to boot.

Le Mary Céleste   Cocktail Bar
(Map p250; www.lemaryceleste.com; 1 rue Commines, 3e; ☺6pm-1.30am; Ⓜ Filles du Calvaire) Predictably, there's a distinct nautical feel to this fashionable, ubercool cocktail bar in the Marais. Snag a stool at the central circular bar or play savvy and reserve one of a handful of tables (in advance online). Cocktails (€12 to €13) are creative and the

perfect partner to a dozen oysters or your pick of tapas-style 'small plates' designed to be shared (€8 to €15).

Le Loir dans La Théière   Cafe
(Map p250; http://leloirdanslatheiere.com; 3 rue des Rosiers, 4e; ☺9am-7.30pm; Ⓜ St-Paul) Its cutesy name (Dormouse in the Teapot) notwithstanding, this is a wonderful old space filled with retro toys, comfy couches and scenes of *Through the Looking-Glass* on the walls. Its dozen different types of tea poured in the company of excellent savoury tarts and crumble-type desserts ensure a constant queue on the street outside. Breakfast and brunch too.

Café Charbon   Bar
(www.facebook.com/cafe.charbon.oberkampf; 109 rue Oberkampf, 11e; ☺9am-2am Mon-Wed & Sun, to 4pm Thu-Sat; ☎; Ⓜ Parmentier) With its post-industrial belle époque ambience, the Charbon was the first of the hip cafes and bars to catch on in Ménilmontant. It's always crowded and worth heading to for the distressed decor with high ceilings, chandeliers and perched DJ booth.

 **Coffee & Tea**

Coffee has always been Parisians' drink of choice to kick-start the day. So it's surprising, particularly given France's fixation on quality, that Parisian coffee has lagged behind world standards, with burnt, poor-quality beans and unrefined preparation methods. But the city is in the throes of a coffee revolution, with local roasteries such as Belleville Brûlerie and Coutume (p181) priming cafes citywide for outstanding brews made by professional baristas, often using cutting-edge extraction techniques. Caffeine fiends are now spoilt for choice, and while there's still plenty of substandard coffee in Paris, you don't have to go far to avoid it.

Tea – often more strongly associated with France's western neighbours, the UK and Ireland – is also extremely popular in Paris. Tearooms offer copious varieties; learn about its history at the tea museum within the original Marais branch of Mariage Frères (p154).

TUUL AND BRUNO MORANDI/ALAMY STOCK PHOTO ©

Le Pick-Clops Bar

(Map p250; 16 rue Vieille du Temple, 4e; ☺7am-2am Mon-Sat, 8am-2am Sun; 🛜; Ⓜ Hôtel de Ville, St-Paul) This buzzy 1950s-styled bar-cafe – all shades of yellow and lit by neon – has formica tables, ancient bar stools and plenty of mirrors. Attracting a friendly flow of locals and passers-by, it's a great place for morning or afternoon coffee, or that last drink alone or with friends.

Gibus Club Club

(Map p250; ☏01 47 00 59 14; www.scream-paris.com; 18 rue du Faubourg du Temple, 11e; ☺11pm-7am Thu-Sat; Ⓜ République) What started out as a summer party thrown by Scream Club has now morphed into a permanent fixture on the city's gay scene, rebranded as Gibus Club and still working hard to stay top dog as one of Paris' biggest gay parties (admission €15 to €20). Follow the gay crowd to the basement of Favela Chic (p190).

La Belle Hortense Bar

(Map p250; www.cafeine.com/belle-hortense; 31 rue Vieille du Temple, 4e; ☺5pm-2am; Ⓜ Hôtel de Ville, St-Paul) This creative wine bar named after a Jacques Roubaud novel fuses shelf after shelf of good books to read with an excellent wine list and an enriching weekly agenda of book readings, signings and art events. A zinc bar and original 19th-century ceiling set the mood perfectly.

Le Petit Fer à Cheval Bar

(Map p250; www.cafeine.com/petit-fer-a-cheval; 30 rue Vieille du Temple, 4e; ☺9am-2am; Ⓜ Hôtel de Ville, St-Paul) A Marais institution, the Little Horseshoe is a minute cafe-bar with an original horseshoe-shaped zinc bar from 1903. The place overflows with regulars from dawn to dark. Great *apéro* (predinner drink) spot and great WC – stainless-steel toilet stalls straight out of a Flash Gordon film (actually inspired by the interior of the *Nautilus* submarine in Jules Verne's *20,000 Leagues under the Sea*).

Wild & the Moon Juice Bar

(Map p250; www.wildandthemoon.com; 55 rue Charlot, 3e; ☺8am-7pm Mon-Fri, 10am-7pm Sat, 11am-5pm Sun; Ⓜ Filles du Calvaire) A beautiful crowd hobnobs over nut milks, vitality shots, smoothies, cold-pressed juices and raw food in this sleek new juice bar in the fashionable Haut Marais. Ingredients are fresh, seasonal and organic, and it is one of the few places in town where you can have moon porridge or avocado slices on almond and rosemary crackers for breakfast.

3w Kafé
Lesbian

(Map p250; 8 rue des Écouffes, 4e; ⏱7pm-3am Wed & Sun, to 4am Thu, to 6.30am Fri & Sat; Ⓜ St-Paul) The name of this flagship cocktail-bar-pub on a street with several lesbian bars means 'women with women'. It's relaxed and there's no ban on men (they must be accompanied by a woman). On weekends there's dancing downstairs with a DJ and themed evenings take place regularly. Check its Facebook page for events.

🍷 Bastille & Eastern Paris

Le Baron Rouge
Wine Bar

(🖉01 43 43 14 32; 1 rue Théophile Roussel, 12e; ⏱10am-2pm & 5-10pm Tue-Fri, 10am-10pm Sat, 10am-4pm Sun; Ⓜ Ledru-Rollin) Just about the ultimate Parisian wine-bar experience, this place has barrels stacked against the bottle-lined walls. As unpretentious as you'll find, it's a local meeting place where everyone is welcome, and it's especially busy on Sunday after the Marché d'Aligre (p85) wraps up. All the usual suspects – cheese, charcuterie and oysters – will keep your belly full.

For a small deposit, you can fill up 1L bottles straight from the barrel for under €5.

Café des Anges
Cafe

(🖉01 73 20 21 10; www.cafedesangesparis.com; 66 rue de la Roquette, 11e; ⏱7.30am-2am; Ⓜ Bastille) With its aqua-blue paintwork and locals sipping coffee beneath a terracotta awning on its busy pavement terrace, Angels Cafe lives up to the 'quintessential Paris cafe' dream. In winter wrap up beneath a ginger blanket outside, or push your way through the crowds at the zinc bar to snag a coveted table inside – for breakfast, a burger lunch, steak dinner (mains €10 to €17) and everything in between.

Concrete
Club

(http://concreteparis.fr; 60 Port de la Rapée, 12e; ⏱10pm-7am; Ⓜ Gare de Lyon) This hugely popular, wild-child club with different dance floors lures a young international set to a boat on the Seine, firmly moored by Gare de Lyon. Notorious for introducing an 'after-hours' element to Paris' somewhat staid clubbing scene, Concrete is the trendy place to party all night until sunrise and beyond. Watch for all-weekend events ie electronic dance music around the clock.

Admission is usually free before midnight. Check for world-class electro DJ events on its Facebook page.

Le Pure Café
Cafe

(www.lepurecafe.fr; 14 rue Jean Macé, 11e; ⏱7am-1am Mon-Fri, 8am-1am Sat, 9am-midnight Sun; Ⓜ Charonne) With vintage wood and zinc bar, this cherry-red Parisian corner cafe is an easy spot to drop in for a morning coffee, aperitif, meal (mains €13 to €16) or copious Sunday brunch (€19). Its selection of natural and organic wines by the glass is particularly good. Film buffs: spot its quaint cinematic façade and traditional interior used in the film *Before Sunset*.

Bar des Ferrailleurs
Bar

(🖉01 48 07 89 12; 18 rue de Lappe, 11e; ⏱5pm-2am Mon-Fri, 3pm-2am Sat & Sun; Ⓜ Bastille) Decorative windsurfers, bicycles, flags and various other vintage bric-a-brac form an organised state of chaos at this throbbing dive bar, the busiest on bar-lined rue de Lappe near Bastille. The bar attracts a mixed crowd of locals and tourists, drinks are well-priced, music is eclectic, and the party action spills onto the street in summer.

Bar des Ferrailleurs is named after the steel- and metalworkers who used to have their ateliers on this ancient street.

Le 49.3
Bar

(🖉06 23 16 92 23; http://le49-3.com; 3 Cité de Phalsbourg, 11e ; ⏱5.30pm-2am Mon-Sat; Ⓜ Charonne) Worn wooden parquet, vintage zinc bar, a leather Chesterfield sofa and old metal chairs picked up at the flea market strike the perfect shabby-chic chord at this appealing new beer bar. The selection of craft beers – 49 to be precise, plus three different types of gin, rum, whisky and tequila – span the globe, and bar staff are clearly *bière* (beer) aficionados.

Paris in a Glass

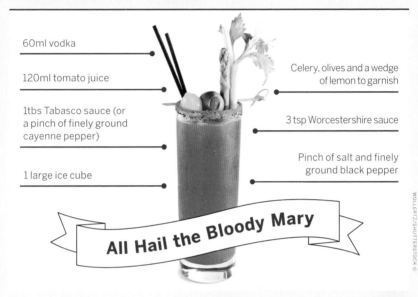

60ml vodka

120ml tomato juice

1tbs Tabasco sauce (or a pinch of finely ground cayenne pepper)

1 large ice cube

Celery, olives and a wedge of lemon to garnish

3 tsp Worcestershire sauce

Pinch of salt and finely ground black pepper

WOLLERTZ/SHUTTERSTOCK ©

All Hail the Bloody Mary

Tasting Notes

Sharp, piquant and refreshingly savoury, a Bloody Mary is ideal at any time of year, with the spicy heat balanced by the cooling tomato juice. Variations involve swapping vodka for gin or adding horseradish. Santé!

The Story Behind the Cocktail

The Bloody Mary was born in 1920s Paris at Harry's New York Bar, when Parisian barman Fernand 'Pete' Petiot experimented with newly available Russian vodka (distilled by immigrants who'd fled the Russian Revolution) and newly invented canned tomato juice. It was christened by Harry's customer American singer/pianist Roy Barton after the Chicago nightclub Bucket of Blood and its waitress, Mary.

★Best Bars for a Bloody Mary

Harry's New York Bar (p171)

Lulu White (p173)

PasDeLoup (p174)

Le Coq (p172)

Little Bastards (p179)

♀ The Islands

Les Jardins du
Pont-Neuf   Cocktail Bar
(Map p250; www.jdp9.com; quai de l'Horloge, 1er;
⊙7pm-2am Tue-Sat; 🐾; ⓂPont Neuf) Island life
became more glamorous with the opening
of this ultra-chic floating cocktail bar
aboard a barge moored by the Pont Neuf.
Decked out with art-nouveau-inspired decor, including rattan furniture and hanging
plants, its two vast terraces overlook the
Seine. There's also a dance floor; check the
website for upcoming soirées.

Taverne Henri IV   Wine Bar
(Map p250; 13 place du Pont Neuf, 1er; ⊙noon-
11pm Mon-Sat, closed Aug; ⓂPont Neuf) Dating
from 1885, this venerable wine bar lures
legal types from the nearby Palais de
Justice (not to mention celeb writers and
actors, as the autographed snaps testify).
A choice of *tartines* (open-faced sandwiches), *charcuterie* (cold cooked meats) and
aromatic cheese platters complement its
extensive wine list.

♀ Latin Quarter

Le Verre à Pied   Cafe
(Map p254; http://leverreapied.fr; 118bis
rue Mouffetard, 5e; ⊙9am-9pm Tue-Sat,
9.30am-4pm Sun; ⓂCensier Daubenton) This
café-tabac is a pearl of a place where little
has changed since 1870. Its nicotine-hued
mirrored wall, moulded cornices and
original bar make it part of a dying breed,
but it epitomises the charm, glamour and
romance of an old Paris everyone loves,
including stallholders from the rue Mouffetard market who yo-yo in and out.

Little Bastards   Cocktail Bar
(Map p254; 5 rue Blainville, 5e; ⊙6pm-2am
Mon-Thu, to 4am Fri & Sat; ⓂPlace Monge) Only
house-creation cocktails are listed on the
menu at uberhip Little Bastards – among
them Fal' in Love (Beefeater gin, cranberry
juice, lime, mint, guava purée and Falernun

clove, ginger and almond-syrup), Be a Beet
Smooth (Jameson, coriander, sherry, egg
white and pepper) and Deep Throat (Absolut
vodka, watermelon syrup and Pernod) – but
they'll also mix up classics if you ask.

Le Pub St-Hilaire   Pub
(Map p254; 2 rue Valette, 5e; ⊙3pm-2am Mon-
Thu, 4pm-5am Fri & Sat; ⓂMaubert-Mutualité)
'Buzzing' fails to do justice to the pulsating
vibe inside this student-loved pub. Generous happy hours last from 5pm to 9pm and
the place is kept packed with a trio of pool
tables, board games, music on two floors,
hearty bar food and various gimmicks to
rev up the party crowd (a metre of cocktails, 'be your own barman' etc).

Caffé Juno   Coffee
(www.caffe-juno.com; 58 rue Henri Barbusse, 5e;
⊙9am-7pm Mon-Sat; 🐾; ⓂRaspail or RER Port
Royal) ◢ Hole-in-the-wall Caffé Juno roasts
its own Ethiopian, Indonesian, Colombian
and Cameroonian beans and specialises in
espressos, filters and lattes. Prices are impressively reasonable to drink on-site in the
industrial-style space strewn with hessian
bags; you can also buy beans to take home.

Mosquée de Paris   Tearoom
(Map p254; www.la-mosquee.com; 39 rue Geoffroy-St-Hilaire, 5e; ⊙9am-11.30pm; ⓂCensier
Daubenton) Sip a sweet mint tea and nibble
on a *pâtisserie orientale* between trees
and chirping birds in the courtyard of the
tearoom of Paris' beautiful mosque, the
Mosquée de Paris (p110).

Le Vieux Chêne   Bar
(Map p254; 69 rue Mouffetard, 5e; ⊙4pm-2am
Sun-Thu, to 5am Fri & Sat; ⓂPlace Monge) This rue
Mouffetard institution is reckoned to be Paris'
oldest bar. Indeed, a revolutionary circle met
here in 1848 and it was a popular *bal musette*
(dancing club) in the late 19th and early 20th
centuries. These days it's a student favourite,
especially during happy hour (4pm to 9pm
Tuesday to Sunday, and from 4pm until
closing on Monday). Resident DJs mix it up
on Friday and Saturday nights.

Au Sauvignon

🍷 St-Germain & Les Invalides

Tiger Bar — Cocktail Bar
(Map p254; www.tiger-paris.com; 13 rue Princesse, 6e; ☺6pm-2am Tue-Sat; MMabillon) Suspended bare-bulb lights and fretted timber make this split-level space a stylish spot for specialist gins (45 different varieties). Its 24 cocktails include a Breakfast Martini (gin, triple sec, orange marmalade and lemon juice) and Oh My Dog (white pepper-infused gin, lime juice, raspberry and rose cordial and ginger ale). You can also sip Japanese sake, wine and craft beer.

Les Deux Magots — Cafe
(Map p250; www.lesdeuxmagots.fr; 170 bd St-Germain, 6e; ☺7.30am-1am; MSt-Germain des Prés) If ever there was a cafe that summed up St-Germain des Prés' early-20th-century literary scene, it's this former hang-out of anyone who was anyone. You will spend *beaucoup* (a lot) to sip a coffee in a wicker chair on the terrace shaded by dark-green awnings and geraniums spilling from window boxes, but it's an undeniable piece of Parisian history. The name refers to the two *magots* (grotesque figurines) of Chinese dignitaries at the entrance.

Au Sauvignon — Wine Bar
(http://ausauvignon.com; 80 rue des Sts-Pères, 7e; ☺8am-11pm Mon-Sat, 9am-10pm Sun; MSèvres-Babylone) Grab a table in the evening light at this wonderfully authentic *bar à vins* or head to the quintessential bistro interior, with an original zinc bar, tightly packed tables and hand-painted ceiling celebrating French viticultural tradition. A plate of *casse-croûtes au pain Poilâne* – toast with ham, pâté, terrine, smoked salmon and foie gras – is the perfect accompaniment.

Café de Flore — Cafe
(Map p250; 172 bd St-Germain, 6e; ☺7am-2am; MSt-Germain des Prés) The red upholstered benches, mirrors and marble walls at this art deco landmark haven't changed much since the days when Jean-Paul Sartre and Simone de Beauvoir essentially set up office here, writing in its warmth during the Nazi occupation. It also hosts a monthly English-language *philocafé* (philosophy discussion) session.

Coutume   Coffee

(http://coutumecafe.com; 47 rue de Babylone, 7e; ⊘8am-7pm Mon-Fri, 10am-7pm Sat & Sun; ☎; Ⓜ St-François Xavier) ✐ The dramatic improvement in Parisian coffee in recent years is thanks in no small part to Coutume, artisan roaster of premium beans for scores of establishments around town. Its flagship cafe – a bright, light-filled, post-industrial space – is ground zero for innovative preparation methods including cold extraction and siphon brews. Fabulous organic fare and pastries too.

La Quincave   Wine Bar

(17 rue Bréa, 6e; ⊘11am-1pm & 5-11.30pm Tue-Thu, 11am-11.30pm Fri & Sat; Ⓜ Vavin) Bar stools at this lively wine bar/shop are fash-ioned from wine barrels, but on summer evenings most of the action spills onto the tiny street out front. Over 200 varieties of natural wines are available by the bottle, ranging from €9 to €35 (corkage costs €7), along with charcuterie and cheese platters to soak them up.

Le 10   Pub

(Map p254; www.lebar10.com; 10 rue de l'Odéon, 6e; ⊘2pm-2am; ☎; Ⓜ Odéon) Plastered with posters, cellar pub 'Le Dix' is a student favourite, not least for its cheap sangria. An eclectic selection emerges from the juke-box – everything from jazz and the Doors to traditional French *chansons* (*à la* Édith Piaf). It's the ideal spot for plotting the next revolution or conquering a lonely heart.

🍴 Montparnasse & Southern Paris

Le Batofar   Club

(www.batofar.org; opposite 11 quai François Mauriac, 13e; ⊘bar noon-midnight, club 11.30pm-6am; Ⓜ Quai de la Gare, Bibliothèque) This much-loved, red-metal tugboat has a rooftop bar that's terrific in summer, and a respected restaurant, while the club underneath provides memorable underwa-ter acoustics between its metal walls and portholes. Le Batofar is known for its edgy, experimental music policy and live perfor-mances from 7pm, mostly electro-oriented but also incorporating hip-hop, new wave, rock, punk or jazz.

Happy hour is 5pm to 8pm. Food is served at the restaurant from noon to 2pm and 7pm to 11pm May to September (shorter hours from October to April).

Le Petit Gorille   Cafe

(46 rue de Cronstadt, 15e; ⊘8.30am-2am Tue-Sun; ☎; Ⓜ Convention) A statue of a gorilla with her baby on her back (the 'little gorilla' of the name) is the first clue to the kitschy-cool vibe at this fun new neighbourhood bar with a marine-blue façade and pavement seating in summer. Inside, the neoretro decor features downlights and a fire-engine-red feature wall. Great cocktails, beers and wines, plus bargain-priced food too.

La Dame de Canton   Club

(www.damedecanton.com; opp 11 quai François Mauriac, 13e; ⊘7pm-2am Tue-Thu, to dawn Fri & Sat; Ⓜ Bibliothèque) This floating *boîte* (club) aboard a three-masted Chinese junk with a couple of world voyages under its belt bobs beneath the Bibliothèque Nationale de France. Concerts cover pop and indie to electro, hip hop, reggae and rock; after-wards DJs keep the crowd hyped. There's also a popular bar and restaurant with wood-fired pizzas served on the terrace from May to September.

Félicie   Bar

(www.felicie.info; 174 av du Maine, 14e; ⊘7.15am-2am Mon-Fri, 8am-2am Sat & Sun; ☎; Ⓜ Lourmel) Chances are your first visit won't be your last at this unpretentious neighbourhood cafe with a big heated pavement terrace, fun-loving staff and a laid-back vibe. It's a quintessentially Parisian spot to hang out any time of day, but especially during Sunday brunch, lunches built around bistro classics like steak tartare, and late at night.

SHOWTIME

Renowned opera, ballet, jazz clubs, street performers and buskers

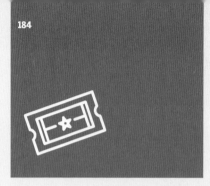

Showtime

Catching a performance in Paris is a treat. French and international opera, ballet and theatre companies and cabaret dancers take to the stage in fabled venues, and a flurry of young, passionate, highly creative musicians, thespians and artists make the city's fascinating fringe art scene what it is.

Paris became Europe's most important jazz centre after WWII and the city has some fantastic jazz clubs, as well as venues for stirring French chansons, dazzling cabarets including the iconic Moulin Rouge, cutting-edge cultural centres, wonderful independent cinemas, and dozens of orchestral, organ and chamber-music concerts each week. In addition to traditional and contemporary theatres and concert halls, Paris' beautiful, centuries-old stone churches have magnificent acoustics and provide a meditative backdrop for classical music concerts.

In This Section

Tickets/Websites

The most convenient place to purchase concert, theatre and other cultural and sporting-event tickets is from electronics and entertainment megashop **Fnac** (☎08 92 68 36 22; www.fnactickets.com), whether in person at the *billeteries* (ticket offices) or by phone or online. There are branches throughout Paris, including in the Forum des Halles (p79). Tickets generally can't be refunded.

Moulin Rouge performers

The Best...

Entertainment Venues

Palais Garnier (p186) Paris' premier opera house.

Point Éphémère (p187) Uber-cool cultural centre.

Moulin Rouge (p188) The razzle-dazzle can-can creator.

Le 104 (p189) Cultural tour de force.

La Flèche d'Or (p191) Renowned for unearthing new musical talent.

Jazz Clubs

Café Universel (p192) Unpretentious vibe and no cover.

New Morning (p188) Solid and varied line-up.

Le Baiser Salé (p187) Focuses on Caribbean and Latin sounds.

Sunset & Sunside (p187) Blues, fusion and world sounds.

Le Caveau des Oubliettes (p193) Dungeon jam sessions.

☆ Eiffel Tower & Western Paris

Maison de la Radio   Live Music
(http://maisondelaradio.fr; 116 av du président Kennedy, 16e; concerts €15; Ⓜ Passy or RER Avenue du Président Kennedy) Catch a classical concert at Radio France's new concert space, opened in December 2014. With some 200 annual performances, expect a wide variety of music, from organ and chamber music to appearances by the national orchestra. To browse performance times on the website, click on 'Agenda'.

If you're fluent in French, check out one of the *émissions en publique* – your chance to sit in on a live radio show.

Yoyo   Music, Cinema
(Map p248; www.yoyo-paris.com; Palais de Tokyo, 13 av du Président Wilson, 16e; ⊘ variable hours; Ⓜ Iéna, Alma Marceau) Be it street-art exhibitions, live-music gigs, fashion shows, club nights or film screenings, this contemporary raw-concrete space inside Palais de Tokyo promises a great night out.

Théâtre National de Chaillot   Theatre
(Map p248; ☎ 01 53 65 30 00; http://theatre-chaillot.fr; 1 place de Trocadéro, 16e; Ⓜ Trocadéro) French national theatre located beneath the Trocadéro esplanade, primarily staging modern dance productions.

☆ Champs-Élysées & Grands Boulevards

Palais Garnier   Opera, Ballet
(☎ 08 92 89 90 90; www.operadeparis.fr; place de l'Opéra, 9e; Ⓜ Opéra) The city's original opera house is smaller than its Bastille counterpart, but has perfect acoustics. Due to its odd shape, some seats have limited or no visibility – book carefully. Ticket prices and conditions (including last-minute discounts) are available from the **box office** (cnr rues Scribe & Auber; ⊘ 11am-6.30pm Mon-Sat; Ⓜ Opéra).

Au Limonaire   Live Music
(Map p250; ☎ 01 45 23 33 33; http://limonaire. free.fr; 18 cité Bergère, 9e; ⊘ 6pm-2am Tue-Sat, from 7pm Sun & Mon; Ⓜ Grands Boulevards) This perfect little wine bar is one of the best places to listen to traditional French *chansons* and local singer-songwriters. Performances begin at 10pm Tuesday to Saturday and 7pm on Sunday. Entry is free; reservations are recommended if you plan on dining.

L'Olympia   Live Music
(Map p248; ☎ 08 92 68 33 68; www.olympiahall. com; 28 bd des Capucines, 9e; Ⓜ Opéra) Opened by the founder of the Moulin Rouge in 1888, the Olympia has hosted all the big names over the years, from Édith Piaf to Jimi Hendrix and Jeff Buckley, though it's small enough to put on a fairly intimate show.

Folies-Bergère   Live Music
(☎ 08 92 68 16 50; www.foliesbergere.com; 32 rue Richer, 9e; Ⓜ Cadet) This is the legendary club where Charlie Chaplin, WC Fields and Stan Laurel appeared on stage together one night in 1911, and where Josephine Baker – accompanied by her diamond-collared pet cheetah and wearing only stilettos and a skirt made from bananas – bewitched audience members, including Hemingway. Today shows span from solo acts such as Ben Harper to musicals.

☆ Louvre & Les Halles

Comédie Française   Theatre
(Map p250; www.comedie-francaise.fr; place Colette, 1er; Ⓜ Palais Royal–Musée du Louvre) Founded in 1680 under Louis XIV, this state-run theatre bases its repertoire around the works of classic French playwrights. The theatre has its roots in an earlier company directed by Molière at the Palais Royal.

Forum des Images   Cinema
(Map p250; www.forumdesimages.fr; 1 Grande Galerie, Porte St-Eustache, Forum des Halles, 1er; ⊘ 1-9pm Tue-Fri, from 2pm Sat & Sun; Ⓜ Les Halles) Cinemas showing films set in Paris are the centrepiece of the city's film

archive. Created in 1988 to establish 'an audiovisual memory bank of Paris', and renovated in dramatic shades of pink, grey and black, the five-screen centre has a library and research centre with newsreels, documentaries and advertising.

Le Grand Rex
Cinema

(Map p250; www.legrandrex.com; 1 bd Poissonnière, 2e; tour adult/child €11/9; ⊙tours 10am-6pm Tue-Sun, 2-6pm Mon; MBonne Nouvelle) A trip to 1932 art deco cinematic icon Le Grand Rex is like no other trip to the flicks. Screenings aside, the cinema runs 50-minute behind-the-scene tours (English soundtracks available) during which visitors – tracked by a sensor slung around their neck – are whisked up (via a lift) behind the giant screen, tour a soundstage and get to have fun in a recording studio.

Le Baiser Salé
Live Music

(Map p250; ☑01 42 33 37 71; www.lebaisersale.com; 58 rue des Lombards, 1er; ⊙daily; MChâtelet) Known for its Afro and Latin jazz, and jazz fusion concerts, the Salty Kiss combines big names and unknown artists. The place has a relaxed vibe, with sets usually starting at 7.30pm or 9.30pm.

Sunset & Sunside
Live Music

(Map p250; ☑01 40 26 46 60; www.sunset-sunside.com; 60 rue des Lombards, 1er; ⊙daily; MChâtelet) Two venues in one at this trendy, well-respected club: electric jazz, fusion and the odd salsa session downstairs; acoustics and concerts upstairs.

Théâtre du Châtelet
Classical Music

(Map p250; ☑01 40 28 28 40; www.chatelet-theatre.com; 1 place du Châtelet, 1er; MChâtelet) This venue hosts concerts as well as operas, musicals, theatre, ballet and popular Sunday-morning concerts.

Opéra Comique
Opera

(Map p250; www.opera-comique.com; 1 place Boïeldieu, 2e; MRichelieu Drouot) This century-old hall (renovated in 2016) has premiered many important French operas and continues to host classic and less-known works.

🎟 Discount Tickets

Pick up half-price tickets for same-day performances of ballet, opera and music at **Kiosque Théâtre Madeleine** (Map p248; opposite 15 place de la Madeleine, 8e; ⊙12.30-8pm Tue-Sat, to 4pm Sun; MMadeleine), a freestanding kiosk by place de la Madeleine.

Join the queue at Kiosque Théâtre Madeleine

☆ Montmartre & Northern Paris

Philharmonie de Paris
Concert Venue

(☑01 44 84 44 84; http://philharmoniedeparis.fr; 221 av Jean Jaurès, 19e; ⊙box office noon-6pm Tue-Fri, 10am-6pm Sat & Sun; MPorte de Pantin) This major complex, comprising the new Philharmonie 1 building by Jean Nouvel and neighbouring Philharmonie 2 building (previously called Cité de la Musique), hosts an eclectic range of concerts in its main 1200-seat Grande Salle and smaller concert halls. There's every imaginable type of music and dance, from classical to North African to Japanese.

Equally entertaining are its atmospheric *ciné* concerts, when a symphonic orchestra, jazz ensemble or organist accompanies a classic film or new box-office film screening.

Point Éphémère
Live Music

(☑01 40 34 02 48; www.pointephemere.org; 200 quai de Valmy, 10e; ⊙12.30pm-2am Mon-Sat, to 11pm Sun; 🛜; MLouis Blanc) This arts and music venue by the Canal St-Martin attracts an underground crowd for drinks, meals, concerts, dance nights and even art exhibitions.

Moulin Rouge — Cabaret

(Map p256; ☎01 53 09 82 82; www.moulinrouge. fr; 82 bd de Clichy, 18e; show €105-130, dinner show from €190; ⊙shows 9pm & 11pm summer, 9pm Sun-Thu, 9pm & 11pm Fri & Sat winter; MBlanche) Immortalised in the posters of Toulouse-Lautrec and later on screen by Baz Luhrmann, Paris' mythical cabaret club twinkles beneath a 1925 replica of its original red windmill. Yes, it's rife with bus-tour crowds. But from the opening bars of music to the last high cancan-girl kick, it's a whirl of fantastical costumes, sets, choreography and Champagne.

Book in advance online and dress smart (jacket and tie is advised for men, but not obligatory). No entry for children under six.

> Now classed as a historical monument, La Cigale dates from 1887

Rosa Bonheur — Dance Hall

(www.rosabonheur.fr; Parc des Buttes Chaumont, 19e; ⊙noon-midnight Thu & Fri, 10am-midnight Sat & Sun; MBotzaris) This self-styled *guinguette* (old-fashioned dance hall) morphs from outdoor cafe by day into a jam-packed dance floor by night. Its setting inside the Parc des Buttes Chaumont is surely the most bucolic getaway in the city, and even if the tapas aren't to die for, good vibes are virtually guaranteed. If the park is closed, enter at 7 rue Botzaris.

New Morning — Jazz, Blues

(www.newmorning.com; 7 & 9 rue des Petites Écuries, 10e; ⊙variable; MChâteau d'Eau) New Morning is a highly regarded auditorium with excellent acoustics that hosts big-name jazz concerts (Ravi Coltrane, Lake Street Dive) as well as a variety of blues, rock, funk, salsa, Afro-Cuban and Brazilian music.

La Cigale — Live Music

(Map p256; ☎01 49 25 89 99; www.lacigale.fr; 120 bd de Rochechouart, 18e; admission €25-75; MAnvers, Pigalle) Now classed as a historical

La Cigale

monument, this music hall dates from 1887 but was redecorated 100 years later by Philippe Starck. Artists who have performed here recently include Rufus Wainwright, Ryan Adams and Ibrahim Maalouf.

Le Divan du Monde   Live Music

(Map p256; ☑01 40 05 06 99; www.divandu-monde.com; 75 rue des Martyrs, 18e; ⊙variable; MPigalle) Take some cinematographic events and *nouvelles chansons françaises* (new French songs). Add in soul/funk fiestas, air-guitar face-offs and rock parties of the Arctic Monkeys/Killers/Libertines persuasion and stir with an Amy Winehouse swizzle stick. You may now be getting some idea of the inventive, open-minded approach at this excellent cross-cultural venue in Pigalle.

Au Lapin Agile   Cabaret

(Map p256; ☑01 46 06 85 87; www.au-lap-in-agile.com; 22 rue des Saules, 18e; adult €28, student except Sat €20; ⊙9pm-1am Tue-Sun; MLamarck-Caulaincourt) This rustic cabaret venue was favoured by artists and intellectuals in the early 20th century and traditional *chansons* are still performed here. The evening-long show includes singing and poetry. Some love it, others feel it's a bit of a trap.

It's named after *Le Lapin à Gill*, a mural of a rabbit jumping out of a cooking pot by caricaturist André Gill, which can still be seen on the western exterior wall.

La Scène du Canal   Concert Venue

(☑01 48 03 33 22; www.lasceneducanal.com; 116 quai de Jemmapes, 10e; MGare de l'Est) French hip hop, slam and *chanson* blasts out on stage inside edgy concert venue Espace Jemmapes within La Scène on Canal St-Martin.

Le 104   Theatre

(☑01 53 35 50 00; www.le104.fr; 104 rue d'Aubervilliers or 5 rue Curial, 19e; ⊙noon-7pm Tue-Fri, 11am-7pm Sat & Sun; ☏; MStalingrad, Crimée) Watch for circus, theatre, music, monthly balls, magic shows and an eclectic range of other events at this former funeral parlour turned city-funded art space. Some shows are free; others require admission.

Studio Le Regard du Cygne   Dance

(☑01 43 58 55 93; www.leregarducygne.com; 210 rue de Belleville, 20e; MPlace des Fêtes) Many of Paris' young and daring talents in movement, music and theatre congregate to perform at this independent, alternative performance space in the creative 20e.

☆ Le Marais, Ménilmontant & Belleville

Le Carreau du Temple   Cultural Centre

(Map p250; ☑01 83 81 93 30; www.carreaudu-temple.eu; 4 rue Eugène Spuller, 3e; ⊙box office 2-6pm Mon-Sat; MTemple) The quarter's old covered market with gorgeous art nouveau ironwork is now the city's most architecturally appealing cultural centre and entertainment venue. The place where silks, lace, leather and other materials were sold in the 19th century is now a vast stage for exhibitions, concerts, sports classes and theatre. Check the program online.

La Maroquinerie   Live Music

(☑01 40 33 64 85; http://lamaroquinerie.fr; 23 rue Boyer, 20e; ⊙7-11.30pm; MMénilmontant) This tiny but trendy venue in Ménilmontant entices a staunchly local, in-the-know set with real cutting-edge gigs – many bands kick off their European tours here. The alfresco courtyard and restaurant render La Maroquinerie an address impossible to resist; to see for yourself, head east along rue de Ménilmontant and take the second right after place de Ménilmontant.

Gaîté Lyrique   Cultural Centre

(Map p250; ☑01 53 01 51 51; www.gaite-lyrique.net; 3bis rue Papin, 3e; exhibitions €7.50, concerts vary; ⊙2-8pm Tue-Sat, noon-6pm Sun; MArts et Métiers, Réaumur-Sébastopol) Unique and fascinating exhibitions – usually art or installation-art oriented – are the mainstay of this vibrant cultural centre in the Marais. Families with teens will find it particularly appealing; post-exhibition, don't miss the video-game room and library.

La Bellevilloise — Cultural Centre
(☎01 46 36 07 07; www.labellevilloise.com; 19-21 rue Boyer, 20e; ⏰7pm-1am Wed & Thu, 7pm-2am Fri, 6pm-2am Sat, 11.30am-midnight Sun; Ⓜ Ménilmontant) Gigs, concerts, theatrical performances, exhibitions, readings, dance classes and workshops: this arts centre is where it all happens after dark in Ménilmontant. Sunday brunch accompanied by live jazz in the trendy cafe-restaurant – gorgeous in summer with its sunlit tables beneath 100-year-old olive trees – packs out the place. Advance reservations recommended.

La Java — World Music
(www.la-java.fr; 105 rue du Faubourg du Temple, 11e; Ⓜ Goncourt) Built in 1922, this is the dance hall where Édith Piaf got her first break, and it now reverberates to the sound of live salsa, rock and world music. Live concerts usually take place at 8pm or 9pm during the week. Afterwards a festive crowd gets dancing to electro, house, disco and Latino DJs.

Le Vieux Belleville — Live Music
(www.le-vieux-belleville.com; 12 rue des Envierges, 20e; ⏰11am-3pm Mon-Fri, 8pm-2am Thu-Sat; Ⓜ Pyrénées) This old-fashioned bistro and *musette* at the top of Parc de Belleville is an atmospheric venue for performances of

La Java

chansons featuring accordions and an organ grinder three times a week. It's a lively favourite with locals, so booking ahead is advised.

Nouveau Casino — Live Music
(☎01 43 57 57 40; www.nouveaucasino.net; 109 rue Oberkampf, 11e; ⏰Tue-Sun; Ⓜ Parmentier) This club-concert annexe of Café Charbon (p175) has made a name for itself amid the bars of Oberkampf with its live-music concerts (usually Tuesday, Thursday and Friday) and lively club nights on weekends. Electro, pop, deep house, rock – the program is eclectic, underground and always up to the minute. Check the website for listings.

Favela Chic — World Music
(Map p250; ☎01 40 21 38 14; www.favelachic.com; 18 rue du Faubourg du Temple, 11e; ⏰7.30pm-2am Tue-Thu, to 5am Fri & Sat; Ⓜ République) It starts as a chic, convivial restaurant and gives way to caipirinha- and mojito-fuelled bumping, grinding, flirting and dancing (mostly on the long tables). The music is traditionally bossa nova, samba, *baile* (dance), funk and Brazilian pop, and it can get very crowded and hot.

L'Alimentation Générale — Live Music
(☎01 43 55 42 50; http://alimentation-generale.net; 64 rue Jean-Pierre Timbaud, 11e; Fri & Sat €10; ⏰7pm-2am Wed, Thu & Sun, to 5am Fri & Sat; Ⓜ Parmentier) This true hybrid, known as the Grocery Store to anglophones, is a massive space, fronted on street level by its achingly cool, in-house Italianate canteen-bar with big glass windows and retro 1960s Belgian furniture. But music is the big deal here, with an impressive line-up of live gigs and DJs spinning pop, rock, electro, soul and funk to a packed dance floor.

Café de la Gare — Theatre, Comedy
(Map p250; ☎01 42 78 52 51; www.cafe-de-la-gare.fr.st; 41 rue du Temple, 4e; Ⓜ Hôtel de Ville) The 'Station Cafe', in the erstwhile mews of a Marais *hôtel particulier* (private mansion) with a fabulous interior courtyard, is one of the best and most innovative cafe-theatres in Paris. Acts range from comic theatre and stand-up to reinterpreted classics.

☆ Bastille & Eastern Paris

La Flèche d'Or   Live Music

(☎01 44 64 01 02; www.flechedor.fr; 102bis rue de Bagnolet, 20e; ⊙variable; MAlexandre Dumas, Gambetta) Just over 1km northeast of place de la Nation in a former railway station on central Paris' outer edge, this awesome music venue hosts both indie rock concerts and house/electro DJ nights. The Golden Arrow – named for the train to Calais in the 1930s – has a solid reputation for promoting new talent.

Opéra Bastille   Classical Music

(☎08 92 89 90 90, 01 40 01 19 70; www.op-eradeparis.fr; 2-6 place de la Bastille, 12e; guided tour €15; ⊙box office 2.30-6.30pm Mon-Sat; MBastille) This 3400-seat venue is the city's main opera hall; it also stages ballet and classical concerts. Tickets go on sale online up to two weeks before they're available by telephone or at the box office. Standing-only tickets (*places débouts;* €5) are available 90 minutes before performances begin. By day, explore the eyesore opera house with a 90-minute guided tour backstage; check hours online.

Badaboum   Live Music

(www.badaboum-paris.com; 2bis rue des Taillandiers, 11e; ⊙cocktail bar 7pm-2am Wed-Sat, club & concerts vary; MBastille, Ledru-Rollin) Formerly La Scène Bastille and freshly refitted, the onomatopoeically named Badaboum hosts a mixed bag of concerts on its up-close-and-personal stage, but focuses on electro, funk and hip-hop. Great atmosphere, super cocktails and a secret room upstairs.

La Cinémathèque Française   Cinema

(www.cinemathequefrancaise.com; 51 rue de Bercy, 12e; ⊙noon-7pm Mon & Wed-Sat, 10am-5pm Sun; MBercy) This national institution is a temple to the 'seventh art' and always screens its foreign offerings in their original versions. Up to 10 movies a day are shown, usually retrospectives (Spielberg, Altman, Eastwood) mixed in with related but more obscure films.

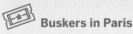 **Buskers in Paris**

Paris' gaggle of clowns, mime artists, living statues, acrobats, inline skaters, buskers and other street entertainers can be loads of fun and cost substantially less than a theatre ticket (a few coins in the hat is appreciated). Some excellent musicians perform in the long echo-filled corridors of the metro, a highly prized privilege that artists audition for. Outside, you can be sure of a good show at the following:

Place Georges Pompidou, 4e The huge square in front of the Centre Pompidou.

Pont St-Louis, 4e The bridge linking Paris' two islands (best enjoyed with a Berthillon ice cream in hand).

Pont au Double, 4e The pedestrian bridge linking Notre Dame with the Left Bank.

Place Joachim du Bellay, 1er Musicians and fire-eaters near the Fontaine des Innocents.

Parc de la Villette, 19e African drummers at the weekend.

Place du Tertre, Montmartre, 18e Montmartre's original main square is Paris' busiest busker stage.

La Chapelle des Lombards   Live Music

(www.la-chapelle-des-lombards.com; 19 rue de Lappe, 11e; admission incl drink €20; ⊙11pm-5am Wed, Thu & Sun, to 6am Fri & Sat; MBastille) World music dominates this perennially popular Bastille dance club, with happening

Cinema

The film-lover's ultimate city, Paris has some wonderful movie houses to catch new flicks, avant-garde cinema and priceless classics.

Foreign films (including English-language films) screened in their original language with French subtitles are labelled 'VO' (*version originale*). Films labelled 'VF' (*version française*) are dubbed in French.

Pariscope and *L'Officiel des Spectacles* list the full crop of Paris' cinematic pickings and screening times; online check out http://cinema.leparisien.fr.

First-run tickets cost around €11.50 for adults (€13.50 for 3D). Students and over 60s get discounted tickets (usually around €8.50) from 7pm Sunday to 7pm Friday. Discounted tickets for children and teens have no restrictions. Most cinemas have across-the-board discounts before noon.

MATTJEACOCK/GETTY IMAGES ©

Latino DJs and reggae, funk and Afro jazz concerts. Performances usually take place on Friday and Saturday. Gals get in free before 2am on Friday and Saturday nights.

Le Balajo   Live Music
(www.balajo.fr; 9 rue de Lappe, 11e; ⊙variable; MBastille) A mainstay of Parisian nightlife since 1936, this ancient ballroom is devoted to salsa classes and Latino music during the week, with an R & B slant on weekends when the dance floor rocks until *aube* (dawn). But the best time to visit is for its old-fashioned

musette (accordion music) gigs on Monday afternoon from 2pm to 7pm.

Le Motel   Live Music
(www.lemotel.fr; 8 passage Josset, 11e; ⊙6pm-2am Tue-Sun; MLedru-Rollin) This hole-in-the-wall venue in the hot-to-boiling-point 11e has become the go-to indie bar around Bastille. It's particularly well loved for its comfy sofas, inexpensive but quality drinks (Belgian beers on tap and indie cocktails) and excellent music. Live bands and DJs throughout the week.

Accor Hotels Arena   Live Music, Stadium
(Palais Omnisports de Paris-Bercy; ☑01 58 70 16 00; www.accorhotelsarena.com; 8 bd de Bercy, 12e; MBercy) This indoor sports arena, one sloping exterior of which is covered with lawns, hosts the largest concerts and events to come through Paris (Cirque du Soleil, Lenny Kravitz, Elton John), as well as various sporting competitions and matches.

☆ Latin Quarter

Café Universel   Jazz, Blues
(Map p254; ☑01 43 25 74 20; www.cafeuniversel.com; 267 rue St-Jacques, 5e; ⊙9pm-2am Mon-Sat; ☎; MCensier Daubenton or RER Port Royal) Café Universel hosts a brilliant array of live concerts, with everything from bebop and Latin sounds to vocal jazz sessions. Plenty of freedom is given to young producers and artists, and its convivial relaxed atmosphere attracts a mix of students and jazz lovers. Concerts are free, but tip the artists when they pass the hat around.

Le Champo   Cinema
(Map p254; www.lechampo.com; 51 rue des Écoles, 5e; tickets adult/child €9/4; MCluny–La Sorbonne) This is one of the most popular of the many Latin Quarter cinemas, featuring classics and retrospectives looking at the films of such actors and directors as Alfred Hitchcock, Jacques Tati, Alain Resnais, Frank Capra, Tim Burton and Woody Allen. One of the two *salles* (cinemas) has wheelchair access.

A couple of times a month Le Champo screens films for night owls, kicking off at midnight (three films plus breakfast €15).

Le Caveau des Oubliettes   Jazz, Blues

(Map p254; ☑01 46 34 24 09; https://le-caveaudesoubliettes.wordpress.com; 52 rue Galande, 5e; ⊗5pm-2am Sun-Tue, to 4am Wed-Sat; MSt-Michel) From the 16th-century ground-floor pub (with a happy hour from 5pm to 9pm), descend to the 12th-century dungeon for jazz, blues and funk concerts, and jam sessions (from 10pm).

Caveau de la Huchette   Jazz, Blues

(Map p250; ☑01 43 26 65 05; www.caveaudela-huchette.fr; 5 rue de la Huchette, 5e; Sun-Thu €13, Fri & Sat €15; ⊗9.30pm-2.30am Sun-Wed, to 4am Thu-Sat; MSt-Michel) Housed in a medieval *caveau* (cellar) used as a courtroom and torture chamber during the Revolution, this club is where virtually all the jazz greats (Georges Brassens, Thibault...) have played since the end of WWII. It attracts its fair share of tourists, but the atmosphere can be more electric than at the more serious jazz clubs. Sessions start at 10pm.

Le Grand Action   Cinema

(Map p254; www.legrandaction.com; 5 rue des Écoles, 5e; tickets €9; MCardinal Lemoine) Cult films both recent (such as the Coen brothers' *Hail, Caesar!*) and not (*Apocalypse Now, East of Eden, 2001 A Space Odyssey* and *The Thing*) screen in their original languages at this cinephiles' favourite.

Le Petit Journal St-Michel   Jazz, Blues

(Map p254; ☑01 43 26 28 59; www.petitjournal-saintmichel.com; 71 bd St-Michel, 5e; admission incl 1 drink €20, with dinner €49-57; ⊗7.30pm-1am Mon-Sat; MCluny–La Sorbonne or RER Luxembourg) Classic jazz concerts kick off at 9.15pm in the atmospheric downstairs cellar of this sophisticated jazz venue across from the Jardin du Luxembourg. Everything ranging from Dixieland and vocals to big band and swing sets patrons' toes tapping. Dinner is served at 8pm (but it's the music that's the real draw).

Église St-Julien le Pauvre   Classical Music

(Map p254; ☑01 42 26 00 00; www.concertin-paris.com; 1 rue St-Julien le Pauvre, 5e; tickets €18-23; MSt-Michel) Piano recitals (Chopin, Liszt) are staged at least two evenings a week in one of the oldest churches in Paris. Higher-priced tickets directly face the stage. Payment is by cash only at the door.

☆ St-Germain & Les Invalides

Chez Papa   Jazz

(Map p250; ☑01 42 86 99 63; www.papajazz-club-paris.fr; 3 rue St-Benoît, 6e; concerts €12; ⊗concerts 9pm-1am Mon-Thu, 9.30pm-1.30am Fri & Sat; MSt-Germain des Prés) The doors of this snug St-Germain jazz club regularly stay open until dawn. Piano duets, blues, sax solos and singers regularly feature on the bill. Its restaurant, serving traditional French dishes opens from noon to 3.30pm and 7.30pm to 10.30pm Monday to Saturday.

Comédie Française Théâtre du Vieux Colombier   Theatre

(☑01 44 58 15 15, tickets 01 44 39 87 00; www.comedie-francaise.fr; 21 rue du Vieux Colombier, 6e; ⊗Sep-Jul; MSt-Sulpice) One of three Comédie Française venues (p186), along with the Right Bank's main Salle Richelieu and Studio Théâtre. Founded in 1680, it presents works by classic French playwrights such as Molière.

Le Lucernaire   Cultural Centre

(☑reservations 01 45 44 57 34; www.lucernaire. fr; 53 rue Notre Dame des Champs, 6e; ⊗bar 11am-9pm Mon, 11am-12.30am Tue-Fri, 4pm-12.30am Sat, 4-10pm Sun; MNotre Dame des Champs) Sunday-evening concerts are a fixture among the impressive offerings at the dynamic Centre National d'Art et d'Essai (National Arts Centre). Whether it's classical guitar, baroque, French *chansons* or east Asian music, these weekly concerts starting from 4pm (hours vary) are a real treat. Art and photography exhibitions, cinema, theatre, lectures, debates and guided walks round off the packed cultural agenda.

ACTIVE PARIS

Picturesque parks, sporting highlights and unique local-led tours

Active Paris

Ready to unwind with the Parisians? Take a break from the concrete and check out the city's glorious parks and two vast forests, the Bois de Boulogne and Bois de Vincennes, which act as its 'green lungs'. The city also has some stunning swimming pools, both historic and new, and a rapidly expanding network of cycling lanes. State-of-the-art facilities will increase as the city prepares its bid to host the 2024 Olympic Games.

As one of the world's most visited cities, Paris is well set up for visitors with a host of guided tours, from bike, boat, bus, scooter and walking tours (including some wonderful local-led options in off-the-beaten-track areas) to more unusual themed options, including photography tours, film-location tours and treasure hunts.

In This Section

What to Watch

From late May to mid-June, the French Open hits up at the Stade Roland Garros. The Tour de France races up the Champs-Élysées at the end of July every year. The main football (soccer) season runs from August through to April.

ARCHITECT: ADRIEN FAINSILBER AND ENGINEER PETER RICE/PHOTO: BRUNO DE HOGUES/GETTY IMAGES ©

Cité des Sciences et le l'Industrie, Parc de la Villette

The Best... ⭐

Sporting Venues

Parc des Princes (p198) Home to local football team Paris St-Germain.

Accor Hotels Arena (p192) Indoor stadium that hosts an array of competitions.

Stade Roland Garros (p198) Prestigious grounds of the French Open.

Hippodrome d'Auteuil (p198) Steeplechases in the Bois de Boulogne.

Outdoor Spaces

Bois de Boulogne (p202) Walk, cycle, row or catch a steeplechase.

Bois de Vincennes (p202) A zoo, a botanical park, playgrounds and pick-up football matches.

Jardin du Luxembourg (p68) Picnic, play tennis and entertain the kids.

Parc des Buttes-Chaumont (p200) Walk the old railway line.

Parc de la Villette (p199) Fifty-five hectares of outdoor-activity bliss.

🎽 Spectator Sports

Stade de France
Stadium

(📞08 92 70 09 00; www.stadefrance.com;
St-Denis La Plaine; stadium tours adult/child
€15/10; ⏲9.30am-6pm Tue-Sun; Ⓜ St-Denis-
Porte de Paris) This 80,000-seat stadium
was built for the 1998 FIFA World Cup,
and hosts major sports and music events.
One-hour stadium tours take you behind
the scenes, providing no event is taking
place. Tours in English depart at 10am and
2.30pm from April to August, and hourly
from 11am to 4pm from September to
March from Gate E.

Stade Roland Garros
Tennis

(www.billetterie.fft.fr; 2 av Gordon Bennett,
Bois de Boulogne, 16e; Ⓜ Porte d'Auteuil) The
French Open is held on clay at the Stade
Roland Garros late May to mid-June. A
much-needed renovation project, which
finally kicked off in 2016 after five years of
delays, will incorporate a new Court No 1
and a retractable roof over the centre court,
among other changes. The project is slated

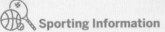

🏀 Sporting Information

Local teams include Paris St-Germain
(football; www.psg.fr) and the pink-clad
Stade Français Paris (rugby; www.stade.
fr). Catch France's national rugby team,
Les Bleus, at the Stade de France.

For upcoming events, click on Sports
& Games (under the Going Out menu) at
http://en.parisinfo.com. Better yet, if you
can read French, sports daily *L'Équipe*
(www.lequipe.fr) will provide more depth.

Stade de France
VIEW PICTURES LTD/ALAMY STOCK PHOTO ©

for completion in 2020; the tournament will
continue during that time.

Parc des Princes
Football

(www.leparcdesprinces.fr; 24 rue du Comman-
dant Guilbaud, 16e; Ⓜ Porte de St-Cloud) Home
ground to Paris' top-division football team
Paris St-Germain (PSG).

Hippodrome d'Auteuil
Horse Racing

(www.france-galop.com; Champ de Courses
d'Auteuil, 16e, Bois de Boulogne; adult weekend/
weekday €8/5, child free; Ⓜ Porte d'Auteuil) This
horse-racing track in the Bois de Boulogne
hosts steeplechases March to June and
September to early December.

🏊 Swimming Pools

Piscine Joséphine Baker
Swimming

(📞01 56 61 96 50; http://equipement.paris.fr/
piscine-josephine-baker-2930; quai François Mauriac, 13e; pool adult/child €3.60/2, sauna €10/5;
⏲7-8.30am & 1-9pm Mon, Wed & Fri, 1-11pm Tue
& Thu, 11am-8pm Sat, 10am-8pm Sun; Ⓜ Quai de
la Gare) Floating on the Seine, this striking
swimming pool is style indeed (named after
the sensual 1920s American singer, what
else could it be?). More of a spot to be seen
than to thrash laps, the two 25m-by-10m
pools lure Parisians like bees to a honey pot
in summer when the roof slides back.

Aquaboulevard
Swimming

(📞01 40 60 10 00; www.aquaboulevard.fr; 4-6
rue Louis Armand, 15e; adult/child €29/15;
⏲9am-11pm Mon-Thu, 9am-midnight Fri,
8am-midnight Sat, 8am-11pm Sun; Ⓜ Balard)
Just outside the *périphérique* (ring road),
this huge tropical 'beach' and aquatic park
is especially worth a visit with kids (note
under threes aren't allowed), with water
slides, waterfalls and wave pools, as well
as tennis, squash, golf, a gym and dance
classes. Last admission is 9pm. Prices are
lower from mid-September to May, when
the outdoor areas close.

Piscine de la Butte
Aux Cailles
Swimming

(📞01 45 89 60 05; http://equipement.paris.fr/
piscine-de-la-butte-aux-cailles.2927; 5 place Paul

Verlaine, 13e; adult/child €3/1.70; ☺hours vary;
Ⓜ Place d'Italie) Built in 1924, this art deco
swimming pool complex takes advantage
of the lovely warm artesian well water
nearby. Its spectacular vaulted indoor pool
was recently restored to its former glory;
come summer, its two outdoor pools buzz
with swimmers frolicking in the sun. Hours
fluctuate; check schedules online.

Piscine Pontoise   Swimming
(Map p254; ☑01 55 42 77 88; http://piscine.
equipement.paris.fr; 19 rue de Pontoise, 5e; adult/
child €4.80/2.90; ☺hours vary; Ⓜ Maubert-
Mutualité) A beautiful art-deco-style indoor
pool in the heart of the Latin Quarter. An
€11.10 evening ticket (from 8pm) covers
entry to the pool, gym and sauna. It has
shorter hours during term time – check
schedules online.

🏃 Inline Skating

Pari Roller   Skating
(http://pari-roller.com; place Raoul Dautry, 14e;
☺10pm-1am Fri, arrive 9.30pm; Ⓜ Montparnasse
Bienvenüe) The world's largest in-line mass
skate, Pari Roller regularly attracts more
than 10,000 bladers. Dubbed 'Friday Night
Fever', this fast-paced skate covers a different
30km-odd route each week. Most incorporate cobblestones and downhill stretches,
and are geared for experienced bladers only
(for your safety and everyone else's). It takes
place year-round except when wet weather
makes conditions treacherous.

Like its gentler counterpart, the Marais-
based **Rollers & Coquillages** (www.
rollers-coquillages.org; 37 bd Bourdon, 4e; Ⓜ Bastille), it's accompanied by yellow-jersey-clad
volunteer marshals, along with police
(some on inline skates) and ambulances.
Wear bright clothes to make yourself visible
to drivers and other skaters.

Nomadeshop (☑01 44 54 07 44; www.
nomadeshop.com; 37 bd Bourdon, 4e; half-/full
day from €5/8; ☺11am-1.30pm & 2.30-7.30pm
Tue-Fri, 10am-7pm Sat, noon-6pm Sun; Ⓜ Bastille)
offers skate rental.

🏀 Swimming Etiquette

If you want to go swimming at either
your hotel or in a public pool, you'll need
to don a *bonnet de bain* (bathing cap) –
even if you don't have any hair. You
shouldn't need to buy one ahead of time
as they are generally sold at most pools.
Men are required to wear skin-tight
trunks (Speedos); loose-fitting Bermu-
da shorts are not allowed.

Piscine Pontoise
LOOK DIE BILDAGENTUR DER FOTOGRAFEN GMBH/ALAMY STOCK PHOTO ©

🏃 Parks

Parc de la Villette   Park
(www.villette.com; 211 av Jean Jaurès, 19e;
☺6am-1am; 👶; Ⓜ Porte de la Villette, Porte de
Pantin) Embracing 55 hectares, this vast city
park is a cultural centre, kids' playground
and landscaped urban space at the inter-
section of two canals, the Ourcq and the
St-Denis. Its futuristic layout includes the
colossal mirror-like sphere of the Géode
cinema and the bright-red cubical pavilions
known as *folies*. Among its themed gardens
are the Jardin du Dragon (Dragon Garden),
with a giant dragon's-tongue slide for kids,
the Jardin des Dunes (Dunes Garden) and
Jardin des Miroirs (Mirror Garden).

Events are staged in the wonderful old
Grande Halle (formerly a slaughterhouse –
the Parisian cattle market was located here
from 1867 to 1974), Le Zénith, the Cabaret
Sauvage, the Cité de la Musique, the Con-
servatoire National Supérieur de Musique
et de Danse and the Philharmonie de Paris.

Promenade Plantée   Park

(La Coulée Verte René-Dumont; cnr rue de Lyon & av Daumesnil, 12e; ⊙8am-9.30pm May-Aug, to 5.30pm Sep-Apr; ⓂBastille, Gare de Lyon) The disused 19th-century Vincennes railway viaduct has been reborn as the world's first elevated park, planted with a fragrant profusion of cherry trees, maples, rose trellises, bamboo corridors and lavender. Three storeys above ground, it provides a unique aerial vantage point on the city. Access is via staircase and it starts just south of place de la Bastille on rue de Lyon. Along the first section, above av Daumesnil, chic art-gallery-workshops squat gracefully beneath the arches to form the Viaduc des Arts (p156).

Walking south, look out for the spectacular art deco police station at the start of rue de Rambouillet, topped with a dozen huge, identical marble caryatids. The viaduct later drops back to street level at Jardin de Reuilly (1.5km), but it's possible to follow the line all the way to the Bois de Vincennes (4.5km). This latter section can also be done on a bike or in-line skates.

At sq Charles Péguy, behind the table-tennis tables, you can access a 200m section of another abandoned Parisian railway-

Parc des Buttes-Chaumont

BRUNO DE HOGUES/GETTY IMAGES ©

turned-park, the Petite Ceinture, here known as the **Petite Ceinture du 12e** (PC 12; 21 rue Rottembourg, 12e; ⊙8.30am-5pm Mon & Tue, 8.30am-10.45pm Wed-Sun; ⓂMichel Bizot), which also has a *jardin partagé* (community garden).

Parc des Buttes-Chaumont   Park

(Rue Manin & rue Botzaris, 19e; ⊙7am-10pm May-Sep, to 8pm Oct-Apr; ⓂButtes-Chaumont, Botzaris) This quirky park is one of the city's largest green spaces; its landscaped slopes hide grottoes, waterfalls, a lake and even an island topped with a temple to Sybil. Once a gypsum quarry and rubbish dump, it was given its present form by Baron Haussmann in time for the opening of the 1867 Exposition Universelle. The tracks of an abandoned 19th-century railway line (La Petite Ceinture, which once circled Paris) run through the park.

It's a favourite with Parisians, who come here to practise t'ai chi, take the kids to a puppet show or simply to relax with a bottle of wine and a sundown picnic.

Jardin de la Nouvelle France   Park

(Map p248; cnr av Franklin D Roosevelt & cours la Reine, 8e; ⊙24hr; ⓂFranklin D Roosevelt) Descending rustic, uneven staircases (by the white-marble Alfred de Musset sculpture on av Franklin D Roosevelt, or the upper garden off cours la Reine) brings you to the tiny 0.7-hectare Jardin de la Nouvelle France, an unexpected wonderland of lilacs, and lemon, orange, maple and weeping beech trees, with a wildlife-filled pond, waterfall, wooden footbridge and benches to soak up the serenity.

Square René Viviani   Park

(Map p254; quai de Montebello, 5e; ⊙24hr; ⓂSt-Michel) Opened in 1928 on the site of the former graveyard of adjoining church Église St-Julien-le-Pauvre, this picturesque little park is home to the oldest tree in Paris. The black locust (*Robinia pseudoacacia*) was planted here in 1602 by Henri III, Henri IV and Louis XII's gardener, Jean Robin, and is now supported by concrete pillars disguised as branches and trunks.

A 1995-installed bronze fountain by Georges Jeanclos depicts the legend of Saint Julien. Roses bloom in spring and summer.

Square du Vert-Galant   Park

(Map p250; place du Pont Neuf; ⊘24hr; M Pont Neuf) Chestnut, yew, black walnut and weeping willow trees grace this picturesque park at the westernmost tip of the Île de la Cité, along with migratory birds including mute swans, pochard and tufted ducks, black-headed gulls and wagtails. Sitting at the islands' original level, 7m below their current height, the waterside park is reached by stairs leading down from the Pont Neuf. It's romantic at any time of day but especially in the evening watching the sun set over the river.

Parc Montsouris   Park

(Av Reille, 14e; ⊘8.30am-9.30pm May-Aug, shorter hours rest of year; M Porte d'Orléans or RER Cité-Universitaire) The name of this sprawling lakeside park – planted with horse-chestnut, yew, cedar, weeping beech and buttonwood trees – derives from *moque souris* (mice mockery) because the area was once overrun with the critters. Today it's a delightful picnic spot and has endearing playground areas, such as a concrete 'road system' where littlies can trundle matchbox cars (BYO cars), as well as a marionette (puppet) theatre and pony rides (Wednesday, Saturday and Sunday afternoons).

An abandoned section of the Petite Ceinture (p#) runs through the park.

The park neighbours the ground-breaking 1920s-built Cité Universitaire (student halls of residence), which you're free to wander.

Parc de Bercy   Park

(Rue Paul Belmondo; ⊘8am-sunset Mon-Fri, from 9am Sat & Sun; M; M Cour St-Émilion, Bercy) Built atop the site of a former wine depot, this large, well-landscaped park is a great place to break for a picnic and let the kids run free. Bercy reached its height as the 'world's wine cellar' in the 19th century: it was right on the Seine, close to Paris yet outside the city walls,

meaning that shipping was convenient and commerce tax-free.

Vestiges of its former incarnation are spread across the park and the Cour St-Émilion, where the warehouses were located. In some spots you'll see the old railroad tracks; in others you'll find grapevines.

Parc Georges Brassens   Park

(http://equipment.paris.fr; 2 place Jacques Marette, 15e; ⊘8am-sunset Mon-Fri, 9am-sunset Sat & Sun; M Convention, ☐ Georges Brassens) Covering 7.74 hectares, Parc Georges Brassens (named for the French singer-song-writer and poet, who lived nearby) has a large central pond bordered by lawns, and gardens featuring roses and medicinal and aromatic plants. The sloping hill is home to a wine-producing vineyard and an apiary; honey is sold on the first Saturday of each month at the entrance. On Wednesday, Saturday and Sunday kids can ride ponies (€3.50; 3pm to 6pm) and watch a mario-nette show (€4; 3.30pm and 4.30pm).

Also here is the Monfort theatre, with dance, circus and theatre performances, and the weekend book market, **Marché Georges Brassens** (104 rue Brancion, 15e; ⊘9am-6pm Sat & Sun; M Porte de Vanves).

A honey and grape-harvest festival takes place on the first weekend in October.

Parc André-Citroën   Park

(2 rue Cauchy, 15e; ⊘8am-9.30pm May-Aug, shorter hours rest of year; M Balard) In 1915 automotive entrepreneur André Citroën built a vast car-manufacturing plant here in the 15e. After it closed in the 1970s, the vacated site was eventually turned into this forward-looking 14-hectare urban park. Its central lawn is flanked by greenhouses, dancing fountains, an elevated reflecting pool, and smaller gardens themed around movement and the (six) senses. The heli-um-filled sightseeing balloon **Le Ballon Air de Paris** (☏01 44 26 20 00; www.ballondeparis. com; Parc André Citroën, 2 rue de la Montagne de la Fage, 15e; adult/child €12/6; ⊘9am-9pm May-Aug, shorter hours Sep-Apr; M Balard, Lourmel) ⚑ is located here. Check seasonal hours signposted at the entrances.

Boules

Don't be surprised to see groups of earnest Parisians playing *boules* (France's most popular traditional game, similar to lawn bowls) in the Jardin du Luxembourg and other parks and squares with suitably flat, shady patches of gravel. The **Arènes de Lutèce** (Map p254; www. arenesdelutece.com; 49 rue Monge, 5e; ⊙8am-9.30pm Apr-Oct, to 5.30pm Nov-Mar; MPlace Monge) FREE *boulodrome* in a 2nd-century Roman amphitheatre in the Latin Quarter is a fabulous spot to absorb the scene. There are usually places to play at Paris Plages.

JAKE WYMAN/GETTY IMAGES ©

Parc de Belleville   Park
(MCouronnes) A few blocks east of blvd de Belleville, this lovely park occupies a hill almost 200m above sea level, set amid 4.5 hectares of urban greenery. From the panoramic terrace at the top of the park, on rue Piat, there are fabulous views of the city. Delve into the park to find fountains, trimmed hedgerows, a gargantuan slide, a toboggan ride and climbing frame for kids.

Petite Ceinture du 15e   Park
(PC 15; www.paris.fr; btwn rue Olivier de Serres & rue St-Charles, 15e; ⊙9am-8.30pm May-Aug, shorter hours rest of year; MBalard or Porte de Versailles) FREE This former railway corridor of Paris' historic Petite Ceinture (p200) steam railway stretches for 1.3km, with biodiverse habitats including forest, grassland and prairies supporting 220 species of flora and fauna. In addition to the end points, there are three lift/elevator-enabled

access points along its route: 397ter rue de Vaugirard; opposite 82 rue Desnouettes; and place Robert Guillemard. Ultimately the goal is to open the entire section of track between Parcs Georges Brassens and André-Citroën, around 3km in all.

🏃 Forests

Bois de Vincennes   Park
(Blvd Poniatowski, 12e; MPorte de Charenton or Porte Dorée) In the southeastern corner of Paris, Bois de Vincennes encompasses some 995 hectares. Originally royal hunting grounds, the woodland was annexed by the army following the Revolution and then donated to the city in 1860 by Napoléon III. A fabulous place to escape the endless stretches of Parisian concrete, Bois de Vincennes also contains a handful of notable sights, including a bona fide royal chateau, **Château de Vincennes** (☎01 48 08 31 20; http://vincennes.monuments-nationaux.fr; av de Paris, Vincennes; guided tour adult/child €8.50/ free; ⊙10am-6pm mid-May–mid-Sep, to 5pm mid-Sep–mid-May; MChâteau de Vincennes), with massive fortifications and a moat.

Paris' largest, now state-of-the-art zoo, the **Parc Zoologique de Paris** (p32), is also here, as is the magnificent **Parc Floral de Paris** (☎01 49 57 24 81; www. parcfloraldeparisjeux.com; Esplanade du Chateau de Vincennes or rte de la Pyramide; adult/child €5.50/2.75; ⊙9.30am-8pm summer, shorter hours rest of year; ⍟; MChâteau de Vincennes), with exciting playgrounds for older children. The wood also has a lovely lake, with boats to rent and ample green lawns to picnic on.

Bois de Boulogne   Park
(Bd Maillot; MPorte Maillot) On the western edge of Paris just beyond the 16e, the 845-hectare Bois de Boulogne owes its informal layout to Baron Haussmann, who was inspired by Hyde Park in London. Be warned that the Bois de Boulogne becomes a distinctly adult playground after dark, especially along the allée de Longchamp, where sex workers cruise for clients.

The southern part of the wood has two horse-racing tracks, the Hippodrome de

Longchamp for flat races and the Hippodrome d'Auteuil for steeplechases.

🏃 Guided Tours & Courses

Parisien d'un Jour – Paris Greeters   Walking Tour
(www.greeters.paris; by donation) See Paris
through local eyes with these two- to three-
hour city tours. Volunteers – mainly knowledgable Parisians passionate about their
city – lead groups (maximum six people) to
their favourite spots. Minimum two weeks'
notice is needed.

Localers   Walking Tour
(📞01 83 64 92 01; www.localers.com) Classic
walking tours and behind-the-scenes urban
discoveries with local Paris experts: *pétanque,* photo shoots, market tours, cooking
classes, foie gras–tasting and more.

Paris Walks   Walking Tour
(📞01 48 09 21 40; www.paris-walks.com; 2hr
tour adult/child €15/8) Long established and
well respected, Paris Walks offers two-hour
thematic walking tours on art, fashion,
chocolate, the French Revolution etc.

Set in Paris   Walking Tour
(Map p254; 📞09 84 42 35 79; http://setinparis.
com; 3 rue Maître Albert, 5e; 2hr tour €25; ⏱2hr
tours 10am & 3pm; Ⓜ Maubert-Mutualité) From
its cinema-style 'box office' HQ in the Latin
Quarter, Set in Paris' two-hour walking tours
take you to locations throughout Paris where
movies including *The Devil Wears Prada, The
Bourne Identity, The Three Musketeers, The
Hunchback of Notre Dame, Ratatouille, Before
Sunset,* several James Bond instalments and
many others were filmed. Advance reservations are recommended.

École Le Cordon Bleu   Cooking Course
(📞01 85 65 15 00; www.cordonbleu.edu;) One of
the world's foremost culinary arts schools.
Prices range from €69 for two-hour classes
to €490 for two-day courses.

Paris Photography Tours   Tour
(📞06 17 08 54 45; www.parisphotographytours.
com; 3hr day/night tours for 1-4 people €150)
Customised tours by professional pho-
tographers take into account your level of
experience and what you most want to capture, such as nature, architecture or street
life. Tours can also incorporate lessons on
how to improve your photographic skills.

THATLou   Tour
(www.thatlou.com; per person excluding museum
admission fees €20-25) Organises treasure
hunts in English and French in the Louvre,
Musée d'Orsay (THATd'Or) and streets of
the Latin Quarter (THATrue). Participants
(two or more people, playing alone or
against another team) have to photograph
themselves in front of 20 to 30 works of
art ('treasure'). Hunts typically last 1½ to 2
hours. Hunts designed for kids (€15) also
available.

Fat Tire Bike Tours   Bicycle Tour
(📞01 85 08 19 76; www.fattirebiketours.com;
tours from €32) Offers both day and night bicycle tours of the city, both in central Paris
and further afield to Versailles and Monet's
Garden in Giverny.

Paris à Vélo, C'est Sympa!   Cycling
(Map p250; 📞01 48 87 60 01; www.parisvelosympa.
com; 22 rue Alphonse Baudin, 11e; Ⓜ St-Sébastien-Froissart) Runs three guided bike tours
(adult/child €35/29; three hours): a Heart
of Paris tour, Unusual Paris (taking in artists'
studios and mansions) and the Contrast tour,
combining nature and modern architecture.
Tours depart from its bike rental shop.

Left Bank Scooters   Tour
(📞06 78 12 04 24; www.leftbankscooters.com;
3hr tours per 1st/2nd passenger from €150/50)
Runs a variety of scooter tours around
Paris, both day and evening, as well as trips
out to Versailles and sidecar tours. Car or
motorcycle licence required. Also rents
scooters (50/125/300cc scooters per 24
hours €70/80/100).

REST YOUR HEAD

Top tips for the best accommodation

Rest Your Head

Paris has a wealth of accommodation for all budgets, from a recently re-invigorated hostel scene that now includes purpose-built, state-of-the-art flashpacker pads to hipster hang-outs, charming old-school hotels, intimate boutique gems, eye-popping designer havens, sleep-drink-dine-dance lifestyle hotels, and deluxe hotels and palaces, some of which rank among the finest in the world. Across all categories, however, accommodation is often complet *(full) well in advance. Reservations are recommended year-round and are essential during the warmer months (April to October) and all public and school holidays. Although marginally cheaper, accom-modation outside central Paris is invariably a false economy given travel time and costs. Choose somewhere within Paris' 20* arrondissements *(city districts) to experience Parisian life the moment you step out the door.*

In This Section

Prices

A 'budget hotel' in Paris generally costs up to €130 for a double room with en suite bathroom in high season (breakfast not included). For a midrange option, plan on spending €130 to €250. Luxury options run €250 and higher.

Tipping

Bellhops usually expect €1 to €2 per bag; it's not necessary to tip the concierge, cleaners or front-desk staff.

MARIOGUTI/GETTY IMAGES ©

Reservations

Reservations are almost always essential – walk-ins are practically impossible and rack rates are unfavourable relative to online deals (usually best directly via hotels' official websites). Reserve your room as early as possible and make sure you understand the cancellation policy. Check-in is generally in the middle of the afternoon and checkout in the late morning.

Useful Websites

Lonely Planet (www.lonelyplanet.com/france/paris/hotels) Reviews of Lonely Planet's top choices.

Paris Hotel Service (www.parishotel-service.com) Boutique hotel gems.

Paris Hotel (www.hotels-paris.fr) Well-organised hotel booking site with lots of user reviews.

Room Sélection (www.room-selection.com) Select apartment rentals centred on Le Marais.

Accommodation Types

Hotels

Hotels in Paris are inspected by government authorities and classified into six categories, from no star to five stars. The vast majority are two- and three-star hotels, which are generally well-equipped. All hotels must display their rates, including TVA (*taxe sur la valeur ajoutée;* valued-added tax), though you'll often get *much* cheaper prices online, especially on the hotels' own websites, which invariably offer the best deals.

Parisian hotel rooms tend to be small by international standards. Families will probably need connecting rooms, but if children are too young to stay in their own room, it's possible to make do with triples, quads or suites in some places.

Cheaper hotels may not have lifts/elevators and/or air-conditioning. Some don't accept credit cards.

Breakfast is rarely included in hotel rates; heading to a cafe often works out to be better value (and more atmospheric).

Hostels

Paris is awash with hostels, and standards are consistently improving. A wave of state-of-the-art hostels have recently opened their doors, such as the design-savvy 950-bed 'megahostel' by leading hostel chain Generator near Canal St-Martin, 10e, and, close by, two by the switched-on St Christopher's group.

Some of the more traditional (ie institutional) hostels have daytime lock-outs and curfews; some have a maximum three-night stay. Places that have upper age limits tend not to enforce them, except at the busiest of times. Only the official *auberges de jeunesse* (youth hostels) require guests to present Hostelling International (HI) cards or their equivalent.

Not all hostels have self-catering kitchens, but rates generally include a basic breakfast.

Room with a view – a hotel overlooking Palais Garnier

MAISANT LUDOVIC/GETTY IMAGES ©

B&Bs & Homestays

Bed-and-breakfast (B&B) accommodation (*chambres d'hôte* in French) is increasingly popular.

Paris Quality Hosts (Hôtes Qualité Paris; www.hotesqualiteparis.fr), a scheme run by the city of Paris, fosters B&Bs, in part to ease the isolation of Parisians, some half of whom live alone. There's often a minimum stay of three or four nights.

Need to Know

Taxe de Séjour

The city of Paris levies a *taxe de séjour* (tourist tax) per person per night on all accommodation, running from €0.22 in budget camping grounds to €1.65 in three-star hotels to €3.30 in five-star properties. If you happen to be staying in a palace or something similarly grand, the tax is €4.40 per night.

Internet Access

Wi-fi (*wee*-fee) is virtually always free of charge at hotels and hostels. You may find that in some hotels, especially older ones, the higher the floor, the less reliable the wi-fi connection.

Smoking

Smoking is officially banned in all Paris hotels.

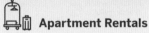 **Apartment Rentals**

Families – and anyone wanting to self-cater – should consider renting a short-stay apartment. Paris has a number of excellent apartment hotels, including the international chain Apart'hotels Citadines (www.citadines.com).

For an even more authentic Parisian experience, websites such as Airbnb (www.airbnb.com) offer private rooms or entire private apartments. Rental agencies (eg Room Sélection, Paris Attitude) also list furnished residential apartments for short stays. Apartments often include facilities such as washing machines, and can be good value. The cheapest rates are usually in local neighbourhoods in outer (higher-numbered) *arrondissements* (city districts). Many older Parisian buildings don't have lifts/elevators; check the *étage* (floor). Parisian apartments are often tiny; confirm the size beforehand. Also establish whether prices include electricity.

Beware of direct-rental scams whereby scammers compile fake apartment advertisements at too-good-to-be-true prices from photos and descriptions on legitimate sites. Whatever you do, never send money via an untraceable money transfer.

Live like a local in a self-catering apartment
BRUNO DE HOGUES/GETTY IMAGES ©

Where to Stay

Neighbourhood	Atmosphere
Eiffel Tower & Western Paris	Close to Paris' iconic tower and museums. Upmarket area with quiet residential streets. Short on budget and midrange options. Limited nightlife.
Champs-Élysées & Grands Boulevards	Luxury hotels, famous boutiques and department stores, gastronomic restaurants, great nightlife. Some areas extremely pricey. Nightlife hot spots can be noisy.
Louvre & Les Halles	Epicentral location, excellent transport links, major museums, shopping galore. Not many bargains. Noise can be an issue.
Montmartre & Northern Paris	Village atmosphere; often views across Paris. Hilly streets, some parts very touristy. Pigalle's red-light district, although well lit and safe, won't appeal to all travellers.
Le Marais, Ménilmontant & Belleville	Buzzing nightlife, hip shopping, fantastic eating options. Lively gay and lesbian scene. Very central. Can be noisy in areas where bars and clubs are concentrated.
Bastille & Eastern Paris	Few tourists, allowing you to see the 'real' Paris up close. Markets, loads of nightlife options. Some areas slightly out of the way.
The Islands	As geographically central as it gets. Accommodation centred on the peaceful Île St-Louis. No metro station on the Île St-Louis. Limited self-catering shops, minimal nightlife.
Latin Quarter	Energetic student area, stacks of eating and drinking options, late-opening bookshops. Rooms hardest to find during conferences and seminars (March to June and October).
St-Germain & Les Invalides	Stylish, central location, superb shopping, sophisticated dining, close to the Jardin du Luxembourg. Limited budget accommodation.
Montparnasse & Southern Paris	Good value, few tourists, excellent links to both major airports. Some areas out of the way and/or not well served by metro.

Paris' skyscraper district, La Défense

In Focus

Paris Today

The Latin motto fluctuat nec mergitur *('tossed but not sunk') was adopted by Paris around 1358. It became emblematic of the city's spirit, however, following the terrorist attacks of 2015. Paris' resilience came to the fore as defiant Parisians, determined to uphold their cherished quality of life, reclaimed cafe terraces and public spaces, and grand-scale plans for the city's infrastructure and greener living surged ahead.*

Greater Paris

The Grand Paris (Greater Paris) redevelopment project got the green light in 2016. The scheme will eventually connect the outer suburbs beyond the traffic-snarled bd Périphérique ring road with the city proper. This is a significant break in the physical and conceptual barrier that the *périphérique* has imposed until now, but, due to the real-estate boom that pushed many middle-class residents and large companies outside the ring road, and the steadily growing suburban population (10.5 million, compared to 2.2 million inside the *périphérique*), a real need to redefine Paris, on both an administrative and infrastructural scale, has arisen.

The crux of Grand Paris is a massive decentralised metro expansion, with 68 new stations and six suburban lines, with a target completion date of 2030. The principal goal is to connect the suburbs with one another, instead of relying on a central inner-city hub from

Aerial view of Paris MATTEO COLOMBO/GETTY IMAGES ©

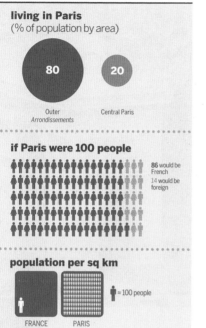

living in Paris
(% of population by area)

80 — Outer Arrondissements
20 — Central Paris

if Paris were 100 people

86 would be French
14 would be foreign

population per sq km

FRANCE   PARIS

≈ 100 people

which all lines radiate outwards. Ultimately, the surrounding suburbs – Vincennes, Neuilly, Issy, St-Denis etc – will lose their autonomy and become part of a much larger Grand Paris governed by the Hôtel de Ville.

Smaller Paris

While Paris is spreading outwards, the city centre itself is – if voted in by parliament – shrinking, administratively at least. One of Mayor Anne Hidalgo's key reforms is to combine the 1er, 2e, 3e and 4e into one *arrondissement* (city district). The move, which would come into operation in 2020, is intended to more evenly distribute services (such as childcare facilities) across the *arrondissements*. While the plan would not do away with the *arrondissements* themselves (the postcodes and identities will stay the same), the four combined epicentral *arrondissements* would have a single mayor.

Greener Paris

Mayor Hidalgo's plans are inextricably tied to greening the city and reducing car traffic and pollution. Her predecessor, Bertrand Delanoë, introduced ground-breaking green transport initiatives during his tenure. These included the Vélib' bike share program, the Autolib' electric-car share program, and the creation of hundreds of kilometres of new bus and bike lanes. Delanoë's outgoing project was to close the riverside roads along the Left Bank and reinvent a new pedestrian-friendly public area, known as Les Berges de Seine. Hidalgo's agenda includes permanently pedestrianising 3.3km of Right Bank expressway between the Tuileries and Bastille, pedestrianising the Champs-Élysées on the first Sunday of each month, and an annual car-free day – along with reducing parking spaces by 55,000 per year, instigating a maximum speed limit of 30km/h on the entire city, investing €150 million in cycling infrastructure and banning diesel cars by 2020.

Transport aside, other green initiatives include a goal of 100 hectares of green roofs, façades and vertical walls, a third of which will be devoted to urban agriculture.

Taller Paris

Architectural change doesn't come easy in Paris, given the need to balance the city's heritage with demands on space. But new projects continue to gather steam. The controversial Tour Triangle, a glittering glass triangular tower designed by Jacques Herzog and Pierre de Meuron, will be the first skyscraper in Paris since Tour Montparnasse in 1973 when it is completed at Porte de Versailles in 2018. Other high-rise projects include Duo, two Jean Nouvel–designed towers (180m and 122m) in the 13e, slated for completion in 2020.

History

With its cobbled streets, terraced cafes and iconic landmarks, Paris evokes a sense of timelessness, yet the city has changed and evolved dramatically over the centuries. And Paris' epic history – from Roman battles to revolution and beyond – is not just consigned to museums and archives: reminders of the city's past can be glimpsed around every corner.

Arc de Triomphe (p42) SACHIN GUPTA/EYEEM/GETTY IMAGES ©

3rd century BC
Celtic Gauls called Parisii arrive in the Paris area and set up wattle-and-daub huts on the Seine.

52 BC
Roman legions under Titus Labienus crush a Celtic revolt on Mons Lutetius and establish the town of Lutetia.

AD 509
Clovis I becomes the first king of the Franks and declares Paris the seat of his new kingdom.

The Beginnings to the Renaissance

Paris was born in the 3rd century BC, when a tribe of Celtic Gauls known as the Parisii settled on what is now the Île de la Cité. Centuries of conflict between the Gauls and Romans ended in 52 BC, when Julius Caesar's legions crushed a Celtic revolt. Christianity was introduced in the 2nd century AD, and Roman rule ended in the 5th century with the arrival of the Germanic Franks. In 508 Frankish king Clovis I united Gaul and made Paris his seat.

France's west coast was beset in the 9th century by Scandinavian Vikings (also known as Norsemen and, later, as Normans). Three centuries later, the Normans started pushing towards Paris, which had risen rapidly in importance: construction had begun on the cathedral of Notre Dame in the 12th century, the Louvre began life as a riverside fortress around 1200, the beautiful Sainte-Chapelle was consecrated in 1248 and the Sorbonne opened in 1253.

The Vikings' incursions heralded the Hundred Years' War between Norman England and Paris' Capetian dynasty, bringing French defeat in 1415 and English control of the capital in 1420. In 1429 the 17-year-old Jeanne d'Arc (Joan of Arc) rallied the French

1163	14 July 1789	1793
Two centuries of nonstop building reaches its zenith with the start of Notre Dame cathedral.	The French Revolution begins when a mob arms itself with stolen weapons and storms the prison at Bastille.	Louis XVI is tried, convicted and executed; Marie Antoinette's turn comes nine months later.

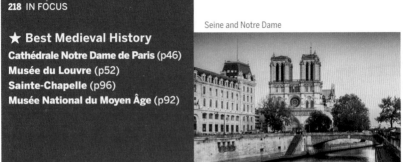

Seine and Notre Dame

troops to defeat the English at Orléans. With the exception of Calais, the English were eventually expelled from France in 1453.

The Renaissance helped Paris get back on its feet in the late 15th century. Less than a century later, however, turmoil ensued as clashes between Huguenot (Protestant) and Catholic groups culminated in the St Bartholomew's Day massacre in 1572.

The Revolution to a New Republic

A five-year-old Louis XIV (later known as the Sun King) ascended the throne in 1643 and ruled until 1715, virtually emptying the national coffers with his ambitious battling and building, including the construction of his extravagant palace at Versailles. The excesses of this grandiose king and his heirs, including Louis XVI and his Vienna-born queen Marie Antoinette, eventually led to an uprising of Parisians on 14 July 1789, kick-starting the French Revolution. Within four years, the Reign of Terror was in full swing.

The unstable post-revolutionary government was consolidated in 1799 under Napoléon Bonaparte, who declared himself First Consul. In 1804 he had the Pope crown him emperor of the French, and went on to conquer most of Europe before his eventual defeat at Waterloo in present-day Belgium in 1815. He was exiled to St Helena, and died in 1821.

France struggled under a string of mostly inept rulers until a coup d'état in 1851 brought Emperor Napoléon III to power. At his behest, Baron Haussmann razed whole tracts of the city, replacing them with sculptured parks, a hygienic sewer system and – strategically – boulevards too broad for rebels to barricade. Napoléon III embroiled France in a costly war with Prussia in 1870, which ended within months with the French army's defeat and the capture of the emperor. When the masses in Paris heard the news, they took to the streets, demanding a republic.

1799	1852–70	1880s
Napoléon Bonaparte overthrows the Directory and seizes control of the government in a coup d'état.	During the Second Empire of Napoléon III much of the city is redesigned or rebuilt by Baron Haussmann as the Paris we know today.	The Third Republic ushers in the belle époque, a creative era that conceives bohemian Paris, with its nightclubs and artistic cafes.

Twentieth-Century History

Out of WWI's conflict came increased industrialisation, confirming Paris' place as a major commercial, as well as artistic, centre and establishing its reputation among freethinking intellectuals.

This was halted by WWII and the Nazi occupation of 1940. During Paris' occupation, almost half the population evacuated, including General Charles de Gaulle, France's undersecretary of war, who fled to London and set up a government-in-exile. In a radio broadcast he appealed to French patriots to continue resisting the Germans, and established the Forces Françaises Libres (Free French Forces) to fight the Germans alongside the Allies. Following Paris' liberation, de Gaulle set up a provisional government, but resigned in 1946; he formed his own party (Rassemblement du Peuple Français) and remained in opposition until 1958, when he was brought back to power. He was succeeded as president in 1969 by Gaullist leader Georges Pompidou.

After the war, Paris regained its position as a creative nucleus and nurtured a revitalised liberalism that peaked with the student-led uprisings of May 1968 – the Sorbonne was occupied, the Latin Quarter blockaded and a general strike paralysed the country.

Under centre-right President Jacques Chirac's watch, the late 1990s saw Paris seize the international spotlight with the rumour-plagued death of Princess Diana in 1997, and France's first-ever World Cup victory in July 1998.

The New Millennium

In May 2001 Socialist Bertrand Delanoë was elected mayor, becoming widely popular for making Paris more liveable through improved infrastructure and green spaces. Chirac's second term in office, starting in 2002, was marred in 2005 by the deaths of two teenagers who were electrocuted while allegedly hiding from police in an electricity substation, which sparked riots that quickly spread across Paris, and then across France.

Contrary to the rigorous economic reform platform on which he'd been elected and against the backdrop of the global recession, Nicolas Sarkozy struggled to keep the French economy buoyant. Attempts to introduce reforms provoked widespread horror and a series of national strikes and protests. Sarkozy's popularity plummeted, paving the way for Socialist Francois Hollande's victory in the 2012 presidential elections.

With France still struggling to restart the economy, Hollande pledged to end austerity measures and reduce unemployment. Many economic policies have thus far proved ineffectual though, and rising anger at Hollande's failure to deliver on campaign promises saw his popularity plunge even faster and further than Sarkozy's and resulted in a near total wipeout for French Socialists in the 2014 municipal elections. The 2014 election of Socialist Anne Hidalgo, Paris' first female mayor, meant the capital was one of the few cities to remain on the political left.

France's next presidential elections are due to take place in May 2017.

1940	**25 August 1944**	**1968**
Germany launches the battle for France, and the four-year occupation of Paris under direct German rule begins.	Spearheaded by Free French units, Allied forces liberate Paris and the city escapes destruction.	Paris is rocked by student-led riots; de Gaulle is forced to resign the following year.

Hôtel des Invalides

Turbulent Times

The year 2015 was a harrowing one for the French capital. On 7 January the offices of magazine *Charlie Hebdo* were attacked in response to satirical images it published of the prophet Muhammad. Eleven staff and one police officer were killed and a further 22 people injured. The attacks shocked the world and on 11 January over two million people, including 40 world leaders, held a rally of national unity in the streets of Paris. Millions more joined demonstrations across France. The hashtag #jesuischarlie ('I am Charlie') became a slogan of support around the globe. The magazine printed 7.95 million copies of its following issue in six languages (compared with its usual 60,000 copies in French only).

But worse was to come. On the night of 13 November 2015 a series of coordinated terrorist attacks occurred in Paris and St-Denis – the deadliest on French soil since WWII. The attacks started at 9.20pm. Three explosions shook the Stade de France stadium during a football friendly match between Germany and France; a series of neighbourhood restaurants and their outdoor terraces in the 10e and 11e *arrondissements* (city districts) were attacked by suicide bombers and gunmen; and, at 9.40pm, three gunmen fired into the audience of Le Bataclan, where American band Eagles of Death Metal were performing. Over the course of the evening's terror 130 people lost their lives (89 in Le Bataclan alone) and 368 were injured. Paris was in lockdown, the army was mobilised and a state of emergency declared. Several of the attackers were linked to atrocities that later took place in Brussels on 22 March 2016.

Parisians responded to the trauma by establishing memorials at the fatality sites and place de la République, which became the focal point for the city's outpouring of grief, and by taking to cafe terraces and other public spaces. The hashtag #jesuisenterrasse ('I am on the terrace') represented Parisians' refusal to live in fear.

The city of Paris also refused to allow daily life to be disrupted. The long-planned United Nations Climate Change Conference (COP21) went ahead from 30 November to 12 December 2015. During the conference leaders from around the world reached an agreement to limit global warming to less than 2°C by the end of the century.

2014	**2015**	**2015**
Spanish-born Anne Hidalgo becomes the first female mayor of Paris.	The year is book-ended by deadly terrorist attacks: at the offices of *Charlie Hebdo* on 7 January, and in multiple locations on 13 November.	Paris successfully hosts the United Nations Climate Change Conference (COP21).

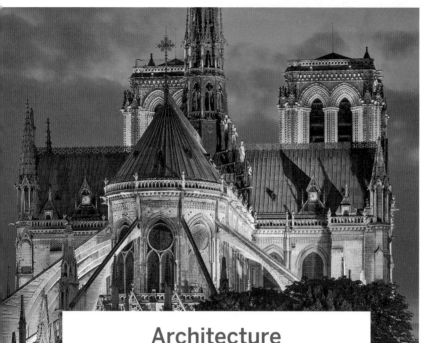

Architecture

It took disease, clogged streets and Baron Georges-Eugène Haussmann to drag architectural Paris out of the Middle Ages and into the modern world – yet ever since Haussmann's radical transformation of the city in the 19th century, Paris has never looked back. Its contemporary skyline shimmers with the whole gamut of architectural styles, from Roman arenas to futuristic skyscrapers.

Gallo-Roman

Traces of Roman Paris can be seen in the residential foundations in the Crypte Archéologique in front of Notre Dame; in the Arènes de Lutèce; and in the *frigidarium* (cooling room) and other remains of Roman baths dating from around AD 200 at the Musée National du Moyen Âge.

The latter museum also contains the *Pillier des Nautes* (Boatsmen's Pillar), one of the most valuable legacies of the Gallo-Roman period. It is a 2.5m-high monument dedicated to Jupiter and was erected by the boatmen's guild during the reign of Tiberius (AD 14–37) on the Île de la Cité. The boat has become the symbol of Paris, and the city's Latin motto is '*Fluctuat Nec Mergitur*' (Tossed by Waves but Does Not Sink).

Cathédrale de Notre Dame (p46) DANITA DELIMONT/GETTY IMAGES ©

Centre Pompidou

Romanesque

A religious revival in the 11th century led to the construction of many *roman* (Romanesque) churches, typically with round arches, heavy walls, few (and small) windows, and a lack of ornamentation that bordered on the austere.

No remaining building in Paris is entirely Romanesque, but several have important representative elements, including Église St-Germain des Prés, the Romanesque bell tower of which, above the west entrance, has changed little since AD 1000.

Gothic

In the 14th century, the Rayonnant – or Radiant – Gothic style, named after the radiating tracery of the rose windows, developed. Interiors became even lighter thanks to broader windows and more translucent stained glass. One of the most influential Rayonnant buildings was Ste-Chapelle, the stained glass of which forms a curtain of glazing on the 1st floor. The two transept façades of Cathédrale de Notre Dame de Paris and the vaulted Salle des Gens d'Armes (Cavalrymen's Hall) in the Conciergerie, the largest surviving medieval hall in Europe, are other fine examples of Rayonnant Gothic style.

By the 15th century, decorative extravagance led to Flamboyant Gothic, so named because the wavy stone carving made the towers appear to be blazing or flaming (*flamboyant*). Several *hôtels particuliers* (private mansions) were built in this style, including Hôtel de Cluny, now the Musée National du Moyen Âge.

Renaissance

The Renaissance set out to realise a 'rebirth' of classical Greek and Roman culture and first affected France at the end of the 15th century, when Charles VIII began a series of invasions of Italy, returning with new ideas. The Early Renaissance style blends a variety of classical components and decorative motifs (columns, tunnel vaults, round arches, domes etc) with the rich decoration of Flamboyant Gothic. Mannerism was introduced around 1530; in 1546 Pierre Lescot designed the richly decorated southwestern corner of the Cour Carrée at the Musée du Louvre.

The Right Bank district of Le Marais remains the best area for Renaissance reminders in Paris proper, with some fine *hôtels particuliers,* such as Hôtel Carnavalet, housing part of the Musée Carnavalet.

Baroque

During the baroque period (tail end of the 16th to late 18th centuries), painting, sculpture and classical architecture were integrated to create structures and interiors of great subtlety, refinement and elegance. With the advent of the baroque, architecture became more pictorial, with painted church ceilings illustrating the Passion of Christ to the faithful, and palaces invoking the power and order of the state. Salomon de Brosse designed the Palais du Luxembourg in the Jardin du Luxembourg in 1615.

Neoclassicism

Neoclassical architecture emerged about 1740 and had its roots in the renewed interest in classical forms – a search for order, reason and serenity through the adoption of forms and conventions of Graeco-Roman antiquity: columns, geometric forms and traditional ornamentation.

Baron Haussmann

The iconic apartment buildings that line the boulevards of central Paris, with their cream-coloured stone and curvy wrought-iron balconies, are the work of Baron Georges-Eugène Haussmann (1809–91), prefect of the Seine *département* between 1853 and 1870.

Among the earliest examples of this style are the Petit Trianon at Versailles, designed by Jacques-Ange Gabriel for Louis XV in 1761. France's greatest neoclassical architect of the 18th century was Jacques-Germain Soufflot, creator of the Panthéon in the Latin Quarter.

Neoclassicism came into its own under Napoléon, who used it to embody the grandeur of imperial France and its capital: the Arc de Triomphe, the Arc de Triomphe du Carrousel and more. The climax to this great 19th-century movement was Palais Garnier, the city's opera house designed by Charles Garnier.

Art Nouveau

Art nouveau, which emerged in Europe and the USA in the second half of the 19th century under various names (Jugendstil, Sezessionstil, Stile Liberty), caught on quickly in Paris, and its influence lasted until about 1910. It was characterised by sinuous curves and flowing, asymmetrical forms reminiscent of creeping vines, water lilies, the patterns on insect wings and the flowering boughs of trees. Influenced by the arrival of exotic objets d'art from Japan, art nouveau's French name came from a Paris gallery that featured works in the 'new art' style. It's expressed to perfection in Paris by Hector Guimard's graceful metro entrances, the Musée d'Orsay and the city's main department stores, Le Bon Marché and Galeries Lafayette.

Modern

Until 1968, French architects were still being trained almost exclusively at the conformist École de Beaux-Arts, reflected in most of the early impersonal and forgettable 'lipstick tubes' and 'upended shoebox' structures erected in the skyscraper district of La Défense and the 210m-tall Tour Montparnasse (1973).

Contemporary

France's leaders sought to immortalise themselves by erecting huge public edifices *('grands projets')* in Paris. Georges Pompidou commissioned the once reviled, now much-loved Centre Pompidou. His successor, Valéry Giscard d'Estaing, was instrumental in transforming the derelict Gare d'Orsay train station into the glorious Musée d'Orsay (1986). François Mitterrand surpassed all of the postwar presidents with monumental projects costing taxpayers €4.6 billion: Jean Nouvel's Institut du Monde Arabe (1987), built during this time, mixes modern Arab and Western elements and is arguably one of the city's most beautiful late 20th-century buildings. Jacques Chirac orchestrated the magnificent Musée du Quai Branly, a glass, wood and sod structure with a 3-hectare experimental garden, also by Jean Nouvel.

Ground-Breaking Designs

Recent years have seen the construction of several modern Parisian landmarks, IM Pei's glass-pyramid Musée du Louvre entrance and the tile-clad Opéra de Paris Bastille, designed by Uruguayan architect Carlos Ott in 1989 among them.

The *grand projet* of the new millennium was Jean Nouvel's long-awaited Philharmonie de Paris, a state-of-the-art creation that took three years to build and cost €381 million.

Recent Renaissance

Some of Paris' loveliest art deco buildings have recently undergone a renaissance: in 2014 a five-star hotel and spa opened in the Molitor swimming pool complex in western Paris, where the bikini made its first appearance in the 1930s. In Le Marais, thermal-baths-turned-1980s-nightclub Les Bain Douches opened as luxury hotel Les Bains after years of being abandoned. Preserving as many of the original art deco features as possible was a characteristic of both projects.

Drawing on the city's long-standing tradition of glass in its architecture, glass is a big feature of the 1970s-eyesore-turned-contemporary-stunner Forum des Halles shopping centre in the 1er – a curvaceous, curvilinear and glass-topped construction by architects Patrick Berger and Jacques Anziutti, completed in 2016.

★ **Best Rooftops**

Grand Palais (p94)

Cathédrale Notre Dame de Paris (p46)

Galeries Lafayette (p148)

Left: Roof of the Grand Palais; Below: Galeries Lafayette

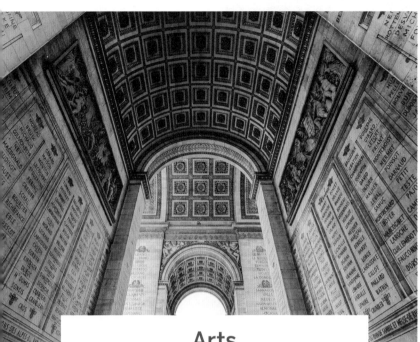

Arts

While art in Paris today means anything and everything – bold installations in the metro, monumental wall frescos, space-invader tags and other gregarious street art – the city's rich art heritage has its roots firmly embedded in the traditional genres of painting and sculpture. Then there are the literary arts, music and film in which Paris plays a starring role.

Visual Arts

Baroque to Neoclassicism

According to philosopher Voltaire, French painting proper began with baroque painter Nicolas Poussin (1594–1665), the greatest representative of 17th-century classicism, who frequently set scenes from ancient Rome, classical mythology and the Bible in ordered landscapes bathed in golden light.

Jean-Baptiste Chardin (1699–1779) brought the humbler domesticity of the Dutch masters to French art, while in 1785, neoclassical artist Jacques Louis David (1748–1825) wooed the public with his vast portraits with clear republican messages. A virtual dictator in matters of art, he advocated a precise, severe classicism.

Detail of the Arc de Triomphe (p42) / GETTY IMAGES ©

Jean-Auguste-Dominique Ingres (1780–1867), David's most gifted pupil in Paris, continued the neoclassical tradition. His historical pictures, such as *Oedipus and the Sphinx,* the 1808 version of which is in the Louvre, are now regarded as inferior to his portraits.

Romanticism

The Raft of the Medusa by Théodore Géricault (1791–1824), one of the Louvre's most gripping paintings, hovers on the threshold of romanticism; if Géricault had not died early (aged 33) he probably would have become a leader of the movement, along with his friend Eugène Delacroix (1798–1863; find him in the Cimetière du Père Lachaise, p80), best known for *Liberty Leading the People,* his masterpiece commemorating the July Revolution of 1830.

In sculpture, the work of Paris-born Auguste Rodin (1840–1917) overcame the conflict between neoclassicism and romanticism. One of Rodin's most gifted pupils was his lover Camille Claudel (1864–1943), whose work can be seen with Rodin's in the Musée Rodin (p66).

Realism

The realists were all about social comment: the paintings of Gustave Courbet (1819–77), a prominent member of the Paris Commune (a group that seized the municipal government of Paris in the French Revolution) whose paintings depicted the drudgery and dignity of working-class lives. In 1850 he broke new ground with *A Burial at Ornans* (in the Musée d'Orsay; p62), painted on a canvas of monumental size reserved until then exclusively for historical paintings.

Édouard Manet (1832–83) used realism to depict Parisian middle classes, yet he included in his pictures numerous references to the old masters. His *Déjeuner sur l'Herbe* and *Olympia* were both scandalous, largely because they broke with the traditional treatment of their subject matter. He was a pivotal figure in the transition from realism to impressionism.

One of the best sculptors of this period was François Rude (1784–1855), creator of the relief on the Arc de Triomphe and several pieces in the Musée d'Orsay. By the mid-19th century, memorial statues in public places had replaced sculpted tombs, making such statues all the rage.

Sculptor Jean-Baptiste Carpeaux (1827–75) began as a romantic, but his work in Paris – such as *The Dance* on the Palais Garnier (p102) and his fountain in the Jardin du Luxembourg (p68) – recalls the gaiety and flamboyance of the baroque era.

Impressionism

Paris' Musée d'Orsay is the crown jewel of impressionism. Initially a term of derision, 'impressionism' was taken from the title of an 1874 experimental painting, *Impression: Soleil Levant* (Impression: Sunrise) by Claude Monet (1840–1926). Monet was the leading figure of the school, and a visit to the Musée d'Orsay unveils a host of other members, among them Alfred Sisley (1839–99), Camille Pissarro (1830–1903), Pierre-Auguste Renoir (1841–1919) and Berthe Morisot (1841–95). The impressionists' main aim was to capture the effects of fleeting light, painting almost universally in the open air – and light came to dominate the content of their painting.

Edgar Degas (1834–1917) was a fellow traveller of the impressionists, but he preferred painting cafe life *(Absinthe)* and in ballet studios *(The Dance Class)* – several beautiful examples hang in the Musée d'Orsay.

Henri de Toulouse-Lautrec (1864–1901) was a great admirer of Degas, but chose subjects one or two notches below: people in the bistros, brothels and music halls of Montmartre (eg *Au Moulin Rouge*). He is best known for his posters and lithographs, in which the distortion of the figures is both satirical and decorative.

Paul Cézanne (1839–1906) is celebrated for his still lifes and landscapes depicting southern France, though he spent many years in Paris after breaking with the impressionists. The name of Paul Gauguin (1848–1903) immediately conjures up studies of Tahitian and Breton women. Both Cézanne and Gauguin were post-impressionists, a catch-all term for the diverse styles that flowed from impressionism.

Pointillism & Symbolism

Pointillism was a technique developed by Georges Seurat (1859–91), who applied paint in small dots or uniform brush strokes of unmixed colour to produce fine 'mosaics' of warm and cool tones. His tableaux *Une Baignade, Asnières* (Bathers at Asnières) is a perfect example.

Metro Art

Art adorns many of the 300-plus stations of the city's world-famous Métropolitain. Themes often relate to the *quartier* (neighbourhood) or name of the station. The following is just a sample of the most interesting stations from an artistic perspective.

Abbesses (line 12 metro entrance) The noodle-like pale-green metalwork and glass canopy of the station entrance is one of the finest examples of the work of Hector Guimard (1867–1942), the celebrated French art nouveau architect whose signature style once graced most metro stations.

Assemblée Nationale (line 12 platform) Gigantic posters of silhouettes in red, white and blue by artist Jean-Charles Blais (b 1956) represent the MPs currently sitting in parliament.

Bastille (line 5 platform) A 180-sq-metre ceramic fresco features scenes taken from newspaper engravings published during the Revolution, with illustrations of the destruction of the infamous prison.

Cluny–La Sorbonne (line 10 platform) A large ceramic mosaic replicates the signatures of intellectuals, artists and scientists from the Latin Quarter through history, including Molière (1622–73), Rabelais (c 1483–1553) and Robespierre (1758–96).

Concorde (line 12 platform) What look like children's building blocks in white-and-blue ceramic on the walls of the station are 45,000 tiles that spell out the text of the *Déclaration des Droits de l'Homme et du Citoyen* (Declaration of the Rights of Man and of the Citizen), the document setting forth the principles of the French Revolution.

Palais Royal–Musée du Louvre (line 1 metro entrance) The zany entrance on place du Palais by Jean-Michel Othoniel (b 1964) is composed of two crown-shaped cupolas (one representing the day, the other night) consisting of 800 red, blue, amber and violet glass balls threaded on an aluminium structure. Sublime.

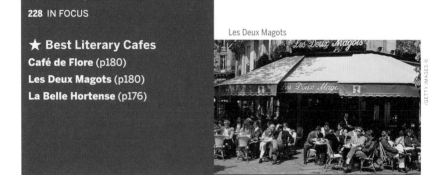

Les Deux Magots

Henri Rousseau (1844–1910) was a contemporary of the post-impressionists, but his 'naive' art was unaffected by them. His dreamlike pictures of the Paris suburbs and of jungle and desert scenes (eg *The Snake Charmer*) – again in Musée d'Orsay – have influenced art right up to this century. The eerie treatment of mythological subjects by Gustave Moreau (1826–98) can be seen in the artist's studio, now within the Musée Gustave-Moreau in the 9e.

Twentieth-Century Art

Twentieth-century French painting is characterised by a bewildering diversity of styles, including Fauvism, named after the slur of a critic who compared the exhibitors at the 1905 Salon d'Automne (Autumn Salon) in Paris with *fauves* (wild animals) because of their wild brush strokes and radical use of intensely bright colours. Among these 'beastly' painters was Henri Matisse (1869–1954).

Cubism was launched in 1907 with *Les Demoiselles d'Avignon* by Spanish prodigy Pablo Picasso (1881–1973). Cubism, as developed by Picasso, Georges Braque (1882–1963) and Juan Gris (1887–1927), deconstructed the subject into a system of intersecting planes and presented various aspects simultaneously.

In the 1920s and '30s the École de Paris (School of Paris) was formed by a group of expressionists, mostly foreign born.

No piece of French art better captures the rebellious, iconoclastic spirit of Dadaism – a Swiss-born literary and artistic movement of revolt – than *Mona Lisa,* by Marcel Duchamp (1887–1968), complete with moustache and goatee. In 1922 German Dadaist Max Ernst (1891–1976) moved to Paris and worked on surrealism, a Dada offshoot that flourished between the wars. Drawing on the theories of Sigmund Freud, it attempted to reunite the conscious and unconscious realms, to permeate everyday life with fantasies and dreams. The most influential of this style in Paris was Spanish-born artist Salvador Dalí (1904–89), who arrived in the French capital in 1929 and painted some of his most seminal works while residing here. To see his work, visit the Dalí Espace Montmartre (p61).

Contemporary Art

Artists in the 1990s turned to the minutiae of daily urban life to express social and political angst, using new mediums to let rip. Conceptual artist Daniel Buren (b 1938) reduced his painting to a signature series of vertical 8.7cm-wide stripes that he applies to every surface imaginable – white-marble columns in the courtyard of Paris' Palais Royal included. Partner-in-crime Michel Parmentier (1938–2000) insisted on monochrome painting – blue in 1966, grey in 1967 and red in 1968.

Street art is the current buzz word. In 2013 the world's largest collective street-art exhibition, La Tour Paris 13 (www.tourparis13.fr), opened in a derelict apartment block in

Panthéon (p93)

the 13e *arrondissement*. Its 36 apartments on 13 floors were covered from head to toe with works by 100 international artists. The blockbuster exhibition ran for just one month, after which the tower was demolished in April 2014.

Another recent high-profile installation featured over 4000 portraits by French photographer JR, which covered the floor and walls of the Panthéon while it underwent renovation. Meanwhile, the famous Pont des Arts, once covered with lovers' padlocks, incorporated temporary panels in 2015 featuring the work of four different street artists.

Literary Arts

Flicking through a street directory reveals just how much Paris honours its literary history, with listings including places Colette and Victor Hugo, avs Marcel Proust and Émile Zola, and rue Balzac. The city has nurtured countless French authors over the centuries, who, together with expat writers from Dickens onwards (including the lost generation's Hemingway, Fitzgerald and Joyce) have sealed Paris' literary reputation. You can leaf through Paris' literary heritage in atmospheric bookshops, hang out in cafes and swish literary bars, visit writers' former-homes-turned-museums, sleep in hotels where writers once holed up, and pay your respects at cemeteries.

Music

From organ recitals in Gothic architectural splendour to a legendary jazz scene, stirring *chansons*, ground-breaking electronica, award-winning world music and some of the world's best rap, music is embedded deep in the Parisian soul. To understand the capital's musical heritage is to enrich your experience of a city where talented musicians have to audition even to perform in the metro.

Film

Paris is one of the world's most cinematic cities. The world's first paying-public film screening was held in Paris' Grand Café on blvd des Capucines, 9e, in December 1895 by the Lumière brothers, inventors of 'moving pictures'. Since that time, the French capital has produced a bevy of blockbuster film-makers and stars and is the filming location of countless box-office hits by both home-grown and foreign directors. Fabulous experiences for film buffs range from exploring behind the scenes at an art deco cinema to catching a classic retrospective in one of the Latin Quarter's many cinemas, or following in the footsteps of iconic screen heroine Amélie Poulain through the streets of Montmartre.

Chansons

The *chanson française* (French song), a tradition dating from troubadours in the Middle Ages, was eclipsed by the music halls of the early 20th century, but was revived in the 1930s by Édith Piaf (1915–63) and Charles Trenet (1913–2001), followed by 'France's Frank Sinatra', Charles Aznavour (b 1924). In the 1950s Left Bank cabarets nurtured singers such as Léo Ferré (1916–63), Georges Brassens (1921–81), Claude Nougaro (1929–2004), Jacques Brel (1929–78), Barbara (1930–97) and the very sexy, very Parisian Serge Gainsbourg (1928–91).

The genre was revived once more in the new millennium as *la nouvelle chanson française* by performers such as Vincent Delerm (b 1976), Bénabar (b 1969), Jeanne Cherhal (b 1978), Camille (b 1978), and Zaz (Isabelle Geffroy; b 1980), who mixes jazz, soul, acoustic and traditional *chansons*.

Survival Guide

Directory A–Z

Discount Cards

Almost all museums and monuments in Paris have discounted tickets (tarif réduit) for students and seniors (generally over 60 years), provided they have valid ID. Children often get in for free; the cut-off age for a child is anywhere between six and 18 years.

EU citizens under 26 years get in for free at national monuments and museums.

○ Paris Museum Pass (www.parismuseumpass.com; 2/4/6 days €48/62/74) Gets you into 50-odd venues in and around Paris; a huge advantage is that pass holders usually enter larger sights at a different entrance meaning you bypass (or substantially reduce) ridiculously long ticket queues.

○ Paris Passlib' (www.parisinfo.com; 2/3/5 days €109/129/155) Sold at the **Paris Convention & Visitors Bureau** (p235) and on its website, this handy city pass covers unlimited public transport in zones 1 to 3, admission to some 50 museums in the Paris region (aka a Paris Museum Pass), a one-hour boat cruise along the Seine,

and a one-day hop-on hop-off open-top bus sightseeing service around central Paris' key sights with **L'Open Tour** (☎01 42 66 56 56; www.paris.opentour.com; 1-day pass adult/child €32/16). There's an optional €15 supplement for a skip-the-line ticket to levels one and two of the Eiffel Tower, or €21.50 for all three Eiffel Tower platforms.

Electricity

230V/50Hz

Emergency

Ambulance (SAMU)	☎15
Fire	☎18
Police	☎17
EU-wide emergency	☎112

Gay & Lesbian Travellers

The city known as 'gay Paree' lives up to its name. Paris is so open that there's less of a defined 'scene' here than in other cities where it's more underground. While Le Marais is the mainstay of gay and lesbian nightlife, you'll find venues right throughout the city attracting a mixed crowd.

The single best source of information for gay and lesbian travellers in Paris is the **Centre Gai et Lesbien de Paris Île de France** (CGL; ☎01 43 57 21 47; www.centrelgbtparis.org; 63 rue Beaubourg, 3e; ⊙centre & bar 3.30-8pm Mon-Fri, 1-7pm Sat, library 6-8pm Mon-Wed, 5-7pm Fri & Sat; Ⓜ Rambuteau, Arts et Métiers), which has a large library of books and periodicals and a sociable bar. Also has details of hotlines, helplines, gay and gay-friendly medical services and politically oriented activist associations.

Health

Hospitals

Paris has some 50 hospitals including the following:
American Hospital of Paris (☎01 46 41 25 25; www.american-hospital.org; 63 bd Victor Hugo, Neuilly-sur-Seine; Ⓜ Pont

de Levallois) Private hospital; emergency 24-hour medical and dental care.

Hertford British Hospital
(📞01 46 39 22 00; www.
british-hospital.org; 3 rue
Barbès, Levallois; Ⓜ Anatole
France) Less expensive, private,
English-speaking option.

Hôpital Hôtel Dieu (📞01 42 34
82 34; www.aphp.fr; 1 place du
Parvis Notre Dame, 4e; Ⓜ Cité)
One of the city's main gov-
ernment-run public hospitals;
after 8pm use the emergency
entrance on rue de la Cité.

Pharmacies

Pharmacies (chemists) are
marked by a large illuminat-
ed green cross outside. At
least one in each neighbourhood is open for extended
hours; find a complete
night-owl listing on the
Paris Convention & Visitors
Bureau website (www.
parisinfo.com).

Insurance

Comprehensive travel insurance to cover theft, loss and
medical problems is highly
recommended.

Worldwide travel
insurance is available at
www.lonelyplanet.com/
travel-insurance. You can
buy, extend and claim online
anytime – even if you're
already on the road.

Internet Access

o Wi-fi (pronounced 'wee-
fee' in France) is available in
most Paris hotels, usually at
no extra cost, and in some
museums.

o Free wi-fi is available in
some 300 public places,
including parks, libraries
and municipal buildings, between 7am and 11pm daily.
For complete details and a
map of hot spots, see www.
paris.fr/wifi.

o Expect to pay around €4
or €5 per hour for online
access in internet cafes;
Milk (www.milklub.com) has
several branches in central
Paris.

Money

o ATMs (*distributeur
automatique de billets* in
French) are widespread.
Unless you have particu-
larly high transaction fees,
ATMs are usually the best
and easiest way to deal
with currency exchange;
French banks don't gener-
ally charge fees to use their
ATMs but check with your
own bank before you travel
to know if/how much they
charge for international
cash withdrawals.

o Visa and MasterCard are
accepted in most hotels,
shops and restaurants;
fewer accept American
Express. Note that France
uses a smartcard with an
embedded microchip and
PIN – few places accept
swipe-and-signature. Some
foreign chip-and-PIN-
enabled cards require a
signature – ask your bank
before you leave.

Opening Hours

The following list shows *ap-
proximate* standard opening
hours for businesses. Hours
can vary by season. Many
businesses close for the
entire month of August for
summer holidays.

Banks 9am to 1pm and 2pm to
5pm Monday to Friday, some
Saturday morning

Bars & Cafes 7am to 2am

Museums 10am to 6pm, closed
Monday or Tuesday

Post Offices 8am to 7pm
Monday to Friday, and until noon
Saturday

Restaurants noon to 2pm and
7.30pm to 10.30pm

Shops (clothing) 10am to 7pm
Monday to Saturday, occasionally close in the early afternoon
for lunch and sometimes all day
Monday

Shops (food) 8am to 1pm and
4pm to 7.30pm, closed Sunday
afternoon and sometimes Monday

Public Holidays

There is close to one public holiday a month in France and, in some years, up to four in May alone. Be aware, though, that unlike in the USA or UK, where public holidays usually fall on (or are shifted to) a Monday, in France a *jour férié* (public holiday) is celebrated strictly on the day on which it falls. Thus if May Day falls on a Saturday or Sunday, no provision is made for an extra day off.

The following holidays are observed in Paris:

New Year's Day (Jour de l'An) 1 January

Easter Sunday & Monday (Pâques & Lundi de Pâques) Late March/April

May Day (Fête du Travail) 1 May

Victory in Europe Day (Victoire 1945) 8 May

Ascension Thursday (L'Ascension) May (celebrated on the 40th day after Easter)

Whit Monday (Lundi de Pentecôte) Mid-May to mid-June (seventh Monday after Easter)

Bastille Day/National Day (Fête Nationale) 14 July

Assumption Day (L'Assomption) 15 August

All Saints' Day (La Toussaint) 1 November

Armistice Day/Remembrance Day (Le Onze Novembre) 11 November

Christmas (Noël) 25 December

Safe Travel

In general, Paris is a safe city and random street assaults are rare. The city is generally well lit and there's no reason not to use the metro until it stops running, at some time between 12.30am and just past 1am (2.15am on weekends). Many women do travel on the metro alone, late at night, in most areas.

Pickpocketing is typically the biggest concern. *Always* be alert and take precautions: don't carry more money than you need, and keep your credit cards, passport and other documents in a concealed pouch, a hotel safe or a safe-deposit box.

Telephone

○ Check with your provider about roaming costs before you leave home, or ensure your phone's unlocked to use a French SIM card (available cheaply in Paris).

○ There are no area codes in France – you always dial the 10-digit number.

○ France's country code is ☏33 and the international access code is ☏00.

Time

○ France is on Central European Time, one hour ahead of GMT.

○ Daylight-saving time (two hours ahead of GMT) runs from the last Sunday in March to the last Sunday in October.

Toilets

○ Public toilets in Paris are signposted *toilettes* or *WC*. The self-cleaning cylindrical toilets you see on Parisian pavements are open 24 hours, are reasonably clean and are free of charge. Look for the words *libre* ('available'; green-coloured) or *occupé* ('occupied'; red-coloured).

○ Cafe owners do not appreciate you using their facilities if you are not a paying customer (a coffee can be a good investment); however, if you have young children they may make an exception (ask first!). Other good bets are major department stores and big hotels.

○ There are free public toilets in front of Notre Dame cathedral, near the Arc de Triomphe, east down the steps at Sacré-Cœur and at the northwestern entrance to the Jardins des Tuileries.

Tourist Information

Paris Convention & Visitors Bureau (Office du Tourisme et des Congrès de Paris; www.parisinfo.com; 27 rue des Pyramides, 1er; ⏲7am-7pm May-Oct, 10am-7pm Nov-Apr; Ⓜ Pyramides) The main branch is 500m northwest of the Louvre. It sells tickets for tours and several attractions, plus museum and transport passes. Also books accommodation.

Travellers with Disabilities

○ For information about which cultural venues in Paris are accessible to people with disabilities, check Accès Culture (www.accesculture.org).

○ Download Lonely Planet's free *Accessible Travel* guide from http://lptravel.to/AccessibleTravel.

Visas

○ Generally no restrictions for EU citizens. Usually not required for most other nationalities for stays of up to 90 days.

Practicalities

○ **Smoking** Smoking is illegal in indoor public spaces, including restaurants and bars (hence the crowds of smokers in doorways and on pavement terraces outside).

○ **Weights and Measures** France uses the metric system.

○ Check www.france.diplomatie.fr for the latest visa regulations and the closest French embassy to your current residence.

Transport

Arriving in Paris

Few roads *don't* lead to Paris, one of the most visited destinations on earth. Practically every major airline flies though one of its three airports, and most European train and bus routes cross it.

Flights, cars and tours can be booked online at lonelyplanet.com.

Charles de Gaulle Airport

Most international airlines fly to **Aéroport de Charles de Gaulle** (CDG; ☎01 70 36 39 50; www.aeroportsdeparis.fr), 28km northeast of central Paris. In French the airport is commonly called 'Roissy' after the suburb in which it is located.

Bus

There are six main bus lines:
Le Bus Direct (line 2) Links the airport with the Arc de Triomphe and Trocadéro (one-way/return €17/30, one hour, every 30 minutes 5.45am to 11pm). Children aged four travel free.

Le Bus Direct (line 4) Links the airport with Gare Montparnasse (80 minutes) in southern Paris via Gare de Lyon (50 minutes) in eastern Paris. Both destinations one-way-return cost €17/30 (children under four travel free) Buses run every 30 minutes from the airport (6am to 10.30pm) and from Montparnasse (5.30am to 10.30pm).

Noctilien bus 140 & 143 Part of the RATP night service, Noctilien has two buses that go to the airport: bus 140 from Gare de l'Est, and 143 from Gare de l'Est and Gare du Nord. The fare is €8 (or four metro tickets) and buses run hourly from 12.30am to 5.30am.

RATP bus 350 Links the airport with Gare de l'Est in northern Paris (€6, 70 minutes, every 30 minutes 5.30am to 11pm).

RATP bus 351 Links the airport with place de la Nation in eastern Paris (€6, 70 minutes, every 30 minutes 5.30am to 11pm).

Roissybus Links the airport with the Opéra (€11, one hour, every 15 minutes 5.30am to 10pm and every 30 minutes 10pm to 11pm from the airport; every 15 minutes 5.15am to 10pm and every 30 minutes 10pm to 12.30am from Paris).

Taxi

o A taxi to the city centre takes 40 minutes. From 2016, fares have been standardised to a flat rate: €50 to the Right Bank and €55 to the Left Bank. The fare increases by 15% between 5pm and 10am and on Sundays.

o Only take taxis at a clearly marked rank. Never follow anyone who approaches you at the airport and claims to be a driver.

Train

The airport is served by the RER B line (€9.75, approximately 50 minutes, every 10 to 20 minutes), which connects with the Gare du Nord, Châtelet–Les Halles and St-Michel–Notre Dame stations in the city centre.

Trains run from 5am to 11pm; there are fewer trains on weekends.

Orly Airport

Aéroport d'Orly (ORY; ☎01 70 36 39 50; www.aeroportsdeparis.fr) is 19km south of central Paris but, despite being closer than CDG, it is not as frequently used by international airlines, and public transport options aren't quite as straightforward.

Orly's south and west terminals are currently being unified into one large terminal suitable for bigger planes such as A380s; completion is due in 2018.

Bus

Two bus lines serve Orly:
Le Bus Direct (line 1) Runs to/from the Arc de Triomphe (one hour) via Gare Montparnasse (40 minutes), La Motte-Picquet and Trocadéro every 20 minuted 5.50am to 11.30pm from Orly, 4.50am to 10.30pm from the Arc de Triomphe. One-way/return tickets to all destinations cost €12/20. Under fours travel free.

Orlybus Runs to/from the metro station Denfert Rochereau in southern Paris, making several stops en route (€7.50, 30 minutes, every 15 minutes 6am to 12.30pm from Orly, 5.35am to midnight from Paris).

Taxi

A taxi to the city centre takes roughly 30 minutes. Standardised flat-rate fares since 2016 mean a taxi costs €30 to the Left Bank and €35 to the Right Bank. The fare increases by 15% between 5pm and 10am and on Sundays.

Train

There is currently no direct train to/from Orly; you'll need to change halfway. Note that while it is possible to take a shuttle to the RER C line, this service is quite long and not recommended.
RER B (€12.05, 35 minutes, every four to 12 minutes) This line connects Orly with the St-Michel–Notre Dame, Châtelet–Les Halles and Gare du Nord stations in the city centre. In order to get from Orly to the RER station (Antony), you must first take the Orlyval automatic train. The service runs from 6am to 11pm (fewer on weekends). You only need one ticket to take the two trains.

Tram

Tramway T7 (€1.80, every six minutes, 40 minutes, 5.30am to 12.30am) This tramway links Orly with Villejuif-Louis Aragon metro station in southern Paris; buy tickets from the machine at the tram stop as no tickets are sold on board.

Climate Change & Travel

Every form of transport that relies on carbon-based fuel generates CO_2, the main cause of human-induced climate change. Modern travel is dependent on aeroplanes, which might use less fuel per kilometre per person than most cars but travel much greater distances. The altitude at which aircraft emit gases (including CO_2) and particles also contributes to their climate change impact. Many websites offer 'carbon calculators' that allow people to estimate the carbon emissions generated by their journey and, for those who wish to do so, to offset the impact of the greenhouse gases emitted with contributions to portfolios of climate-friendly initiatives throughout the world. Lonely Planet offsets the carbon footprint of all staff and author travel.

Beauvais Airport

Aéroport de Beauvais (BVA; ☎ 08 92 68 20 66; www. aeroportbeauvais.com) is 75km north of Paris and is served by a few low-cost flights. Before you snap up that bargain, consider if the post-arrival journey is worth it.

Shuttle (€17, 1¼ hours) The Beauvais shuttle bus links the airport with metro station Porte de Maillot. See the airport website for details and tickets.

Gare du Nord

Gare du Nord (rue de Dunkerque, 10e; Ⓜ Gare du Nord), located in northern Paris, is the terminus for northbound domestic trains as well as several international services.

Eurostar (www.eurostar.com) The London–Paris line runs from St-Pancras International to Gare du Nord. Voyages take 2¼ hours.

Thalys (www.thalys.com) Trains pull into Paris' Gare du Nord from Brussels, Amsterdam and Cologne.

Other Mainline Train Stations

Paris has five other stations for long-distance trains, each with its own metro station: Gare d'Austerlitz, Gare de l'Est, Gare de Lyon, Gare Montparnasse and Gare St-Lazare; the station used depends on the direction from Paris.

Contact Voyages SNCF (www.voyages-sncf.com) for connections throughout France and continental Europe.

Gare Routiére Internationale de Paris-Galliéni

Eurolines (www.eurolines. fr) connects all major European capitals to Paris' international bus terminal, **Gare Routiére Internationale de Paris-Galliéni** (☎ 08 92 89 90 91; 28 av du Général de Gaulle; Ⓜ Galliéni). The terminal is in the eastern suburb of Bagnolet; it's about a 15-minute metro ride to the more central République station.

Getting Around

Arrondissements

Paris is divided into 20 *arrondissements* (city districts), which spiral clockwise from the centre. *Arrondissement* numbers (1er, 2e

etc) form an integral part of all Parisian addresses.

Train

Paris' underground network is run by RATP and consists of two separate but linked systems: the metro and the Réseau Express Régional (RER) suburban train line. The metro has 14 numbered lines; the RER has five main lines (but you'll probably only need to use A, B and C). When buying tickets consider how many zones your journey will cover; there are five concentric transportation zones rippling out from Paris (5 being the furthest); if you travel from Charles de Gaulle airport to Paris, for instance, you will have to buy a zone 1–5 ticket.

For information on the metro, RER and bus systems, visit www.ratp.fr. Metro maps of various sizes

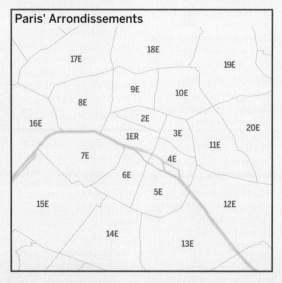

Paris' Arrondissements

and degrees of detail are available for free at metro ticket windows; several can also be downloaded for free from the RATP website.

Metro

○ Metro lines are identified by both their number (eg ligne 1; line 1) and their colour, listed on official metro signs and maps.

○ Signs in metro and RER stations indicate the way to the correct platform for your line. The *direction* signs on each platform indicate the terminus. On lines that split into several branches (such as lines 7 and 13), the terminus of each train is indicated on the cars and on signs on each platform giving the number of minutes until the next and subsequent train.

○ Signs marked *correspondance* (transfer) show how to reach connecting trains. At stations with many intersecting lines, like Châtelet and Montparnasse Bienvenüe, walking from one platform to the next can take a very long time.

○ Different station exits are indicated by white-on-blue *sortie* (exit) signs. You can get your bearings by checking the *plan du quartier* (neighbourhood maps) posted at exits.

○ Each line has its own schedule, but trains usually start at around 5.30am, with the last train beginning its run between 12.35am and

1.15am (2.15am on Friday and Saturday).

RER

○ The RER is faster than the metro, but the stops are much further apart. Some attractions, particularly those on the Left Bank (eg the Musée d'Orsay, Eiffel Tower and Panthéon), can be reached far more conveniently by the RER than by the metro.

○ If you're going out to the suburbs (eg Versailles, Disneyland), ask for help on the platform – finding the right train can be confusing. Also make sure your ticket is for the correct zone.

Tickets & Fares

○ The same RATP tickets are valid on the metro, the RER (for travel within the city limits), buses, trams and the Montmartre funicular.

○ A ticket – white in colour and called *Le Ticket t+* – costs €1.80 (half price for children aged four to nine years) if bought individually and €14.10 for adults for a *carnet* (book) of 10.

○ Tickets are sold at all metro stations. Ticket windows accept most credit cards; however, automated machines do not accept credit cards without embedded chips (and even then, not all foreign chip-embedded cards).

○ One ticket lets you travel between any two metro stations (no return journeys)

for a period of 1½ hours, no matter how many transfers are required. You can also use it on the RER for travel within zone 1, which encompasses all of central Paris.

○ Transfers from the metro to bus or vice-versa are not possible.

○ Always keep your ticket until you exit from your station; if you are stopped by a ticket inspector, you will have to pay a fine if you don't have a valid ticket.

Bicycle

Vélib'

The **Vélib'** (01 30 79 79 30; www.velib.paris.fr; day/week subscription €1.70/8, bike hire up to 30min/60min/90min/2hr free/€1/2/4) bike share scheme puts 23,600 bikes at the disposal of Parisians and visitors to get around the city. There are some 1800 stations throughout the city, each with anywhere from 20 to 70 bike stands. The bikes are accessible around the clock.

○ To get a bike, you first need to purchase a one- or seven-day subscription. There are two ways to do this: either at the terminals found at docking stations or online.

○ The terminals require a credit card with an embedded smartchip (which precludes many North American cards), and, even then, not all foreign chip-embedded cards will work. Alternatively, you can purchase a subscription online before you leave your hotel.

○ After you authorise a deposit (€150) to pay for the bike should it go missing, you'll receive an ID number and PIN code and you're ready to go.

○ Bikes are rented in 30-minute intervals. If you return a bike before a half-hour is up and then take a new one, you will not be charged.

○ If the station you want to return your bike to is full, log in to the terminal to get 15 minutes for free to find another station.

○ Bikes are geared to cyclists aged 14 and over, and are fitted with gears, an anti-theft lock with key, reflective strips and front/rear lights. Bring your own helmet (they are not required by law).

○ P'tits Vélib' is a bike-sharing scheme for children aged two to 10 years, with bike stations at seven sites, including Bois de Bologne, Bois de Vincennes and Les Berges de Seine. Child helmets are always provided.

Rentals

Most rental places will require a deposit (usually €150). Take ID and bank card/credit card.

Au Point Vélo Hollandais
(☏01 43 54 85 36; www.point-velo.com; 83 bd St-Michel, 5e; per day €15; ⏰10.30am-7.30pm Mon-Sat; Ⓜ Cluny-La Sorbonne or RER Luxembourg)

Freescoot (☏01 44 07 06 72; www.freescoot.com; 63

Tourist Transport Passes

The Mobilis and Paris Visite passes are valid on the metro, RER, SNCF's suburban lines, buses, night buses, trams and Montmartre funicular railway. No photo is needed, but write your card number on the ticket. Passes are sold at larger metro and RER stations, SNCF offices in Paris, and the airports.

○ **Mobilis** cards allow unlimited travel for one day and cost €7 (two zones) to €16.60 (five zones). Buy at any metro, RER or SNCF station in the Paris region. Depending on how many times you plan to hop on/off the metro in a day, a *carnet* might work out cheaper.

○ **Paris Visite** allows unlimited travel as well as discounted entry to certain museums and other discounts and bonuses. The 'Paris+Suburbs+Airports' pass includes transport to/from the airports and costs €23.50/35.70/50.05/61.25 for one/two/three/five days. The cheaper 'Paris Centre' pass, valid for zones 1 to 3, costs €11.15/18.15/24.80/35.70. Children aged four to 11 years pay half price.

quai de la Tournelle, 5e; bike/tandem/electric bike per day from €20/35/40; ⏰9am-1pm & 2-7pm mid-Apr–mid-Sep, closed Sun & Wed mid-Sep–mid-Apr; Ⓜ Maubert-Mutualité)

Gepetto et Vélos (☏01 43 54 19 95; www.gepetto-velos.com; 59 rue du Cardinal Lemoine, 5e; per day €16, child seat €5; ⏰9am-2pm & 3-7pm Tue-Sat year-round plus 10am-2pm & 3-7pm Sun mid-Apr–mid-Sep; Ⓜ Cardinal Lemoine)

Paris à Vélo, C'est Sympa (☏01 48 87 60 01; www.parisvelosympa.com; 22 rue Alphonse Baudin, 11e; half-day/full day/24 hours from €12/15/20, electric bikes per half-day/full day/24 hours €20/30/40; ⏰9.30am-1pm & 2-6pm Mon-Fri, 9am-7pm Sat & Sun Apr-Oct, shorter hours winter; Ⓜ St-Sébastien-Froissart)

Boat

Glassed-in trimarans that dock every 20 to 25 minutes at small piers along the Seine are run by **Batobus** (www.batobus.com; adult/child 1-day pass €17/10, 2-day pass €19/10; ⏰10am-9.30pm Apr-Aug, to 7pm Sep-Mar). Key stops include the Eiffel Tower, Musée d'Orsay, St-Germain des Prés, Notre Dame, Jardin des Plantes/Cité de la Mode et du Design, Hôtel de Ville, Musée du Louvre and Champs-Élysées.

Buy tickets online, at ferry stops or tourist offices. You can also buy a Pass+ that includes L'Open Tour buses, to be used on consecutive days. A two-day pass per adult/child costs €46/21; a three-day pass is €50/21.

Bus

Buses can be a scenic way to get around – and there are no stairs to climb, meaning they are more widely accessible – but they're slower and less intuitive to figure out than the metro.

Local Buses

Paris' bus system, operated by RATP, runs from 5.30am to 8.30pm Monday to Saturday; after that, certain evening-service lines continue until between midnight and 12.30am. Services are drastically reduced on Sunday and public holidays, when buses run from 7am to 8.30pm.

Night Buses

o The RATP runs 47 night bus lines known as Noctilien (www.vianavigo.com), which depart hourly from 12.30am to 5.30am. The services pass through the main *gares* (train stations) and cross the major axes of the city before heading out to the suburbs. Look for navy-blue N or Noctilien signs at bus stops. There are two circular lines within Paris (the N01 and N02) that link four main train stations – St-Lazare, Gare de l'Est, Gare de Lyon and Gare Montparnasse – as well as popular nightlife areas (Bastille, Champs-Elysées, Pigalle, St-Germain).

o Noctilien services are included on your Mobilis or Paris Visite pass for the zones in which you are travelling. Otherwise you pay a certain number of standard €1.80 metro/bus tickets,

depending on the length of your journey.

Tickets & Fares

o Normal bus rides embracing one or two bus zones cost one metro ticket; longer rides require two or even three tickets. Transfers to other buses – but not the metro – are allowed on the same ticket as long as the change takes place 1½ hours between the first and last validation. This does not apply to Noctilien services.

o Whatever kind of single-journey ticket you have, you must validate it in the ticket machine near the driver. If you don't have a ticket, the driver can sell you one for €2 (correct change required). If you have a Mobilis or Paris Visite pass, flash it at the driver when you board.

Taxi

o The *prise en charge* (flagfall) is €2.60. Within the city limits, it costs €1.04 per kilometre for travel between 10am and 5pm Monday to Saturday (*Tarif A;* white light on taxi roof and meter).

o At night (5pm to 10am), on Sunday from 7am to midnight, and in the inner suburbs the rate is €1.27 per kilometre (*Tarif B;* orange light).

o Travel in the city limits and inner suburbs on Sunday night (midnight to 7am Monday) and in the outer suburbs is at *Tarif C,* €1.54 per kilometre (blue light).

o The minimum taxi fare for a short trip is €6.86.

o Flat fees have been introduced for taxis to/from the major airports, Charles de Gualle and Orly.

o There's a €3 surcharge for taking a fourth passenger, but drivers sometimes refuse for insurance reasons. The first piece of baggage is free; additional pieces over 5kg cost €1 extra.

o Flagging down a taxi in Paris can be difficult; it's best to find an official taxi stand.

o To order a taxi, call or reserve online with **Taxis G7** (✆01 41 27 66 99, 3607; www. taxisg7.com), **Taxis Bleus** (✆08 91 70 10 10, 3609; www. taxis-bleus.com) or **Alpha Taxis** (✆01 45 85 85 85; www. alphataxis.fr).

o An alternative is the private driver system, Uber (www. uber.com/cities/paris). Official taxis continue to protest about the service and there have been instances of Uber drivers and passengers being harassed.

Car & Motorcycle

Driving in Paris is defined by the triple hassle of navigation, heavy traffic and limited parking. Petrol stations are also difficult to locate and access. It doesn't make sense to use a car to get around, but if you're heading out of the city on an excursion, then your own set of wheels can certainly be useful. If you plan on hiring a car, it's best to do so online and in advance.

Language

The sounds used in spoken French can almost all be found in English. There are a couple of exceptions: nasal vowels (represented in our pronunciation guides by 'o' or 'u' followed by an almost inaudible nasal consonant sound 'm', 'n' or 'ng'), the 'funny' *u* sound ('ew' in our guides) and the deep-in-the-throat *r*. Bearing these few points in mind and reading our pronunciation guides below as if they were English, you'll be understood just fine. The markers (m) and (f) indicate the forms for male and female speakers respectively.

To enhance your trip with a phrasebook, visit **lonelyplanet.com**. Lonely Planet iPhone phrasebooks are available through the Apple App store.

Basics

Hello.
Bonjour. — bon·zhoor
Goodbye.
Au revoir. — o·rer·vwa
How are you?
Comment allez-vous? — ko·mon ta·lay·voo
I'm fine, thanks.
Bien, merci. — byun mair·see
Please.
S'il vous plaît. — seel voo play
Thank you.
Merci. — mair·see
Excuse me.
Excusez-moi. — ek·skew·zay·mwa
Sorry.
Pardon. — par·don
Yes./No.
Oui./Non. — wee/non
I don't understand.
Je ne comprends pas. — zher ner kom·pron pa
Do you speak English?
Parlez-vous anglais? — par·lay·voo ong·glay

Shopping

I'd like to buy ...
Je voudrais acheter ... — zher voo·dray ash·tay ...

I'm just looking.
Je regarde. — zher rer·gard
How much is it?
C'est combien? — say kom·byun
It's too expensive.
C'est trop cher. — say tro shair
Can you lower the price?
Vous pouvez baisser le prix? — voo poo·vay bay·say ler pree

Eating & Drinking

..., please.
..., s'il vous plaît. — ... seel voo play
  A coffee *un café* — un ka·fay
  A table for two *une table pour deux* — ewn ta·bler poor der
  Two beers *deux bières* — der bee·yair

I'm a vegetarian.
Je suis végétarien/végétarienne. (m/f) — zher swee vay·zhay·ta·ryun/vay·zhay·ta·ryen
Cheers!
Santé! — son·tay
That was delicious!
C'était délicieux! — say·tay day·lee·syer
The bill, please.
L'addition, s'il vous plaît. — la·dee·syon seel voo play

Emergencies

Help!
Au secours! — o skoor
Call the police!
Appelez la police! — a·play la po·lees
Call a doctor!
Appelez un médecin! — a·play un mayd·sun
I'm sick.
Je suis malade. — zher swee ma·lad
I'm lost.
Je suis perdu/perdue. (m/f) — zhe swee pair·dew
Where are the toilets?
Où sont les toilettes? — oo son lay twa·let

Transport & Directions

Where's ...?
Où est ...? — oo ay ...
What's the address?
Quelle est l'adresse? — kel ay la·dres
I want to go to ...
Je voudrais aller à ... — zher voo·dray a·lay a ...

Behind the Scenes

Acknowledgements

Climate map data adapted from Peel MC, Finlayson BL & McMahon TA (2007) 'Updated World Map of the Koppen-Geiger Climate Classification', *Hydrology and Earth System Sciences*, 11, 163344

Illustrations pp50-1, pp56-7 and pp88-9 by Javier Zarracina.

This Book

This book was curated by Catherine Le Nevez who also researched and wrote for it along with Christopher Pitts and Nicola Williams. This guidebook was commissioned in Lonely Planet's Melbourne office, and produced by the following:

Destination Editor Helen Elfer
Associate Product Director Liz Heynes
Series Designer Katherine Marsh
Cartographic Series Designer Wayne Murphy
Senior Product Editor Catherine Naghten
Product Editor Anne Mason
Book Designer Wendy Wright
Cartographer Hunor Csutoros
Assisting Editors Victoria Harrison, Charlotte Orr, Gabrielle Stefanos, Saralinda Turner
Cover Researcher Naomi Parker
Thanks to Cam Ashley, James Hardy, Indra Kilfoyle, Valentina Kremenchutskaya, Kate Mathews, Campbell McKenzie, Jenna Myers, Kirsten Rawlings, Alison Ridgway, Kathryn Rowan, Dianne Schallmeiner, Vicky Smith, Luna Soo, Lyahna Spencer, Angela Tinson, Tony Wheeler

Send Us Your Feedback

We love to hear from travellers – your comments keep us on our toes and help make our books better. Our well-travelled team reads every word on what you loved or loathed about this book. Although we cannot reply individually to postal submissions, we always guarantee that your feedback goes straight to the appropriate authors, in time for the next edition. Each person who sends us information is thanked in the next edition, the most useful submissions are rewarded with a selection of digital PDF chapters.

Visit lonelyplanet.com/contact to submit your updates and suggestions or to ask for help. Our award-winning website also features inspirational travel stories, news and discussions.

Note: We may edit, reproduce and incorporate your comments in Lonely Planet products such as guidebooks, websites and digital products, so let us know if you don't want your comments reproduced or your name acknowledged. For a copy of our privacy policy visit lonelyplanet.com/privacy.

A – Z
Index

Paris City Maps

Western Paris, Champs-Élysées, St-Germain & Les Invalides

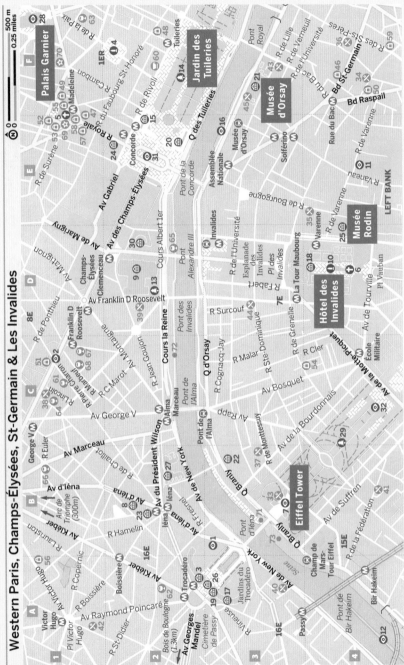

Western Paris, Champs-Élysées, St-Germain & Les Invalides

Les Halles, Le Marais & The Islands

9E

Galerie des Galeries (600m);
Galeries Lafayette
(600m)

Pl de
l'Opéra

Bd des Italiens

A **B** **C** **D**

M Richelieu
Drouot

Bd Montmartre

M Grands Boulevards
119

Bd Poissonnière

Bonne
Nouvelle

R de Marivaux

R de la Michodière

R de Choiseul

128

52

R St-Marc

R Feydeau

86

40

R d'Uzès

R St-Fiacre

107

127

R du Sentier

R Poissonnière

R de Cléry

Quatre
Septembre

R St-Augustin

Pl de la
Bourse

Bourse M

R de l'Opéra

Av de l'Opéra

R Ste-Anne

R des Petits Champs

116

R St-Joseph

R de Réaumur

113

34

R d'Aboukir

Sentier M

2E

33

R du Caire

R de Réaumur

2

R St-Roch

Pyramides M

Paris Convention
& Visitors Bureau

32

57 44

61

74

Pl des
Victoires

R Étienne Marcel

R d'Aboukir

R du Mail

R Léopold Bellan

84

108

R Mandar

56

97

R Dussoubs

3

60

64

15

R Molière

R de Valois

**RIGHT
BANK**

69

R Montorgueil

43

114 83

Étienne
Marcel M

R aux Ours

65

123 Pl Colette

8

68

R Croix des Petits Champs

R du Louvre

10

R Rambuteau

Les
Halles

13

51

R de la Grande
Truanderie

R Rambuteau

R de Rivoli

62

Palais Royal –
Musée du Louvre M

R du Faubourg St-Honoré

R Berger

23

38

R Berger

Châtelet –
Les Halles M

R de Sébastopol

R St-Denis

Jardin du
Carrousel

2

14

Jardin de
l'Oratoire

58 102

53

Louvre
Rivoli M

Pl du
Louvre

1ER

R du Pont Neuf

129

Châtelet M

125

R St-Martin

**Musée du
Louvre**

17

Cour
Carrée

Châtelet M

1

Q du Louvre

Jardin de
l'Infante

Pont du
Carroussel

Pont des
Arts

Seine

Pont
Neuf

Pont
Neuf M

Q de la Mégisserie

130 Châtelet

Sq de la
Tour
St-Jacques

Châtelet M

5

77

Q Malaquais

20

133

117 111

48

Q de l'Horloge

Pont au
Change

Q des Gesvres

R Bonaparte

Q de Conti

54

16

Pont
Neuf

46

41

R de l'Horloge

Pont
Notre
Dame

Q de la Corse

Pont
Notre Dame

Hôpital
Hôtel Dieu

Pont
d'Arcole

122

67

R Visconti

R Jacob

22

35

55

R de Seine

6E

R de Nevers

R Dauphine

R Mazarine

7

Cité M

Île de
la Cité

R de Lutèce

79

Q du Marché Neuf

9

**Cathédrale
Notre Dame
de Paris**

93

110

11

R de l'Abbaye

71

R de Buci

St-Germain
des Prés M

Bd St-Germain

Mabillon M

36

47

R Suger

St-Michel–
Notre Dame M

St-Michel M

121

Q St-Michel

18

5

Sainte-Chapelle

19

6

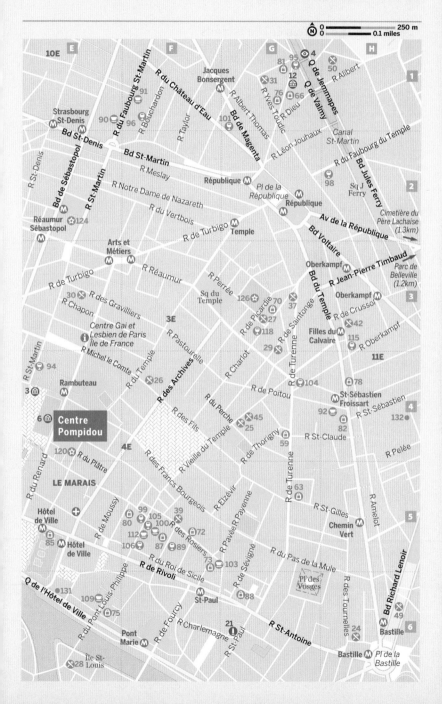

Les Halles, Le Marais & The Islands

Latin Quarter

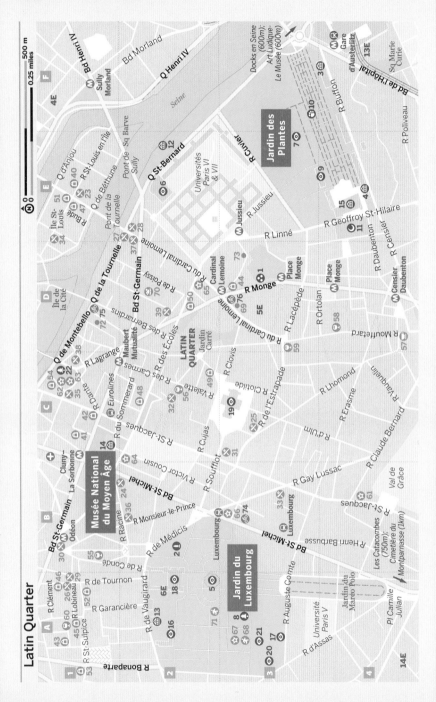

Latin Quarter

Montmartre

◎ Sights
1 Basilique du Sacré-Cœur C1
2 Brasserie de la Goutte d'Or D2
3 Clos Montmartre B1
4 Dalí Espace Montmartre B2
5 Moulin Blute Fin A1
6 Musée de Montmartre B1
7 Place du Tertre B2

⊗ Eating
8 Le Grenier à Pain A2
9 Le Miroir B2
10 Le Pantruche B3
11 L'Été en Pente Douce C2
12 Soul Kitchen B1

⊜ Shopping
13 Belle du Jour B2

14 Jeremie Barthod B2
15 Maison Kitsuné B3
16 Pigalle B3
17 Spree B2

⊝ Drinking & Nightlife
18 La Fourmi B3
19 Le Progrès B2
20 Le Très Particulier A1
21 L'Entrée des Artistes B3
22 Lulu White B3

✪ Entertainment
23 Au Lapin Agile B1
24 La Cigale B3
25 Le Divan du Monde B3
26 Moulin Rouge A2

Symbols & Map Key

Look for these symbols to quickly identify listings:

- ◎ Sights
- ✪ Activities
- ☻ Courses
- ☺ Tours
- ❀ Festivals & Events
- ✦ Eating
- ❶ Drinking
- ✪ Entertainment
- ❻ Shopping
- ❶ Information & Transport

These symbols and abbreviations give vital information for each listing:

- ⚑ Sustainable or green recommendation
- **FREE** No payment required

- ☏ Telephone number
- ⊙ Opening hours
- P Parking
- ⊖ Nonsmoking
- ❄ Air-conditioning
- @ Internet access
- ⧈ Wi-fi access
- ⧖ Swimming pool

- ⊟ Bus
- ⊠ Ferry
- ⊟ Tram
- ⊠ Train
- ⬚ English-language menu
- ◈ Vegetarian selection
- ⧊ Family-friendly

Find your best experiences with these Great For... icons.

- ▣ Budget
- ▢ Short Trip
- ⦿ Food & Drink
- ⧉ Detour
- ⦚ Drinking
- ⧍ Walking
- ⬡ Cycling
- ⦂ Local Life
- ⬚ Shopping
- ⬙ History
- ⬢ Sport
- ⬙ Entertainment
- ⬜ Art & Culture
- ≈ Beaches
- ✧ Events
- ❄ Winter Travel
- ⬚ Photo Op
- ♨ Cafe/Coffee
- ⬚ Scenery
- ⬚ Nature & Wildlife
- ⬚ Family Travel

Sights

- ◎ Beach
- ◉ Bird Sanctuary
- ◭ Buddhist
- ◉ Castle/Palace
- ✛ Christian
- ⬚ Confucian
- ⬚ Hindu
- ◉ Islamic
- ◉ Jain
- ✡ Jewish
- ❶ Monument
- ⬛ Museum/Gallery/ Historic Building
- ⬚ Ruin
- ⬚ Shinto
- ◉ Sikh
- ◉ Taoist
- ◉ Winery/Vineyard
- ◉ Zoo/Wildlife Sanctuary
- ◎ Other Sight

Points of Interest

- ⦿ Bodysurfing
- ⦿ Camping
- ⦿ Cafe
- ⦿ Canoeing/Kayaking
- ● Course/Tour
- ⦿ Diving
- ⦿ Drinking & Nightlife
- ⦿ Eating
- ⦿ Entertainment
- ⦿ Sento Hot Baths/ Onsen
- ⦿ Shopping
- ⦿ Skiing
- ⦿ Sleeping
- ⦿ Snorkelling
- ⦿ Surfing
- ⦿ Swimming/Pool
- ⦿ Walking
- ⦿ Windsurfing
- ⦿ Other Activity

Information

- ⑤ Bank
- ⦿ Embassy/Consulate
- ⊕ Hospital/Medical
- @ Internet
- ⦿ Police
- ⊠ Post Office
- ⦿ Telephone
- ⦿ Toilet
- ⦿ Tourist Information
- ● Other Information

Geographic

- ⦿ Beach
- ⊷ Gate
- ⦿ Hut/Shelter
- ⦿ Lighthouse
- ⦿ Lookout
- ▲ Mountain/Volcano
- ⦿ Oasis
- ⦿ Park
-)(Pass
- ⦿ Picnic Area
- ⦿ Waterfall

Transport

- ⦿ Airport
- Ⓑ BART station
- ⦿ Border crossing
- ⦿ Boston T station
- ⦿ Bus
- +⦿+ Cable car/Funicular
- ⦿ Cycling
- ⦿ Ferry
- Ⓜ Metro/MRT station
- ⦿ Monorail
- Ⓟ Parking
- ⦿ Petrol station
- ⑤ Subway/S-Bahn/ Skytrain station
- ⦿ Taxi
- +⦿+ Train station/Railway
- ⨯⨯⨯⨯ Tram
- ⦿ Tube Station
- Ⓤ Underground/ U-Bahn station
- ● Other Transport

Our Story

A beat-up old car, a few dollars in the pocket and a sense of adventure. In 1972 that's all Tony and Maureen Wheeler needed for the trip of a lifetime – across Europe and Asia overland to Australia. It took several months, and at the end – broke but inspired – they sat at their kitchen table writing and stapling together their first travel guide, Across Asia on the Cheap. Within a week they'd sold 1500 copies. Lonely Planet was born.

Today, Lonely Planet has offices in Melbourne, London, Oakland, Franklin, Delhi and Beijing, with more than 600 staff and writers. We share Tony's belief that 'a great guidebook should do three things: inform, educate and amuse'.

Our Writers

Catherine Le Nevez

An award-winning, Paris-based travel writer, Catherine first lived in the French capital aged four and has been hitting the road at every opportunity, completing her Doctorate of Creative Arts in Writing, Masters in Professional Writing, and postgrad qualifications in Editing and Publishing along the way. Over the last dozen-plus years she's written scores of Lonely Planet guides, along with numerous print and online articles, covering Paris, France, Europe and far beyond. Wanderlust aside, Paris remains her favourite city on earth.

Christopher Pitts

Christopher Pitts first moved to Paris in 2001. He initially began writing about the city as a means to buy baguettes – and to impress a certain Parisian (it worked, they're now married with two kids). Over the past decade, he has written for various publications, in addition to working as a translator and editor. Visit him online at www.christopherpitts.net.

Nicola Williams

British writer and editorial consultant Nicola Williams has lived in France and written about it for more than a decade. From her hillside house on the southern shore of Lake Geneva, it's an easy hop to Paris where she has spent endless years revelling in its extraordinary art, urban architecture, boutique shopping and cuisine. Nicola has worked on numerous titles for Lonely Planet, including *France* and *Discover France*. Find Nicola on Twitter at @Tripalong.

EUROPE Unit E, Digital Court, The Digital Hub, Rainsford St, Dublin 8, Ireland

AUSTRALIA Levels 2 & 3 551 Swanston St, Carlton, Victoria 3053
☎ 03 8379 8000,
fax 03 8379 8111

USA 150 Linden Street, Oakland, CA 94607
☎ 510 250 6400,
toll free 800 275 8555,
fax 510 893 8572

UK 240 Blackfriars Road, London SE1 8NW
☎ 020 3771 5100,
fax 020 3771 5101

 twitter.com/ lonelyplanet
 facebook.com/ lonelyplanet
 instagram.com/ lonelyplanet
youtube.com/ lonelyplanet
lonelyplanet.com/ newsletter